New Perspectives on

Microsoft®

PowerPoint® 97

INTRODUCTORY

The New Perspectives Series

The New Perspectives Series consists of texts and technology that teach computer concepts and microcomputer applications (listed below). You can order these New Perspectives texts in many different lengths, software releases, custom-bound combinations, CourseKits™ and Custom Editions®. Contact your Course Technology sales representative or customer service representative for the most up-to-date details.

The New Perspectives Series

Computer Concepts

Borland® dBASE®

Borland® Paradox®

Corel® Presentations™

Corel® Quattro Pro®

Corel® WordPerfect®

DOS

HTML

Lotus® 1-2-3®

Microsoft® Access

Microsoft® Excel

Microsoft® Internet Explorer

Microsoft® Office Professional

Microsoft® PowerPoint®

Microsoft® Windows® 3.1

Microsoft® Windows® 95

Microsoft® Windows NT® Server 4.0

Microsoft® Windows NT® Workstation 4.0

Microsoft® Word

Microsoft® Works

Netscape Navigator™

Netscape Navigator™ Gold

Microsoft® Visual Basic® 4 and 5

New Perspectives on
Microsoft®
PowerPoint® 97

Beverly B. Zimmerman
Brigham Young University

S. Scott Zimmerman
Brigham Young University

COURSE
TECHNOLOGY

ONE MAIN STREET, CAMBRIDGE, MA 02142

an International Thomson Publishing company I(T)P®

Cambridge • Albany • Bonn • Boston • Cincinnati • London • Madrid • Melbourne • Mexico City
New York • Paris • San Francisco • Singapore • Tokyo • Toronto • Washington

New Perspectives on Microsoft® PowerPoint® 97 — Introductory is published by Course Technology.

Associate Publisher	Mac Mendelsohn
Series Consulting Editor	Susan Solomon
Acquisitions Editor	Mark Reimold
Developmental Editor	Terry Ann Kremer
Production Editor	Daphne Barbas
Text and Cover Designer	Ella Hanna
Cover Illustrator	Douglas Goodman

© 1997 by Course Technology
A Division of International Thomson Publishing Inc. — I(T)P®

For more information contact:

Course Technology
One Main Street
Cambridge, MA 02142

International Thomson Publishing Europe
Berkshire House 168-173
High Holborn
London WCIV 7AA
England

Thomas Nelson Australia
102 Dodds Street
South Melbourne, 3205
Victoria, Australia

Nelson Canada
1120 Birchmount Road
Scarborough, Ontario
Canada M1K 5G4

International Thomson Editores
Campos Eliseos 385, Piso 7
Col. Polanco
11560 Mexico D.F. Mexico

International Thomson Publishing GmbH
Königswinterer Strasse 418
53227 Bonn
Germany

International Thomson Publishing Asia
211 Henderson Road
#05-10 Henderson Building
Singapore 0315

International Thomson Publishing Japan
Hirakawacho Kyowa Building, 3F
2-2-1 Hirakawacho
Chiyoda-ku, Tokyo 102
Japan

ISBN 0-7600-5276-X

Printed in the United States of America

10 9 8 7 6 5 4 3 2 1

At Course Technology we have one foot in education and the other in technology. We believe that technology is transforming the way people teach and learn, and we are excited about providing instructors and students with materials that use technology to teach about technology.

Our development process is unparalleled in the higher education publishing industry. Every product we create goes through an exacting process of design, development, review, and testing.

Reviewers give us direction and insight that shape our manuscripts and bring them up to the latest standards. Every manuscript is quality tested. Students whose backgrounds match the intended audience work through every keystroke, carefully checking for clarity and pointing out errors in logic and sequence. Together with our own technical reviewers, these testers help us ensure that everything that carries our name is error-free and easy to use.

We show both how and why technology is critical to solving problems in college and in whatever field you choose to teach or pursue. Our time-tested, step-by-step instructions provide unparalleled clarity. Examples and applications are chosen and crafted to motivate students.

As the New Perspectives Series team at Course Technology, our goal is to produce the most timely, accurate, creative, and technologically sound product in the entire college publishing industry. We strive for consistent high quality. This takes a lot of communication, coordination, and hard work. But we love what we do. We are determined to be the best. Write to us and let us know what you think. You can also e-mail us at NewPerspectives@course.com.

The New Perspectives Series Team

Joseph J. Adamski	Jessica Evans	Dan Oja
Judy Adamski	Marilyn Freedman	David Paradice
Roy Ageloff	Kathy Finnegan	June Parsons
David Auer	Robin Geller	Harry Phillips
Dirk Baldwin	Donna Gridley	Sandra Poindexter
Daphne Barbas	Roger Hayen	Mark Reimold
Rachel Bunin	Charles Hommel	Ann Shaffer
Joan Carey	Janice Jutras	Karen Shortill
Patrick Carey	Chris Kelly	Susan Solomon
Sharon Caswell	Mary Kemper	Susanne Walker
Barbara Clemens	Terry Ann Kremer	John Zeanchock
Rachel Crapser	John Leschke	Beverly Zimmerman
Kim Crowley	Mac Mendelsohn	Scott Zimmerman
Michael Ekedahl	William Newman	

Preface The New Perspectives Series

What is the New Perspectives Series?

Course Technology's **New Perspectives Series** is an integrated system of instruction that combines text and technology products to teach computer concepts and microcomputer applications. Users consistently praise this series for innovative pedagogy, creativity, supportive and engaging style, accuracy, and use of interactive technology. The first New Perspectives text was published in January of 1993. Since then, the series has grown to more than 100 titles and has become the best-selling series on computer concepts and microcomputer applications. Others have imitated the New Perspectives features, design, and technologies, but none have replicated its quality and its ability to consistently anticipate and meet the needs of instructors and students.

What is the Integrated System of Instruction?

New Perspectives textbooks are part of a truly Integrated System of Instruction: text, graphics, video, sound, animation, and simulations that are linked and that provide a flexible, unified, and interactive system to help you teach and help your students learn. Specifically, the *New Perspectives Integrated System of Instruction* includes a Course Technology textbook in addition to some or all of the following items: Course Labs, Course Test Manager, Online Companions, and Course Presenter. These components—shown in the graphic on the back cover of this book—have been developed to work together to provide a complete, integrative teaching and learning experience.

How is the New Perspectives Series different from other microcomputer concepts and applications series?

The **New Perspectives Series** distinguishes itself from other series in at least four substantial ways: sound instructional design, consistent quality, innovative technology, and proven pedagogy. The applications texts in this series consist of two or more tutorials, which are based on sound instructional design. Each tutorial is motivated by a realistic case that is meaningful to students. Rather than learn a laundry list of features, students learn the features in the context of solving a problem. This process motivates all concepts and skills by demonstrating to students *why* they would want to know them.

Instructors and students have come to rely on the high quality of the **New Perspectives Series** and to consistently praise its accuracy. This accuracy is a result of Course Technology's unique multi-step quality assurance process that incorporates student testing in at least two stages of development, using hardware and software configurations appropriate to the product. All solutions, test questions, and other supplements are tested using similar procedures. Instructors who adopt this series report that students can work through the tutorials independently with minimum intervention or "damage control" by instructors or staff. This consistent quality has meant that if instructors are pleased with one product from the series, they can rely on the same quality with any other New Perspectives product.

The **New Perspectives Series** also distinguishes itself by its innovative technology. This series innovated Course Labs, truly *interactive* learning applications. These have set the standard for interactive learning.

How do I know that the New Perspectives Series will work?

Some instructors who use this series report a significant difference between how much their students learn and retain with this series as compared to other series. With other series, instructors often find that students can work through the book and do well on homework and tests, but still not demonstrate competency when asked to perform particular tasks outside the context of the text's sample case or project. With the **New Perspectives Series**, however, instructors report that students have a complete, integrative learning experience that stays with them. They credit this high retention and competency to the fact that this series incorporates critical thinking and problem-solving with computer skills mastery.

How does this book I'm holding fit into the New Perspectives Series?

New Perspectives applications books are available in the following categories:

Brief books are typically about 150 pages long, contain two to four tutorials, and are intended to teach the basics of an application.

Introductory books are typically about 300 pages long and consist of four to seven tutorials that go beyond the basics. These books often build out of the Brief editions by providing two or three additional tutorials. The book you are holding is an Introductory book.

Comprehensive books are typically about 600 pages long and consist of all of the tutorials in the Introductory books, plus additional tutorials covering higher-level topics. Comprehensive books also include two Windows tutorials and three or four Additional Cases.

Advanced books cover topics similar to those in the Comprehensive books, but go into more depth. Advanced books present the most high-level coverage in the series.

Custom Books The New Perspectives Series offers you two ways to customize a New Perspectives text to fit your course exactly: *CourseKits*™, two or more texts packaged together in a box, and *Custom Editions*®, your choice of books bound together. Custom Editions offer you unparalleled flexibility in designing your concepts and applications courses. You can build your own book by ordering a combination of titles bound together to cover only the topics you want. Your students save because they buy only the materials they need. There is no minimum order, and books are spiral bound. Both CourseKits and Custom Editions offer significant price discounts. Contact your Course Technology sales representative for more information.

New Perspectives Series Microcomputer Applications

- ■ **Brief Titles or Modules**
- ■ **Introductory Titles or Modules**
- ■ **Intermediate Tutorials**
- ■ **Advanced Titles or Modules**
- ▢ **Other Modules**

Brief	Introductory	Comprehensive	Advanced	Custom Editions
2 to 4 tutorials	6 or 7 tutorials, or Brief + 2 or 3 more tutorials	Introductory + 3 to 6 more tutorials. Includes Brief Windows tutorials and Additional Cases	Quick Review of basics + in-depth, high-level coverage	Choose from any of the above to build your own Custom Editions® or CourseKits™

In what kind of course could I use this book?

This book can be used in any course in which you want students to learn all the most important topics of Microsoft PowerPoint 97. It is particularly recommended for a "short" course on PowerPoint. This book assumes that students have learned basic Windows 95 navigation and file management skills from Course Technology's *New Perspectives on Microsoft Windows 95—Brief* or an *equivalent* book.

This book has been approved by Microsoft as courseware for the Certified Microsoft Office User (CMOU) program. After completing the tutorials and exercises in this book, you will be prepared to take the Expert level CMOU Exam for Microsoft PowerPoint 97. By passing the certification exam for a Microsoft software program you demonstrate your proficiency in that program to employers. CMOU exams are offered at participating test centers, participating corporations, and participating employment agencies. For more information about certification, visit the CMOU program World Wide Web site at http://www.microsoft.com/office/train_cert/.

How do the Windows 95 editions differ from the Windows 3.1 editions?

Sessions We've divided the tutorials into sessions. Each session is designed to be completed in about 45 minutes to an hour (depending, of course, upon student needs and the speed of your lab equipment). With sessions, learning is broken up into more easily assimilated portions. You can more accurately allocate time in your syllabus, and students can better manage the available lab time. Each session begins with a "session box," which quickly describes the skills students will learn in the session. Furthermore, each session is numbered, which makes it easier for you and your students to navigate and communicate about the tutorial. Look on page P 3.4 for the session box that opens Session 3.1.

Quick Checks Each session concludes with meaningful, conceptual Quick Check questions that test students' understanding of what they learned in the session. Answers to the Quick Check questions in this book are provided beginning on pages P 2.29 and P 4.39.

New Design We have retained the best of the old design to help students differentiate between what they are to *do* and what they are to *read*. The steps are clearly identified by their shaded background and numbered steps. Furthermore, this new design presents steps and screen shots in a larger, easier to read format. Some good examples of our new design are pages P 3.7 and P 3.26.

What features are retained in the Windows 95 editions of the New Perspectives Series?

"Read This Before You Begin" Page This page is consistent with Course Technology's unequaled commitment to helping instructors introduce technology into the classroom. Technical considerations and assumptions about software are listed to help instructors save time and eliminate unnecessary aggravation. See pages P 1.2 and P 3.2 for the "Read This Before You Begin" pages in this book.

Tutorial Case Each tutorial begins with a problem presented in a case that is meaningful to students. The problem turns the task of learning how to use an application into a problem-solving process. The problems increase in complexity with each tutorial. These cases touch on multicultural, international, and ethical issues—so important to today's business curriculum. See page P 1.3 for the case that begins Tutorial 1.

Step-by-Step Methodology This unique Course Technology methodology keeps students on track. They enter data, click buttons, or press keys always within the context of solving the problem posed in the tutorial case. The text constantly guides students, letting them know where they are in the course of solving the problem. In addition, the numerous screen shots include labels that direct students' attention to what they should look at on the screen. On almost every page in this book, you can find an example of how steps, screen shots, and labels work together.

TROUBLE?

TROUBLE? Paragraphs These paragraphs anticipate the mistakes or problems that students are likely to have and help them recover and continue with the tutorial. By putting these paragraphs in the book, rather than in the Instructor's Manual, we facilitate independent learning and free the instructor to focus on substantive conceptual issues rather than on common procedural errors. Some representative examples of TROUBLE? paragraphs appear on page P 3.5.

REFERENCE window

Reference Windows Reference Windows appear throughout the text. They are succinct summaries of the most important tasks covered in the tutorials. Reference Windows are specially designed and written so students can refer to them when doing the Tutorial Assignments and Case Problems, and after completing the course. Page P 3.5 contains the Reference Window for inserting slides from another presentation.

Task Reference The Task Reference contains a summary of how to perform common tasks using the most efficient method, as well as references to pages where the task is discussed in more detail. It appears as a table at the end of the book.

Tutorial Assignments, Case Problems, and Lab Assignments Each tutorial concludes with Tutorial Assignments, which provide students with additional hands-on practice of the skills they learned in the tutorial. See page P 4.34 for examples of Tutorial Assignments. The Tutorial Assignments are followed by four Case Problems that have approximately the same scope as the tutorial case. In the Windows 95 applications texts, the last Case Problem of each tutorial typically requires students to solve the problem independently, either "from scratch" or with minimum guidance. See page P 4.35 for examples of Case Problems. Finally, if a Course Lab accompanies a tutorial, Lab Assignments are included after the Case Problems.

Exploration Exercises The Windows environment allows students to learn by exploring and discovering what they can do. Exploration Exercises can be Tutorial Assignments or Case Problems that challenge students, encourage them to explore the capabilities of the program they are using, and extend their knowledge using the Help facility and other reference materials. Page P 4.35 contains Exploration Exercises for Tutorial 4.

What supplements are available with this textbook?

Course Test Manager: This cutting-edge Windows-based testing software helps instructors design and administer tests and pre-tests. The full-featured online program permits students to take tests at the computer where their grades are computed immediately following the completion of the exam. Automatic statistics collection, student study guides customized to the students performance, and printed tests are only a few of the features.

Course Presenter: This lecture presentation tool allows instructors to create electronic slide shows or traditional overhead transparencies using the figure files from the book. Instructors can customize, edit, save, and display the figures from the text in order to illustrate key topics or concepts in class.

Online Companions: Dedicated to Keeping You and Your Students Up-To-Date When you use a New Perspectives product, you can access Course Technology's faculty sites and student sites on the World Wide Web. You can browse the password-protected Faculty Online Companions to obtain online Instructor's Manuals, Solution Files, Student Files, and more. Please see your Instructor's Manual or call your Course Technology customer service representative for more information. Student and Faculty Online Companions are accessible by clicking the appropriate links on the Course Technology home page at http://www.course.com.

Student Files Student Files contain all of the data that students will use to complete the tutorials, Tutorial Assignments, and Case Problems. A Readme file includes technical tips for lab management. See the inside covers of this book and the "Read This Before You Begin" page before Tutorial 1 and before Tutorial 3 for more information on Student Files.

Instructor's Manual New Perspectives Series Instructor's Manuals contain instructor's notes and printed solutions for each tutorial. Instructor's notes provide tutorial overviews and outlines, technical notes, lecture notes, and extra Case Problems. Printed solutions include solutions to Tutorial Assignments and Case Problems.

Internet Assignments The Instructor's Manual that accompanies this text includes additional assignments that integrate the World Wide Web with the presentation graphics skills students learn in the tutorials. To complete these assignments, students will need to search the Web and follow the links from the New Perspectives on Microsoft Office 97 home page. The Office 97 home page is accessible through the Student Online Companions link found on the Course Technology home page at http\\:www.course.com. Please refer to the Instructor's Manual for more information.

Solution Files Solution Files contain every file students are asked to create or modify in the tutorials, Tutorial Assignments, and Case Problems.

The following supplements are included in the Instructor's Resource Kit that accompanies this textbook:

- Instructor's Manual
- Solution Files
- Student Files
- Course Test Manager Release 1.1 Test Bank
- Course Test Manager Release 1.1 Engine
- Course Presenter

Some of the supplements listed above are also available over the World Wide Web through Course Technology's password-protected Faculty Online Companions. Please see your Instructor's Manual or call your Course Technology customer service representative for more information.

Acknowledgments

The authors would like to thank the following reviewers for their valuable feedback on this very exciting project: Linda Wise Miller, University of Idaho; Suzanne Nordhaus, Lee College; and Suzanne Tomlinson, Iowa State University.

Also special thanks to: Susan Solomon, Series Consulting Editor; Mac Mendelsohn, Associate Publisher; Mark Reimold, Acquisitions Editor; Daphne Barbas, Production Editor; Greg Bigelow, Quality Assurance Supervisor; and student tester John McCarthy.

Finally, we would like to thank Terry Ann Kremer, our developmental editor, for her cheerful encouragement, expert assistance, and friendly support.

Beverly B. Zimmerman
S. Scott Zimmerman

Preface   iii

Microsoft PowerPoint 97

Level I Tutorials   **P 1.1**

Read This Before You Begin   **P 1.2**

TUTORIAL 1

Creating a PowerPoint Presentation

Presentation to Reach Potential Customers of Inca Imports International   **P 1.3**

Using the Tutorials Effectively   **P 1.4**

Session 1.1   **P 1.5**

What Is PowerPoint?   **P 1.5**

Planning a Presentation   **P 1.5**

Starting PowerPoint   **P 1.6**

Using the AutoContent Wizard to Create an Outline   **P 1.7**

The PowerPoint Window   **P 1.10**

Common Windows Elements   P 1.10

The Toolbars   P 1.10

Adapting an AutoContent Outline   **P 1.11**

Saving the Presentation and Exiting PowerPoint   **P 1.13**

Quick Check   **P 1.14**

Session 1.2   **P 1.14**

Editing the Presentation in Outline View   **P 1.14**

Moving Text Up and Down in Outline View   P 1.15

Promoting and Demoting the Outline Text   P 1.16

Deleting Slides   **P 1.17**

Viewing Slides in Slide View   **P 1.18**

Editing the Presentation in Slide View   **P 1.19**

Moving Text Using Cut and Paste   P 1.19

Adding a New Slide and Choosing a Layout   P 1.21

Changing the Design Template   **P 1.22**

Getting Help   **P 1.24**

Finding Information with the Office Assistant   P 1.24

Creating Speaker Notes   **P 1.25**

Viewing the Completed Slide Show   **P 1.26**

Previewing and Printing the Presentation   **P 1.27**

Quick Check   **P 1.29**

Tutorial Assignments   **P 1.29**

Case Problems   **P 1.30**

TUTORIAL 2
Creating Graphics for Your Slides
Creating a Sales Presentation for Inca Imports   P 2.1

Session 2.1   P 2.2

Planning the Presentation   P 2.2

Resizing and Moving Text Boxes   P 2.2

Removing a Background Graphic from a Slide   P 2.6

Inserting a Picture into a Slide   P 2.7

Changing the Slide Layout   P 2.8

Inserting Clip Art   P 2.10

Quick Check   P 2.13

Session 2.2   P 2.14

Inserting an Organization Chart   P 2.14

Creating and Manipulating a Shape   P 2.17

Adding a Text Box   P 2.19

Rotating Text Boxes   P 2.20

Viewing and Printing the Completed Slide Show   P 2.22

Quick Check   P 2.23

Tutorial Assignments   P 2.23

Case Problems   P 2.25

Microsoft PowerPoint 97
Level II Tutorials   P 3.1

Read This Before You Begin   P 3.2

TUTORIAL 3
Presenting a Slide Show
Annual Report of Inca Imports International   P 3.3

Session 3.1   P 3.4

Planning the Presentation   P 3.4

Inserting Slides from Another Presentation   P 3.4

Applying a Design Template from Another Presentation   P 3.7

Using the Slide Master   P 3.7

Changing the Slide Color Scheme   P 3.9

Modifying Fonts and Bullets   P 3.10

Changing Text Alignment   P 3.12

Adding a Scanned Image to the Title Master   P 3.13

Finding and Replacing Text   P 3.14

Hiding Slides and Adding a Black Final Slide   P 3.16

Quick Check   P 3.17

Session 3.2   P 3.17

Building a Graph (Chart)   P 3.17

Adding a New Slide	P 3.20
Creating a Table	P 3.21
Entering Information into the Table	P 3.21
Formatting the Table	P 3.22
Editing the Table	P 3.24
Adding Special Effects	P 3.25
Adding Slide Transitions	P 3.26
Adding Animation and Sound	P 3.27
Starting the Slide Show in the Middle	P 3.28
Checking the Presentation Style	P 3.29
Preparing Presentation Materials	P 3.31
Preparing 35mm Slides	P 3.31
Preparing Overheads	P 3.32
Printing the Slide Show in Color	P 3.33
Preparing the Presentation to Run on Another Computer	P 3.34
Quick Check	P 3.35
Tutorial Assignments	P 3.35
Case Problems	P 3.37

TUTORIAL 4

Integrating PowerPoint with Other Programs and with the WorldWide Web

Presenting a Proposal to the Executive Officers P 4.1

Session 4.1	**P 4.2**

Planning the Presentation	P 4.2
Using Integration Techniques: Importing, Embedding, and Linking	P 4.2
Importing an Outline from Word	P 4.3
Modifying and Exporting the Outline	P 4.5
Embedding and Modifying Clip-Art Images	4.7
Searching for a Clip-Art Image	P 4.7
Positioning the Image Using Guides	P 4.9
Recoloring the Image	P 4.11
Changing the Stacking Order of Objects	P 4.12
Embedding a Video Clip	P 4.13
Embedding a Sound File	P 4.14
Quick Check	P 4.15
Session 4.2	**P 4.16**
Linking an Excel Chart	P 4.16
Modifying a Linked Chart	P 4.17
Viewing the Completed Slide Show	P 4.19
Adding Tab Stops	P 4.20
Using the Slide Navigator	P 4.23
Generating Meeting Notes and Action Items	P 4.23
Creating and Editing Hyperlinks	P 4.25
Setting Up a Self-Running Presentation	P 4.27
Running a Presentation Conference	P 4.29

Publishing a Presentation on the World Wide Web   **P 4.30**

Saving a Presentation as an
HTML Document   P 4.30

Viewing the Presentation in a
Web Browser   P 4.32

Quick Check   **P 4.33**

Tutorial Assignments   **P 4.34**

Case Problems   **P 4.35**

Answers to Quick Check Questions   **P 4.39**

Index   **P Index 1**

Task Reference

Design Windows

Principles for Creating Effective
Text Presentations   P 1.11

Using Graphics Effectively   P 2.2

Selecting an Appropriate Type
of Graphic   P 2.10

Tips on Electronic Presentations   P 3.25

Giving Effective Slide Show
Presentations   P 3.35

Reference Windows

Cutting and Pasting (Moving) Text   P 1.20

Using the Office Assistant   P 1.24

Resizing and Moving an Object   P 2.4

Inserting a Picture into a Slide   P 2.7

Changing the Layout of a Slide   P 2.8

Inserting an Organization Chart   P 2.14

Preparing for a Presentation Meeting   P 3.4

Inserting Slides from Another
Presentation   P 3.5

Using the Slide Master   P 3.8

Changing Bullet Style   P 3.11

Inserting a Chart   P 3.17

Adding Transition Effects   P 3.26

Adding Animation   P 3.27

Using Genigraphics to Prepare
35mm Slides   P 3.31

Preparing a Pack and Go Disk
and Running the Viewer   P 3.34

Importing a Word Outline   P 4.4

Using Guides   P 4.9

Using Sound Effectively   P 4.14

Linking an Object   P 4.16

Setting Up and Running a
Conference Presentation   P 4.30

Microsoft
PowerPoint 97

LEVEL I

TUTORIALS

TUTORIAL 1

Creating a PowerPoint Presentation
**Presentation to Reach Potential Customers of
Inca Imports International**

P 1.3

TUTORIAL 2

Creating Graphics for Your Slides
Creating a Sales Presentation for Inca Imports

P 2.1

Read This **Before You Begin**

STUDENT DISKS

To complete PowerPoint 97 Tutorials 1 and 2, you need 2 Student Disks. Your instructor will either provide you with Student Disks or ask you to make your own.

If you are supposed to make your own Student Disks, you will need 2 blank, formatted high-density disks. You will need to copy a set of folders from a file server or standalone computer onto your disks. Your instructor will tell you which computer, drive letter, and folders contain the files you need. The following table shows you which folders go on each of your disks, so that you will have enough disk space to complete all the tutorials, Tutorial Assignments, and Case Problems:

Student Disk	Write this on the disk label	Put these folders on the disk
1	Student Disk 1: PowerPoint 97 Tutorial 1	Tutorial.01
2	Student Disk 2: PowerPoint 97 Tutorial 2	Tutorial.02

When you begin each tutorial, be sure you are using the correct Student Disk. See the inside front or inside back cover of this book for more information on Student Disk files, or ask your instructor or technical support person for assistance.

USING YOUR OWN COMPUTER

If you are going to work through this book using your own computer, you need:

■ **Computer System** Microsoft Windows 95 or Microsoft Windows NT Workstation 4.0 (or a later version) and Microsoft PowerPoint 97 must be installed on your computer. This book assumes a typical installation of PowerPoint 97.

■ **Student Disks** Ask your instructor or lab manager for details on how to get the Student Disks. You will not be able to complete the tutorials or end-of-tutorial assignments in this book using your own computer until you have Student Disks. The Student Files may also be obtained electronically over the Internet. See the inside front or inside back cover of this book for more details.

To complete PowerPoint 97 Tutorials 1 and 2, your students must use a set of files on 2 Student Disks. These files are included in the Instructor's Resource Kit, and they may also be obtained electronically over the Internet. See the inside front or inside back cover of this book for more details. Follow the instructions in the Readme file to copy the files to your server or standalone computer. You can view the Readme file using WordPad. Once the files are copied, you can make Student Disks for the students yourself, or you can tell students where to find the files so they can make their own Student Disks.

COURSE TECHNOLOGY STUDENT FILES

You are granted a license to copy the Student Files to any computer or computer network used by students who have purchased this book.

Creating a PowerPoint Presentation

Presentation to Reach Potential Customers of Inca Imports International

OBJECTIVES

In this tutorial you will:

- Start and exit PowerPoint

- Create an outline with the AutoContent Wizard

- Identify the components of the PowerPoint window

- Edit text of the presentation in Outline View and Slide View

- Open an existing presentation

- Insert and delete slides

- Change the design template

- Use the PowerPoint Help system

- Create speaker notes

- Preview, print, and save a presentation

CASE

Inca Imports International

Three years ago Patricia Cuevas and Angelena Cristenas began an import business called Inca Imports International. Working with suppliers in South America, particularly in Ecuador and Peru, the company imports fresh fruits and vegetables to North America during the winter and spring (which are summer and fall in South America) and sells them to small grocery stores in the Los Angeles area.

Inca Imports now has 34 employees and is healthy and growing. The company has recently made plans to construct a distribution facility in Quito, Ecuador, and to launch a marketing campaign to position itself for further expansion. Patricia (President of Inca Imports) assigned Carl Vetterli (Vice President of Sales and Marketing) the task of identifying potential customers and developing methods to reach them. Carl has scheduled a meeting with Patricia, Angelena (Vice President of Operations), Enrique Hoffmann (Director of Marketing), and other colleagues to review the results of his market research.

For his presentation Carl will use an electronic slide show that will include a demographic profile of Inca Imports' current customers, the results of a customer satisfaction survey, a vision statement of the company's future growth, a list of options for attracting new clients, and recommendations for a marketing strategy. Carl asks you to help create the slides for his presentation by using Microsoft PowerPoint 97 (or simply PowerPoint).

Using the Tutorials Effectively

These tutorials are designed to be used at a computer. Each tutorial is divided into sessions. Watch for the session headings, such as "Session 1.1" and "Session 1.2." Each session is designed to be completed in about 45 minutes, but take as much time as you need. When you've completed a session, it's a good idea to exit the program and take a break. You can exit Microsoft PowerPoint by clicking the Close button in the top-right corner of the program window.

Before you begin, read the following questions and answers. They are designed to help you use the tutorials effectively.

Where do I start?

Each tutorial begins with a case, which sets the scene for the tutorial and gives you background information to help you understand what you will be doing in the tutorial. Read the case before you go to the lab. In the lab, begin with the first session of the tutorial.

How do I know what to do on the computer?

Each session contains steps that you will perform on the computer to learn how to use Microsoft PowerPoint. The steps are numbered and are set against a colored background. Read the text that introduces each series of steps, and read each step carefully and completely before you try it.

How do I know if I did the step correctly?

As you work, compare your computer screen with the corresponding figure in the tutorial. Don't worry if your screen display is somewhat different from the figure. The important parts of the screen display are labeled in each figure. Check to make sure these parts are on your screen.

What if I make a mistake?

Don't worry about making mistakes—they are part of the learning process. Paragraphs labeled "**TROUBLE?**" identify common problems and explain how to get back on track. Follow the steps in a **TROUBLE?** paragraph *only* if you are having the problem described. If you run into other problems, carefully consider the current state of your system, the position of the pointer, and any messages on the screen.

How do I use the Reference Windows?

Reference Windows summarize the procedures you learn in the tutorial steps. Do not complete the actions in the Reference Windows when you are working through the tutorial. Instead, refer to the Reference Windows while you are working on the assignments at the end of the tutorial.

How can I test my understanding of the material I learned in the tutorial?

At the end of each session, you can answer the Quick Check questions. If necessary, refer to the Answers to Quick Check Questions to check your work.

After you have completed the entire tutorial, you should complete the Tutorial Assignments and Case Problems. These exercises are carefully structured so you will review what you have learned and then apply your knowledge to new situations.

What if I can't remember how to do something?

You should refer to the Task Reference at the end of the book; it summarizes how to accomplish commonly performed tasks.

Now that you've seen how to use the tutorials effectively, you are ready to begin.

SESSION

1.1

In this session you will learn how to start and exit PowerPoint, use the AutoContent Wizard to create an outline of Carl's presentation, and identify the parts of the PowerPoint window. You will also learn how to use Outline View to insert and edit text in an outline.

What Is PowerPoint?

PowerPoint is a powerful presentation graphics program that provides everything you need to produce an effective presentation in the form of black-and-white or color overheads, 35mm photographic slides, or on-screen slides. You may have already seen your instructors use PowerPoint presentations to enhance their classroom lectures.

Using PowerPoint, you can prepare each component of a presentation: individual slides, speaker notes, an outline of the presentation, and audience handouts. Carl's presentation will include slides, speaker notes, and handouts. In addition, you can easily create a consistent format for your presentation by using a slide master. A **slide master** is a slide that contains the text and graphics that will appear on every slide of a particular kind in the presentation. For example the company's name, the date, and the company's logo can be put on the slide master so this information will appear on every slide in the presentation.

As you create Carl's slides, you'll learn to use many of PowerPoint's features. Before you begin creating the slides, however, you should make sure the presentation is carefully planned.

Planning a Presentation

Planning a presentation before you create it improves the quality of your presentation, makes your presentation more effective and enjoyable, and, in the long run, saves you time and effort. As you plan your presentation, you should answer several questions: What is my purpose or objective for this presentation? What type of presentation is needed? Who is the audience? What information does that audience need? What is the physical location of my presentation? What is the best format for presenting the information contained in this presentation, given the location of the presentation?

In planning his presentation, Carl identifies the following elements of the presentation:

- **Purpose of the presentation:** To identify potential customers and ways to reach them

- **Type of presentation:** Recommend a strategy for the new marketing campaign

- **Audience for the presentation:** Patricia, Angelena, Enrique, and other key staff members in a weekly executive meeting

- **Audience needs:** To understand who our current clients are and to determine the best way to reach similar new clients

- **Location of the presentation:** Small boardroom

- **Format:** Oral presentation; electronic slide show of five to seven slides

Carl has carefully planned his presentation; you can now use PowerPoint to create it. You begin by starting PowerPoint.

Starting PowerPoint

You start PowerPoint in the same way that you start other Windows 95 programs—using the Start button on the taskbar.

To start PowerPoint:

1. Make sure Windows 95 is running on your computer and the Windows 95 desktop appears on your screen.

   TROUBLE? If you're running Windows NT Workstation 4.0 (or a later version) on your computer or network, don't worry. Although the figures in this book were created while running Windows 95, Windows NT 4.0 and Windows 95 share the same interface, and PowerPoint 97 runs equally well under either operating system.

2. Click the **Start** button on the taskbar to display the Start menu, and then point to **Programs** to display the Programs menu.

3. Point to **Microsoft PowerPoint** on the Programs menu. See Figure 1-1.

Figure 1-1 ◀
Starting
Microsoft
PowerPoint

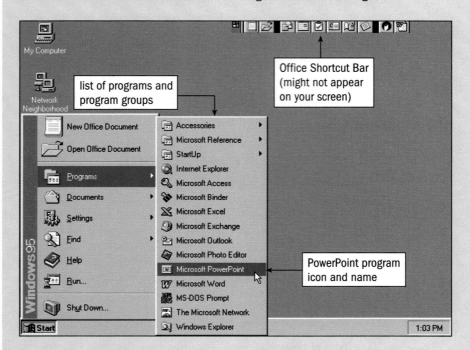

   TROUBLE? If you don't see Microsoft PowerPoint on the Programs menu, ask your instructor or technical support person for help.

   TROUBLE? The Office Shortcut Bar, which appears along the top border of the desktop in Figure 1-1, might look different on your screen or it might not appear at all, depending on how your system is set up. The steps in these tutorials do not require that you use the Office Shortcut Bar; therefore, the remaining figures do not display the Office Shortcut Bar.

4. Click **Microsoft PowerPoint**. After a short pause the PowerPoint dialog box appears on the screen. See Figure 1-2.

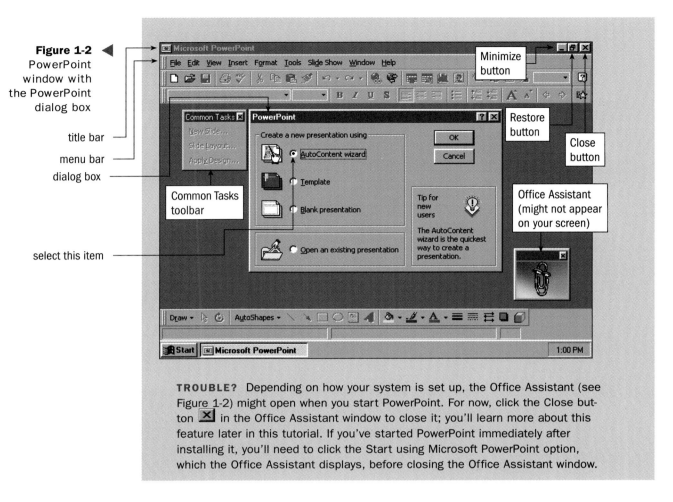

Figure 1-2
PowerPoint
window with
the PowerPoint
dialog box

title bar

menu bar

dialog box

Common Tasks
toolbar

select this item

TROUBLE? Depending on how your system is set up, the Office Assistant (see Figure 1-2) might open when you start PowerPoint. For now, click the Close button ⊠ in the Office Assistant window to close it; you'll learn more about this feature later in this tutorial. If you've started PowerPoint immediately after installing it, you'll need to click the Start using Microsoft PowerPoint option, which the Office Assistant displays, before closing the Office Assistant window.

Now that you've started PowerPoint, you're ready to create Carl's presentation. Your first step will be using the AutoContent Wizard.

Using the AutoContent Wizard to Create an Outline

PowerPoint helps you quickly create effective presentations by using wizards, which ask you a series of questions to determine the organizational structure and style for your presentation. The **AutoContent Wizard** lets you choose a presentation category such as "Product/Services Overview," "Recommending a Strategy," or "Generic." After you have selected the type of presentation you want, the AutoContent Wizard creates a general outline for you to follow.

If you open a new presentation without using the AutoContent Wizard, you must create your own outline, one slide at a time (though creating your own outline is more efficient if it doesn't fall into one of PowerPoint's predefined types). Carl, however, asks you to use the AutoContent Wizard because his presentation topic is a common one: recommending a strategy. The AutoContent Wizard will automatically create a title slide and standard outline, which you can then edit to fit Carl's presentation.

To create a presentation with the AutoContent Wizard:

1. With the PowerPoint startup dialog box on the screen, click the **AutoContent wizard** radio button, then click the **OK** button. The first of several AutoContent Wizard dialog boxes appears. See Figure 1-3.

Figure 1-3 ◄
AutoContent
Wizard dialog
box

current topic of
AutoContent Wizard

click to go to next
AutoContent Wizard
dialog box

TROUBLE? If the PowerPoint startup dialog box doesn't appear on your screen, click File, then click New. When the New Presentation dialog box opens, click the Presentations tab, click the AutoContent Wizard button, and then click the OK button.

TROUBLE? If the Office Assistant opens to ask if you want help with the AutoContent Wizard, click "No, don't provide help now."

2. Read the information in the AutoContent Wizard dialog box, then click the **Next** button to display the next dialog box of the AutoContent Wizard.

This dialog box allows you to select the type of presentation that you're going to give. Carl wants you to select a general presentation on recommending a strategy.

3. Make sure the **All** button is selected, if necessary click **Recommending a Strategy** in the list box, then click the **Next** button to display the next AutoContent Wizard dialog box.

This dialog box displays the question "How will this presentation be used?"

4. Make sure the **Presentations, informal meetings, handouts** radio button is selected, because Carl's presentation will be for an informal meeting. It will not be a presentation for the Internet or for a kiosk (a stand-alone booth or demonstration). Then click the **Next** button.

The next AutoContent dialog box allows you to specify the presentation style, that is, the mode of the presentation. See Figure 1-4.

Figure 1-4 ◄
AutoContent
Wizard dialog
box to specify
presentation
style

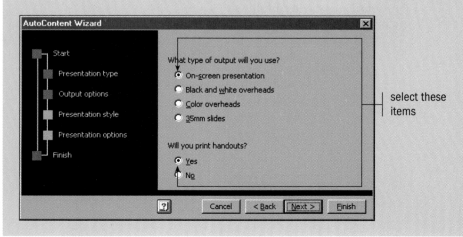

select these
items

PowerPoint

Carl wants you to create an on-screen presentation; he will make his presentation directly from a computer screen. Carl will also want you to print handouts for his presentation.

5. If necessary click the **On-screen presentation** radio button, make sure the **Yes** radio button is selected below the question "Will you print handouts?" then click the **Next** button to display the next AutoContent dialog box.

Here you'll specify the title and author of the presentation.

6. Drag I across all the text in the Presentation title text box, type **Reaching Potential Customers**, press the **Tab** key, type **Carl Vetterli** in the Your name text box, and then press the **Tab** key. If any text in the Additional information text box is highlighted, press the **Delete** key. See Figure 1-5.

Figure 1-5 ◀
AutoContent Wizard dialog box with presentation title and author

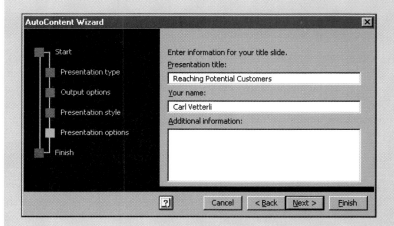

7. Click the **Next** button. The final AutoContent Wizard dialog box appears, letting you know that you have completed the AutoContent Wizard.

8. Click the **Finish** button. PowerPoint now displays the outline of the presentation that the AutoContent wizard automatically created, as well as a slide miniature of slide 1. If necessary drag the Common Tasks floating toolbar to the right side of the presentation window so it doesn't cover any text of the outline. See Figure 1-6.

Figure 1-6 ◀
PowerPoint window with outline of presentation

Standard toolbar

Formatting toolbar

presentation window

Outlining toolbar

View toolbar
status bar

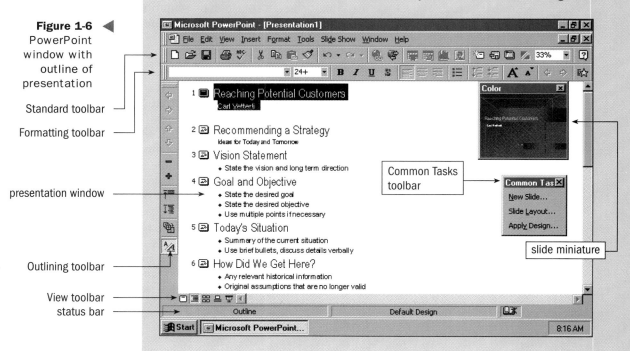

TROUBLE? If the presentation window doesn't fill the entire screen as in Figure 1-6, click the Maximize button in the upper-right corner of the presentation window, and, if necessary, drag the horizontal scroll button to the far left so you can see the left edge of the outline text.

You'll need to edit the outline that the AutoContent Wizard created to fit Carl's presentation, but first you should make sure that you're familiar with the PowerPoint window.

The PowerPoint Window

The PowerPoint window contains features common to all Windows programs, as well as features specific to PowerPoint, such as the options available on the toolbars.

Common Windows Elements

Several elements of the PowerPoint window are common to other Windows 95 programs. For example, as shown in Figure 1-2, the PowerPoint window has a title bar, menu bar, and window sizing buttons. These elements function the same way in PowerPoint as they do in other Windows programs. However, the PowerPoint window also includes items that are specific to PowerPoint, such as the toolbars.

The Toolbars

Like many Windows programs, PowerPoint supplies several toolbars, as shown in Figure 1-6. A **toolbar** is a horizontal or vertical ribbon of icons that provides menu shortcuts. When you move the mouse pointer over one of the icons on the toolbar, the outline of the button appears, followed by a **ToolTip**, which is a yellow box containing the name of the button. You will learn to use the toolbars for tasks that are repeated often, such as opening or saving a file.

The toolbar immediately below the menu bar is the **Standard toolbar**, which allows you to use many of the standard Windows and PowerPoint commands, such as opening an existing presentation, saving the current presentation to disk, printing the presentation, and cutting and pasting text and graphics. Below the Standard toolbar is the **Formatting toolbar**, which allows you to format the text of your presentations. The vertical toolbar on the left edge of the PowerPoint window is the **Outlining toolbar**, which allows you to change the view of or make modifications to the outline.

Finally the small toolbar immediately above the status bar is the **View toolbar**, which contains buttons that allow you to change the way you view a slide presentation. Each way of seeing a presentation is called a **view**, and the status bar indicates which view you are in. Notice that you are currently in Outline View. Clicking the **Slide View button** 🔲 allows you to see and edit text and graphics on an individual slide. In Slide View the Drawing toolbar is automatically displayed at the bottom of the screen instead of the Outlining toolbar. Clicking the **Slide Sorter View button** 🔳 changes the view to miniature images of all the slides at once. You use this view to change the order of the slides or set special features for your slide show. Clicking the **Notes Page View button** 🔲 changes the view so you can see and edit your presentation notes on individual slides. To present your slide show, you can click the **Slide Show button** 🖳.

As with other Windows programs, PowerPoint lets you select commands by using the menus with the keyboard or the mouse, by using shortcut keys, or by using toolbar buttons. Because the toolbar buttons are usually the easiest and fastest method of selecting commands, in these tutorials you will use the toolbars more often than the menus or keyboard.

Now that you're familiar with the PowerPoint window, you're ready to adapt PowerPoint's default outline to fit Carl's presentation.

Adapting an AutoContent Outline

After you complete the AutoContent Wizard, PowerPoint displays the outline with the title and Carl Vetterli's name in slide 1. PowerPoint also automatically includes other slides with suggested text located in placeholders. A **placeholder** is a region of a slide or a location in an outline reserved for inserting text or graphics. Furthermore, in Outline View, each main heading of the outline, or the **title** of each slide, appears to the right of the slide icon and slide number, as shown in Figure 1-6. The **main text** of each slide is indented and bulleted under the title.

To adapt the AutoContent outline to fit Carl's presentation, you must **select**, or high-light, the placeholders one at a time, and then replace them with other text.

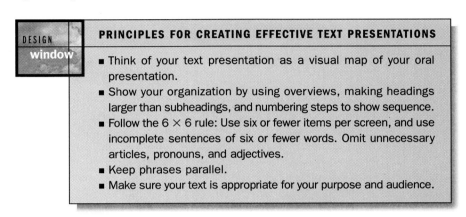

DESIGN window

PRINCIPLES FOR CREATING EFFECTIVE TEXT PRESENTATIONS

- Think of your text presentation as a visual map of your oral presentation.
- Show your organization by using overviews, making headings larger than subheadings, and numbering steps to show sequence.
- Follow the 6 × 6 rule: Use six or fewer items per screen, and use incomplete sentences of six or fewer words. Omit unnecessary articles, pronouns, and adjectives.
- Keep phrases parallel.
- Make sure your text is appropriate for your purpose and audience.

You'll now begin to replace the main text to fit Carl's presentation. Later, you'll need to edit it further to make sure it conforms with the 6 x 6 rule (see the Design Window above).

To replace the main text in a slide:

1. Position the pointer on the bullet that is located just beneath the title of slide 3. The text to the right of this bullet is "State the vision and long term direction." The pointer changes to ⊕.

2. Click ⊕ on the bullet to select the text. See Figure 1-7. By clicking a bullet, you can quickly select all the text in a bulleted item of the main text of a slide. (You could also select the text by positioning I before the "S" in the sentence "State the vision and long term direction" and dragging I over the text while holding down the mouse button.) Once the text is selected, you can begin typing to replace it.

Figure 1-7 ◀
Outline after
selecting item

slide icon ————

title of slide 3 ————

pointer on bullet ————

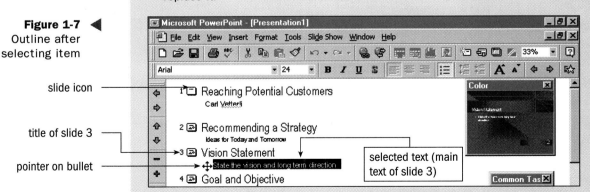

selected text (main text of slide 3)

3. Type **Inca can improve the quality of its produce**, then press the **Enter** key. Your screen should now look like Figure 1-8. Notice that as soon as you started typing, the selected text disappeared. Notice also that when you press the Enter key, PowerPoint automatically inserts a bullet for the next item in the list, and the insertion point appears to the right of the bullet.

Figure 1-8 ◀
New text in
outline

marked word not
found in the
PowerPoint dictionary

new bulleted item

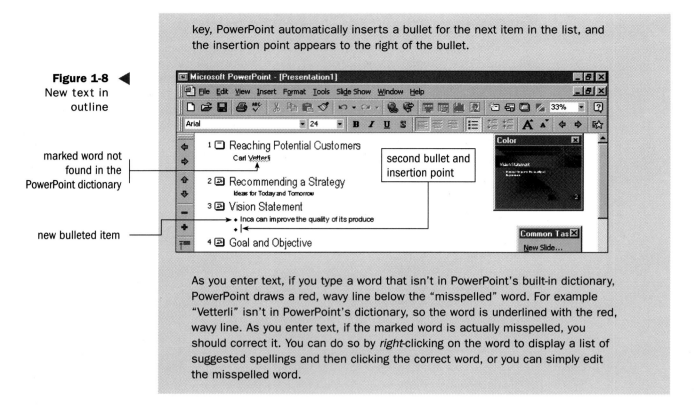

As you enter text, if you type a word that isn't in PowerPoint's built-in dictionary, PowerPoint draws a red, wavy line below the "misspelled" word. For example "Vetterli" isn't in PowerPoint's dictionary, so the word is underlined with the red, wavy line. As you enter text, if the marked word is actually misspelled, you should correct it. You can do so by *right*-clicking on the word to display a list of suggested spellings and then clicking the correct word, or you can simply edit the misspelled word.

Carl has two more bullets he wants you to add to the Vision Statement slide. You'll do that now.

To add new text to the outline:

1. Type **Inca can sell more produce to more customers**, then press the **Enter** key.

2. Type **Inca can become the clear market leader in southern California**, then press the **Enter** key. Your screen should now look like Figure 1-9.

Figure 1-9 ◀
Outline after
inserting new
text

new text

bullet to be deleted

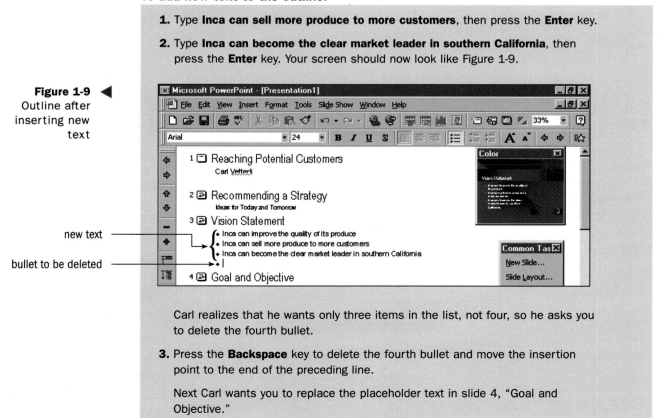

Carl realizes that he wants only three items in the list, not four, so he asks you to delete the fourth bullet.

3. Press the **Backspace** key to delete the fourth bullet and move the insertion point to the end of the preceding line.

Next Carl wants you to replace the placeholder text in slide 4, "Goal and Objective."

4. Make the changes to slide 4 using the text shown in Figure 1-10.

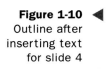

Figure 1-10 ◄
Outline after
inserting text
for slide 4

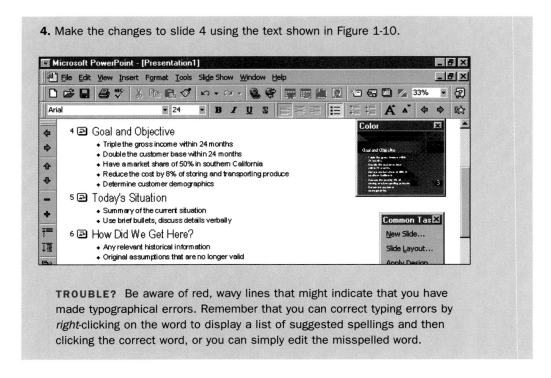

TROUBLE? Be aware of red, wavy lines that might indicate that you have made typographical errors. Remember that you can correct typing errors by *right*-clicking on the word to display a list of suggested spellings and then clicking the correct word, or you can simply edit the misspelled word.

Your presentation window should now look like Figure 1-10. You have made substantial progress on Carl's presentation but realize that you need to attend a meeting in a few minutes. Therefore you'll need to save your work and then exit PowerPoint.

Saving the Presentation and Exiting PowerPoint

In addition to saving your work before you exit PowerPoint, you should also save about every 15 minutes, so you won't lose all your work if, for example, a power failure occurs.

To save a presentation for the first time:

1. Place your Student Disk into the appropriate drive.

TROUBLE? If you don't have a Student Disk, you need to get one before you can proceed. Your instructor will either give you one or ask you to make your own by following the instructions on the "Read This Before You Begin" page before this tutorial. See your instructor or technical support person for more information.

2. Click the **Save** button 🖫 on the Standard toolbar. The Save dialog box opens.

3. Click the **Save in** list arrow, then click the drive that contains your Student Disk.

4. Double-click the **Tutorial.01** folder to open that folder.

5. Click in the **File name** text box, type **Reaching Potential Customers**, and then click the **Save** button.

PowerPoint saves the presentation to the disk using the filename Reaching Potential Customers. That name now appears in the title bar.

Having saved your work, you're now ready to exit PowerPoint.

To exit PowerPoint:

1. Click the **Close** button ⊠ in the upper-right corner of the PowerPoint window. (You could also click **File** on the menu bar, then click **Exit**.)

Quick Check

1 In one to three sentences, describe the purpose of the PowerPoint program and the components of a presentation that you can create with it.

2 Why should you plan a presentation before you create it? What are some of the presentation elements that should be considered?

3 Describe the purpose of the AutoContent Wizard.

4 Define the following terms:
   a. slide master
   b. placeholder
   c. title (on a slide)
   d. main text (on a slide)

5 What is the 6 × 6 rule?

6 What does a red, wavy line indicate?

7 Why is it important to save your work frequently?

When you return from your meeting, you'll continue to edit the text of Carl's presentation, as well as create speaker notes.

SESSION

1.2

In this session you will learn how to open an existing presentation, edit and change text in Outline View and Slide View, add and delete slides, and change the design template. You will also learn how to use PowerPoint's Help system, create speaker notes, and preview and print a presentation.

Editing the Presentation in Outline View

When you return from your meeting, Carl has already looked at the text of the first four slides. Reviewing the 6 × 6 rule, he realizes that in a slide presentation, each text item should be as short as possible. It's easier for the audience to read short phrases. In addition Carl knows that he'll be conveying most of the information orally, so the main text doesn't have to be in complete sentences.

Carl decides he wants you to apply the 6 × 6 rule as much as possible. To simplify the text in slide 3, you'll omit the company name because the audience will know Carl is talking about Inca Imports. Similarly, articles (for example, the, a), many possessive pronouns (for example, your, its), and most adjectives (for example, high, clear, very) can safely be left out of titles and the main text. Therefore Carl asks you to change "Inca can improve the quality of its produce" to "Improve quality of produce." Carl also realizes that by changing the title of slide 4 from "Goal and Objective," to "Two-Year Goals," he can delete the words "within 24 months" from the bulleted list.

You'll now make Carl's changes. First you need to start PowerPoint and open the presentation you worked on in the last session.

To start PowerPoint and open an existing presentation:

1. Using the steps described in Session 1.1, start PowerPoint.

2. With the PowerPoint startup dialog box on the screen, click the **Open an existing presentation** radio button, then click the **OK** button to display the Open dialog box.

3. Click the **Look in** list arrow to display the list of available drives, then click the drive that contains your Student Disk.

4. Double-click the **Tutorial.01** folder to open that folder, click **Reaching Potential Customers** in the Name list box, then click the **Open** button. Carl's presentation should now appear on your screen. If necessary click the **Maximize** button 🔲 so the presentation window fills the screen.

Now that you've opened Carl's presentation, you're ready to edit the outline.

To edit the outline:

1. Using Figure 1-11 as a guide, change the text of slides 3 and 4 of Carl's presentation by dragging I to select the text and then deleting or retyping it as necessary.

Figure 1-11 ◀
Text of slides
3 and 4

revised text ——

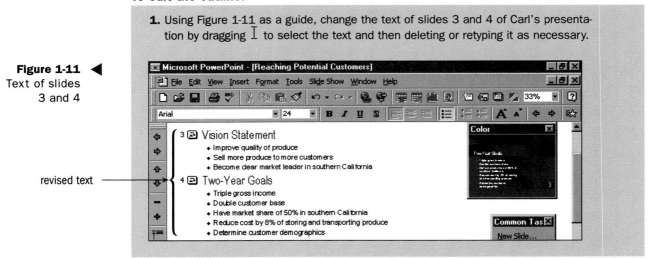

Carl reads through the text of the edited slides 3 and 4. He decides to switch the second and third items under "Two-Year Goals" (slide 4) and asks you to make this change.

Moving Text Up and Down in Outline View

In PowerPoint it's easy to switch main text items in Outline View. You'll reverse the order of the second and third items in slide 4 now.

To move an item of text in Outline View:

1. Click ✛ on the bullet to the left of the text "Have market share of 50% in southern California" in slide 4 to highlight the text.

2. Click the **Move Up** button 🔼 on the Outlining toolbar. The highlighted item is now moved up one position in the list, so the second and third items are switched. See Figure 1-12.

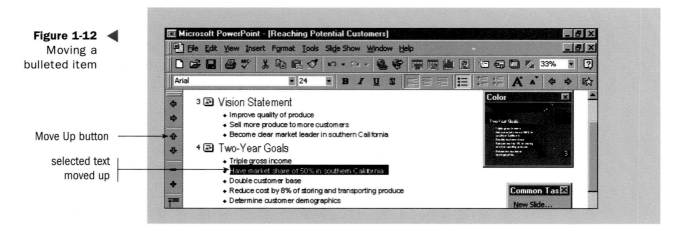

Figure 1-12 ◀
Moving a
bulleted item

Move Up button

selected text
moved up

You can also use this same method to move entire slides. You'll have a chance to practice moving an entire slide in both Outline View and Slide Sorter View in the Tutorial Assignments and Case Problems.

Carl reviews the change you made to slide 4 and realizes that he also needs to present more information on his customer demographics study. He decides the demographic information should be a separate slide and asks you to create it. Instead of deleting the bulleted item and then retyping it as a new slide title, you can promote the item from main text to slide title.

Promoting and Demoting the Outline Text

To **promote** an item means to increase the outline level of an item, for example, to change a bulleted item into a slide title. To **demote** an item means to decrease the outline level, for example, to change a slide title into a bulleted item within another slide.

You'll now promote the item "Determine customer demographics" to create the new slide.

To promote an item:

1. Click I anywhere within the bulleted item "Determine customer demographics" in slide 4.

2. Click the **Promote** button ◆ on either the Outlining toolbar or the Formatting toolbar. "Determine customer demographics" is now the title of a new slide 5, and "Today's Situation" becomes slide 6, as shown in Figure 1-13.

Figure 1-13 ◀
Outline text
after promoting
item
Promote button
(dimmed)

Demote button

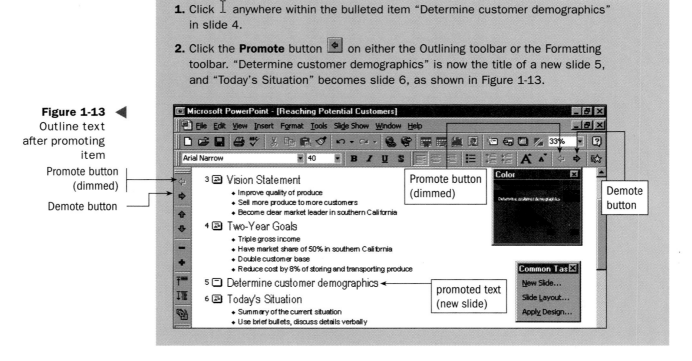

Because the title of slide 5 is wordy, Carl asks you to edit it.

3. Change the title "Determine customer demographics" to "Customer Demographics."

You're now ready to add the bulleted items beneath the title of slide 5. However, because the current outline level is a slide title, any text that you type will be at the same outline level, that is, a slide title. To add main text, therefore, you must move down a level in the outline. You can do this by using the Demote command.

To demote an item:

1. Click I at the end of the title "Customer Demographics," then press the **Enter** key. PowerPoint creates a new slide 6.

2. Click the **Demote** button [⇨] on the Outlining or Formatting toolbar to change the outline level from slide title to main text. PowerPoint creates a bullet, with the insertion point appearing to the right of it.

3. Type the main text of slide 5, as shown in Figure 1-14. Make sure you have typed the information correctly. Watch for any words that PowerPoint marks with a red, wavy line, indicating that the word isn't in PowerPoint's built-in dictionary. Make any necessary corrections.

Figure 1-14 ◀
Outline after
inserting text

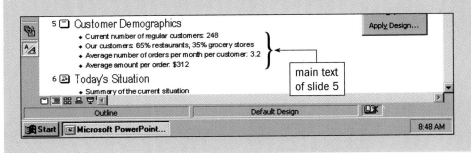

You have now created a new fifth slide for Carl's presentation. After reviewing the changes you've made to his presentation, Carl decides several slides are unnecessary. He asks you to delete these unnecessary slides that the AutoContent Wizard automatically created.

Deleting Slides

Carl decides that he doesn't need slides on "Recommending a Stategy," "Today's Situation," "How Did We Get Here?" or "Available Options." You can delete slides in any view except Slide Show View. However it's often easiest to delete slides in Outline View, which is the view you're currently in.

To delete slides in Outline View:

1. Click the **up arrow** on the vertical scroll bar until you can see all the text of slide 2 on the screen.

2. Click ✛ on the slide icon for slide 2. The title and the main text of slide 2 are selected. See Figure 1-15.

Figure 1-15 ◀
Selected text
to be deleted

selected slide icon ——

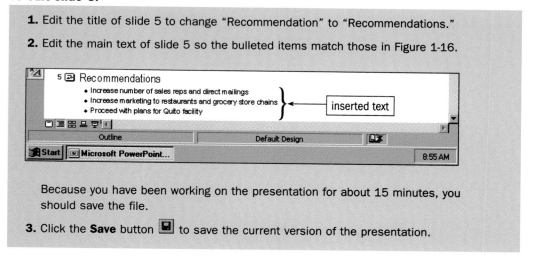

3. Click **Edit**, then click **Delete Slide**. (You could also press the **Backspace** key or the **Delete** key after selecting the slide to delete it.) The selected slide is deleted, and all the slides after it are renumbered.

4. To delete slides 5 ("Today's Situation"), 6 ("How Did We Get Here?"), and 7 ("Available Options") at the same time, scroll until you can see slide 7, click ✛ on the slide 5 icon, press and hold the **Shift** key, click ✛ on the slide 7 icon, and then press the **Backspace** key. When you get a warning dialog box, click the **OK** button to delete all three slides.

The new slide 5 in Carl's presentation is now "Recommendation." Carl asks you to edit that slide also.

To edit slide 5:

1. Edit the title of slide 5 to change "Recommendation" to "Recommendations."

2. Edit the main text of slide 5 so the bulleted items match those in Figure 1-16.

Figure 1-16 ◀
Text of slide 5

Because you have been working on the presentation for about 15 minutes, you should save the file.

3. Click the **Save** button 🔲 to save the current version of the presentation.

You have adapted and edited Carl's presentation in Outline View and completed the five slides of his presentation. Carl now wants you to use Slide View to see how his presentation looks.

Viewing Slides in Slide View

Viewing your presentation in Outline View doesn't show you how each of your slides will look during an actual presentation. You can get a better idea of how the slides will look from the Slide Miniature, but the miniature is too small to see the details and read the text. To see the slides as they will appear in a presentation, you must change to one of the other views. You'll now view the slides in Slide View.

To see slides in Slide View:

1. Scroll the presentation window so you can see the beginning of the outline, then click the pointer anywhere within the text of slide 1. This makes slide 1 the

current slide, so that when you switch to Slide View, slide 1 will appear on the screen first.

2. Click the **Slide View** button ⬚ on the View toolbar to display slide 1 in the presentation window. After looking over the slide, you will view the next slide.

3. Click the **Next Slide** button ⬚ at the bottom of the vertical scroll bar to display slide 2, "Vision Statement."

4. To view slide 3, drag the scroll box down until the message by the scroll box says that you're on slide 3, then release the mouse button. See Figure 1-17.

Figure 1-17 ◀
Moving scroll
box to slide 3

presentation
window in
Slide View

Drawing toolbar

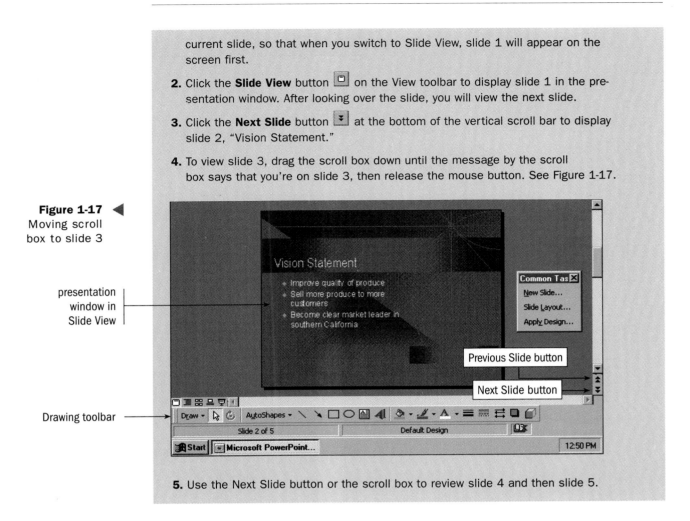

5. Use the Next Slide button or the scroll box to review slide 4 and then slide 5.

Carl has also viewed the presentation and decides further changes are necessary. He asks you to move text and add a new slide. You can make these changes in Slide View.

Editing the Presentation in Slide View

The advantage of editing in Outline View is that you can see much (or even all) of the text of your entire presentation at once. The disadvantage is that you can't see exactly how the text will appear in the completed slide show. For example in Outline View you can't see the text color, the background color, or the background graphics on the slides, but you can see these things in Slide View.

As Carl reviews slide 3 ("Two-Year Goals") of his PowerPoint presentation, he decides that the text of the fourth bullet is awkward. He wants to move the phrase "by 8%" to the end of the fourth item, so that it becomes "Reduce cost of storing and transporting produce by 8%." Carl asks you to change the text using the cut-and-paste method.

Moving Text Using Cut and Paste

Cut and paste is an important way to move text in PowerPoint. To **cut** means to remove text (or some other item) from the document and place it on the Windows Clipboard. The **Clipboard** is an area where text and graphics that have been cut or copied are stored until you act on them further. To **paste** means to transfer a copy of the text from the Clipboard into the document. To perform a cut-and-paste operation, you simply highlight the material you want to move, cut it, and then paste the material where you want it.

REFERENCE window	**CUTTING AND PASTING (MOVING) TEXT**
	■ Select the text you want to move. ■ Cut the selected text by clicking the Cut button on the Standard toolbar. ■ Move the insertion point to the target location in the presentation. ■ Paste the text back into the presentation by clicking the Paste button on the Standard toolbar.

You'll now change the text using the cut-and-paste method.

To move text using cut and paste:

1. In Slide View use the Previous Slide button or the scroll box to move to slide 3.

2. Select the phrase "by 8%" in the fourth item of slide 3 by dragging I over it. See Figure 1-18.

Figure 1-18 ◄
Selecting text
for cut and
paste

Cut button ———

Paste button ———

selected text ———

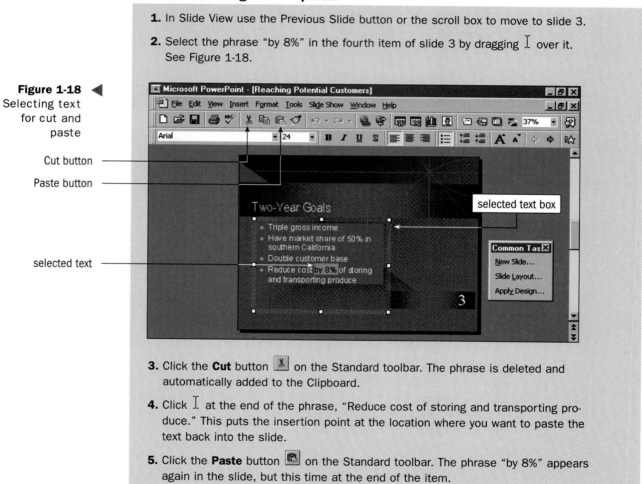

3. Click the **Cut** button on the Standard toolbar. The phrase is deleted and automatically added to the Clipboard.

4. Click I at the end of the phrase, "Reduce cost of storing and transporting produce." This puts the insertion point at the location where you want to paste the text back into the slide.

5. Click the **Paste** button on the Standard toolbar. The phrase "by 8%" appears again in the slide, but this time at the end of the item.

You can also use the cut-and-paste method to copy selected text instead of moving it; simply click the Copy button on the Standard toolbar instead of the Cut button. Then you can paste a copy of the text anywhere in the presentation.

Furthermore, in addition to cut and paste, you can use **drag and drop** to move text in PowerPoint. You simply select the text by dragging the pointer over it, move the pointer into the selected area, press and hold down the left mouse button while you drag the text, and then release the mouse button when the selected text is positioned where you want it. You'll have a chance to use drag and drop at the end of this tutorial.

Now that you've completed the changes for slide 3, you're ready to add a new slide to Carl's presentation.

Adding a New Slide and Choosing a Layout

Carl decides his presentation needs a slide that summarizes Inca Imports' new marketing plan, so he asks you to add a new slide. You'll add the slide in Slide View now.

To add a slide in Slide View:

1. With slide 3 still in the presentation window, click **New Slide** on the Common Tasks toolbar. (You could also click the **New Slide** button ⊡ on the Standard toolbar.) PowerPoint displays the New Slide dialog box. See Figure 1-19.

Figure 1-19 ◀
New Slide
dialog box

select this layout ——

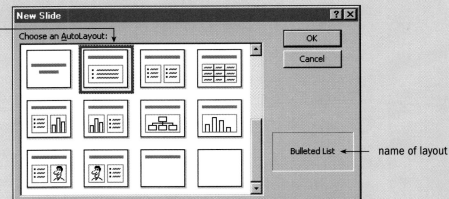

name of layout

Before adding a new slide, you must decide where you want the placeholders for titles, text, and graphics to go. PowerPoint gives you the option of selecting from a variety of AutoLayout slides, which are preformatted slides with placeholders already in them. You can also choose a Blank layout.

2. Click on a few of the AutoLayouts, and read their names in the lower-right corner of the dialog box. If you wanted to start with a blank slide, you would click the Blank layout, which is in the fourth column of the third row. However Carl wants his new slide to be a bulleted list.

3. If necessary scroll up in the Choose an AutoLayout list box, then click the second layout in the top row, titled Bulleted List. See Figure 1-19.

4. Click the **OK** button. PowerPoint inserts a new slide containing a title and main text placeholder for the bulleted list.

5. Click the title placeholder (where the slide says "Click to add title"), then type **Our New Marketing Campaign**.

6. Click the main text placeholder, then type the three bulleted items shown in Figure 1-20.

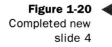

Figure 1-20 ◄
Completed new
slide 4

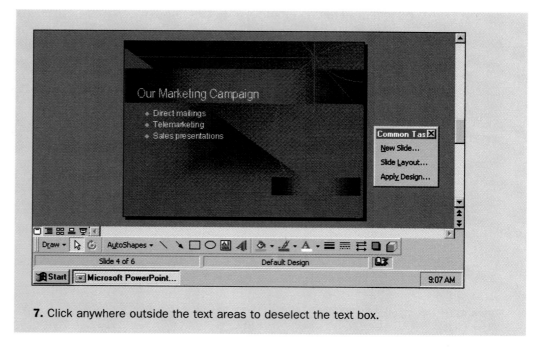

7. Click anywhere outside the text areas to deselect the text box.

You have now added a new slide, with a new layout. Carl is almost satisfied with the slides, but he thinks the design template should be changed to one that is more appropriate for his presentation.

Changing the Design Template

When you use the AutoContent Wizard or open a blank presentation, PowerPoint provides a predetermined **design template**, that is, the colors and format of the background and the type style of the titles, accents, and other text. The default design template that PowerPoint uses with the "Recommending a Strategy" option in the AutoContent Wizard is titled Default Design, with certain colors for the text, background, and graphics. You can easily change the default design template to one of many more that PowerPoint provides. To change the design template, you click the Apply Design button on the Standard toolbar.

Carl wants you to change the template for his presentation to the one titled Ribbons.

To change the template:

1. Click the **Apply Design** button 🔲 on the Standard toolbar. (You could also click **Apply Design** on the Common Tasks toolbar.) The Apply Design dialog box opens. See Figure 1-21.

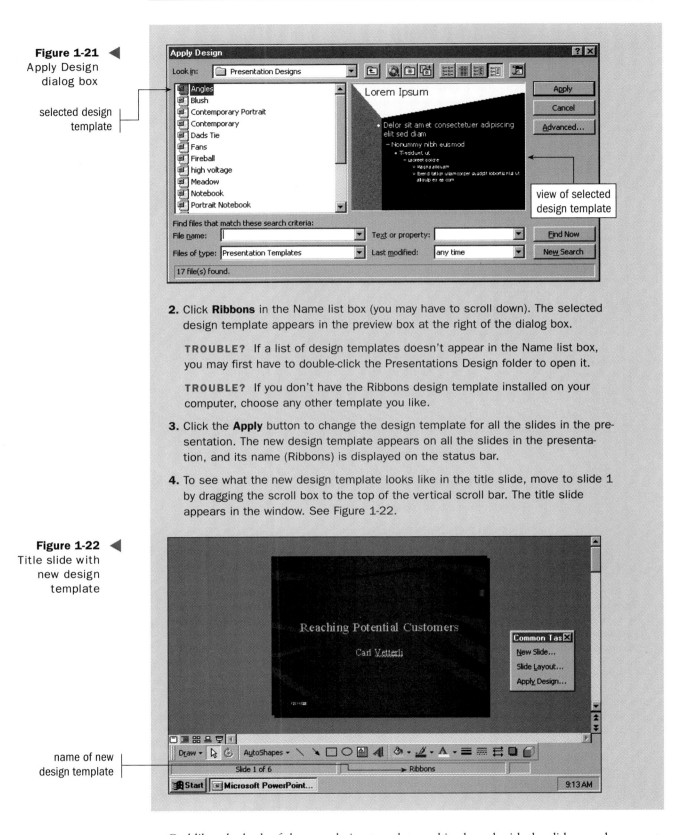

Figure 1-21
Apply Design
dialog box

selected design
template

view of selected
design template

Figure 1-22
Title slide with
new design
template

name of new
design template

2. Click **Ribbons** in the Name list box (you may have to scroll down). The selected design template appears in the preview box at the right of the dialog box.

   TROUBLE? If a list of design templates doesn't appear in the Name list box, you may first have to double-click the Presentations Design folder to open it.

   TROUBLE? If you don't have the Ribbons design template installed on your computer, choose any other template you like.

3. Click the **Apply** button to change the design template for all the slides in the presentation. The new design template appears on all the slides in the presentation, and its name (Ribbons) is displayed on the status bar.

4. To see what the new design template looks like in the title slide, move to slide 1 by dragging the scroll box to the top of the vertical scroll bar. The title slide appears in the window. See Figure 1-22.

Carl likes the look of the new design template and is pleased with the slides you have created for his presentation. You're now ready to prepare the other parts of Carl's presentation: the speaker notes and audience handouts (which are simply a printout of the slides). **Speaker notes** are printed pages that contain a picture of and notes about each slide to help the speaker remember what to say while a particular slide is displayed during the presentation. Because you aren't sure how to create speaker notes, you consult the PowerPoint Help system.

Getting Help

The PowerPoint Help system provides the same options as the Help system in other Windows programs—the Help Contents, the Help Index, and the Find feature, which are available on the Help menu. The PowerPoint Help system also provides additional ways to get help as you work—the Office Assistant and the What's This? command.

You'll learn how to use the Office Assistant next in this section. The What's This? 〈？ command provides context-sensitive help information. When you choose this command from the Help menu, the pointer changes to the Help pointer, which you can then use to click any object or option on the screen to see a description of the object.

Finding Information with the Office Assistant

The **Office Assistant** is an interactive guide to finding information in the Help system. You can ask the Office Assistant a question, and it will look through the Help system to find an answer.

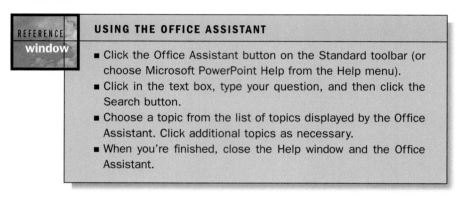

REFERENCE window	**USING THE OFFICE ASSISTANT**
	■ Click the Office Assistant button on the Standard toolbar (or choose Microsoft PowerPoint Help from the Help menu).
	■ Click in the text box, type your question, and then click the Search button.
	■ Choose a topic from the list of topics displayed by the Office Assistant. Click additional topics as necessary.
	■ When you're finished, close the Help window and the Office Assistant.

You'll use the Office Assistant to get help about creating speaker notes in PowerPoint.

To get help about speaker notes:

1. Click the **Office Assistant** button 〔図〕 on the Standard toolbar. The Office Assistant appears and displays a dialog box with several options. See Figure 1-23. The Office Assistant dialog box shown on your screen may not display all the options shown in the figure.

Figure 1-23 ◄
Office
Assistant
dialog box

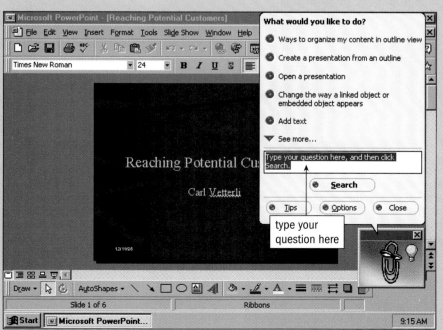

You can now type a question in the text box and have the Office Assistant look for an answer to your question.

2. Type **How do I create speaker notes?** and then click the **Search** option. The Office Assistant displays a list of relevant topics.

3. Click the topic **Create speaker notes and handouts**. The Office Assistant displays the text for the topic in the Help window. See Figure 1-24.

Figure 1-24 ◀
Help window
after clicking
topic "Create
speaker notes
and handouts"

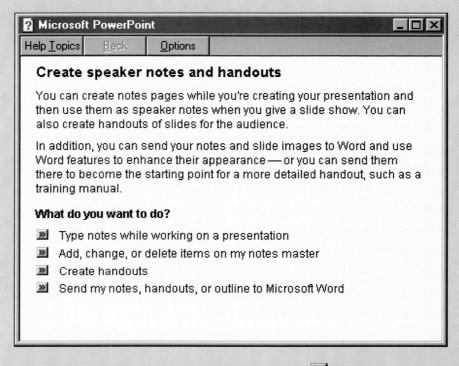

4. After reading the information, click the **Close** button ⊠ on the Help window and then on the Office Assistant window to close both windows.

After reading about speaker notes, you're now ready to create them for Carl's presentation.

Creating Speaker Notes

You'll create speaker notes for three of the slides in Carl's presentation.

To create speaker notes:

1. Make sure slide 1 still appears in the presentation window, then click the **Notes Page View** button ▣. PowerPoint now displays a page for the speaker notes for slide 1, with the placeholder "Click to add text" in a blank text box.

2. Click the **Zoom** list arrow on the Standard toolbar and click **100%** so that you can see the speaker notes at full size, and then, if necessary, scroll so you can see the "Click to add text" placeholder.

3. Click the placeholder and type **Welcome the participants**, press the **Enter** key, type **Thank them for coming**, press the **Enter** key, and type **State need for this meeting: to find ways to increase customer base**.

This completes the notes for slide 1. See Figure 1-25.

Figure 1-25 ◀
Notes Page
View of slide 1

partial view of slide

text of
speaker notes

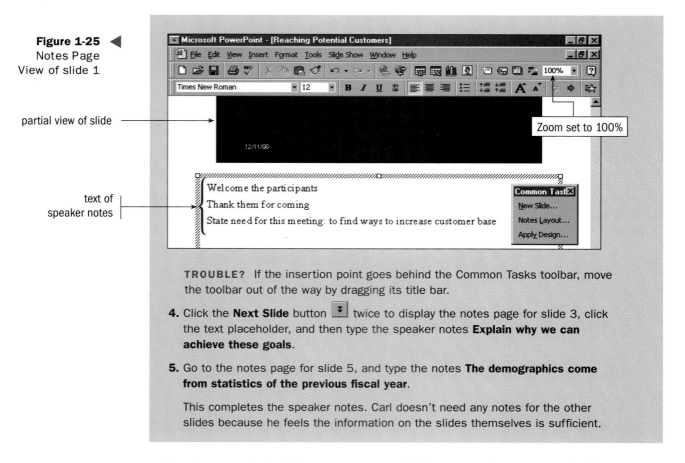

TROUBLE? If the insertion point goes behind the Common Tasks toolbar, move the toolbar out of the way by dragging its title bar.

4. Click the **Next Slide** button twice to display the notes page for slide 3, click the text placeholder, and then type the speaker notes **Explain why we can achieve these goals**.

5. Go to the notes page for slide 5, and type the notes **The demographics come from statistics of the previous fiscal year**.

This completes the speaker notes. Carl doesn't need any notes for the other slides because he feels the information on the slides themselves is sufficient.

You have made significant progress on Carl's presentation, so you should now save your work. Because you saved the presentation previously, you can simply click the Save button to save the current version of the file over the now obsolete version.

To save a file that has been saved previously:

1. Make sure your Student Disk is still in the disk drive.

2. Click on the Standard toolbar to save the file using its current filename, Reaching Potential Customers.

A copy of the updated presentation is now on your Student Disk.

Viewing the Completed Slide Show

You now want to look over Carl's completed presentation.

To view the completed presentation as a slide show:

1. Change to Slide View and scroll up to view slide 1, click the **Zoom** list arrow on the Standard toolbar, and then click **Fit**. Now the slide fits into the presentation window.

2. Click the **Slide Show** button on the View toolbar.

3. After you read a slide, click the left mouse button or press the **spacebar** to advance to the next slide. Continue advancing until you have seen the entire slide show and PowerPoint returns to Slide View. You can also exit the slide show at any time by pressing the Esc key.

Carl is satisfied with the presentation; you can now print the handouts and speaker notes.

Previewing and Printing the Presentation

Usually, before you print or present a slide show, you should do a final spell check of all the slides and speaker notes by using PowerPoint's Spell Checker feature. You'll have a chance to use the spell checker in the Tutorial Assignments and Case Problems at the end of this tutorial.

Before printing on your black-and-white printer, you should preview the presentation to make sure the text is legible in black and white.

To preview the presentation in black and white:

1. Make sure slide 1, in Slide View, appears on your screen, then click the **Black and White View** button 🔳 on the Standard toolbar. See Figure 1-26.

Figure 1-26 ◀
Slide in black-and-white view

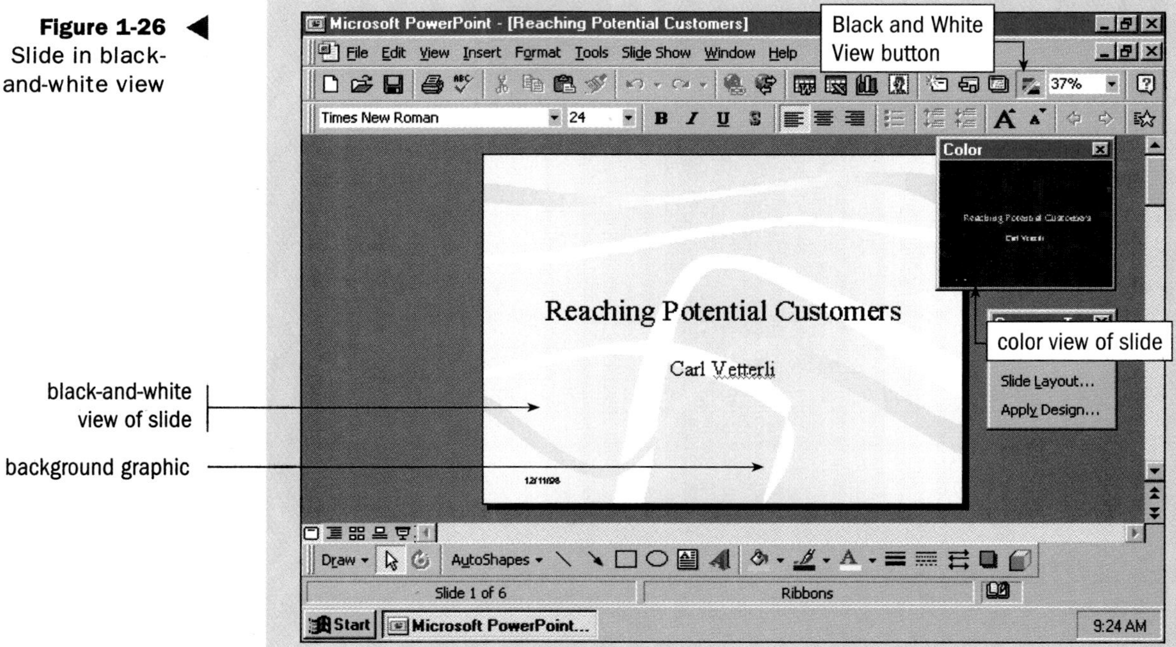

black-and-white view of slide

background graphic

2. Look at the text on each slide to make sure it is legible. Depending on your Windows printer driver, the background graphics of the Ribbons design template might make some of the text hard to read, so you might want to omit the graphics from the slides.

3. Click **Format**, click **Background** to display the Background dialog box, click the **Omit background graphics from master** check box, and then click the **Apply to all** button. The slide appears as before, except without the background graphics.

4. Click **File**, then click the **Print** button to open the Print dialog box. Don't click the Print button on the Standard toolbar or PowerPoint will immediately start printing without letting you change the print settings.

5. Click the **Print what** list arrow and select **Handouts (3 slides per page)**. If you're using a black-and-white printer, make sure the **Black & white** check box is selected. See Figure 1-27.

Figure 1-27 ◀
Print dialog box

item to print ────────

select this ────────

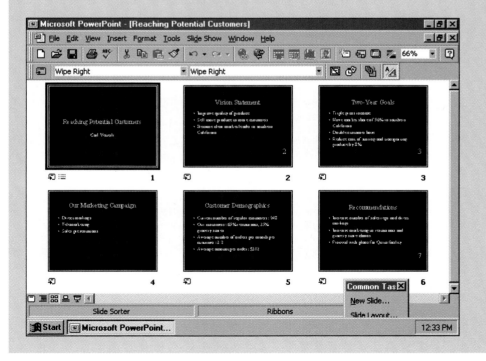

6. Click the **OK** button to print the handouts. Be patient. Graphics usually take a long time to print, even on a fast printer. You should have two handout pages, each containing three slides.

You're now ready to print the speaker notes.

7. Again, click the **Print what** list arrow, but this time select **Notes Pages**. Then click the **OK** button to print the speaker notes.

8. To see how the slides look as a group, first click the **Black and White View** button 🖼 to return to color view, then click the **Slide Sorter View** button 🖼. If necessary drag the Common Tasks toolbar so it doesn't cover any of the slides. Compare your handouts with the six slides shown in Figure 1-28.

Figure 1-28 ◀
Completed
presentation in
Slide Sorter
View

Now that you have created, edited, saved, and printed Carl's presentation, you can exit PowerPoint.

To exit PowerPoint:

1. Click ☒ in the upper-right corner of the PowerPoint window. Because you have made changes since the last time you saved the presentation, PowerPoint displays a dialog box with the message "Do you want to save the changes you made to Reaching Potential Customers?"

2. Click the **Yes** button to save the current version and exit PowerPoint.

Quick Check

1 Explain how to do the following in Outline View:
a. move text up
b. delete a slide
c. change placeholder text
d. edit text

2 What does it mean to promote a slide in Outline View? To demote a slide?

3 Explain a benefit of Outline View over Slide View and a benefit of Slide View over Outline View.

4 Explain how to do the following:
a. move text using cut and paste in any view
b. add a slide in Slide View

5 What is a design template? How do you change the template in a presentation?

6 How does the Office Assistant provide help?

7 What are speaker notes? How do you create them?

8 Why is it necessary to preview a presentation before printing it?

You have created a presentation using the AutoContent Wizard, edited it to fit Carl's presentation, and created and printed speaker notes and handouts. Carl thanks you for your help; he believes that your work will allow him to make an effective presentation.

Tutorial Assignments

After Carl presents his market research to his colleagues, Enrique Hoffman (Director of Marketing) decides he needs to present a new marketing campaign, based on Carl's research. Before presenting to his colleagues at Inca Imports, Enrique asks you to finalize his slides by doing the following:

1. Start PowerPoint and make sure your Student Disk is in the disk drive.

2. Click the Open an existing file radio button, open the file Campaign in the Tutorial.01 TAssign folder on your Student Disk, and save the file as New Marketing Campaign. (To save a file with a different filename, click File, click Save As, type the new filename in the File name text box, and then click the Save button.)

3. In Outline View, delete the unnecessary articles "a," "an," and "the" from each main text slide.

4. In slide 2, move (using drag and drop) the phrase "by telephone" so it immediately follows the phrase "Follow up" in the same item of the main text.
a. Select the phrase "by telephone."

   b. Move the pointer within the region of the selected text, press and hold the mouse button, drag the pointer to the right of the words "Follow up," and then release the mouse button.

   c. Click anywhere outside the text area to deselect the text.

5. Move the second item in slide 3, "Will develop slide presentation," down so that it becomes the third (last) item in the main text.

6. In slide 4, the third item of the main text is "Step #2. Establishing Contact with Potential Customers." Promote that item to become a slide title (new slide 5).

7. In the new slide 6, demote the second, third, and fourth bulleted items so they appear indented beneath the first item, "Organize data for our market advantage."

8. Edit the main text of slide 8 so the phrase "Must hire" becomes simply "Hire."

9. Move the entire slide 9 ("Key Issues") up to become slide 8, so that "Becoming More Effective" is the last slide. *Hint:* Remember that to move an entire slide, you click on the slide icon and then click the Move Up button.

10. Spell check the presentation by clicking Tools, then clicking Spelling. When PowerPoint stops at a word that is misspelled, click the correctly spelled word from within the Suggestions, so that it becomes the "Change To" word, and then click the Change button. If PowerPoint stops at a word that is actually spelled correctly but that it doesn't recognize, click the Ignore button.

11. View the entire presentation in Slide Show View.

12. Use the Save command to save the presentation to your Student Disk using the default filename.

13. Use the Office Assistant to find out how to print the outline of the presentation, and then do so.

14. Close the file.

Case Problems

1. New Weave Fashions Shaunda Shao works for New Weave Fashions, a clothing supplier for specialty retail stores in the Northwest. New Weave contracts with wholesale fashion centers to supply New Weave retailers with women's shoes, sports fashions, and boutique merchandise. Shaunda's job is to provide training for New Weave's fledgling retailers. She asks you to help her finalize a presentation she'll use as part of training. Do the following:

1. Open the file Newweave in the Tutorial.01 Cases folder on your Student Disk and save the file as New Weave.

2. In the first bulleted item in slide 2, use cut and paste to move the year ("1998") from the end of the line of text to the beginning, delete the word "in" that now appears at the end of the line, and change "Sales" to "sales."

3. In the second bulleted item in slide 2, use drag and drop to move "increased only 5.5%" from the middle of the line to the end of the line of text. *Hint:* See Tutorial Assignment 4 for instructions for using drag and drop.

4. In slide 4, divide the second item into two separate items, and then revise the results so that they become "Obtaining volume discounts," and "Obtaining quick, reliable delivery."

5. Also in slide 4, move the last item ("Competing with well-known stores") so it becomes the second item in the main text of slide 2.

6. In slide 6, promote the phrase "Telephone follow-ups" so that it is on the same level as the bulleted item above it.

7. Spell check the presentation by using the Spelling button on the Standard toolbar or by clicking Tools, then clicking Spelling. *Hint*: See Tutorial Assignment 10 for more details on spell checking the presentation.

8. View all the slides of the presentation in Slide Show View.

9. Preview the slides in Black and White View. If some of the text is illegible, change the design template to make the text readable or delete the background graphics.

10. Save the file using its default filename.

11. Use the Help Index to find out how to print only slide 5, and then do so. *Hint*: Click Help on the menu bar, click Contents and Index, click the Index tab, type "printing" in the text box labeled 1, click handouts, and then click the Display button to display the Topics Found dialog box.

12. Print handouts of all the slides (3 slides per page) in black and white, and close the file.

2. InfoTech Pratt Deitschmann is seeking venture capital in the amount of $2.5 million for his startup company, InfoTech. InfoTech provides mailroom, word processing, in-house printing, and other information-output services for large corporations and law practices. Pratt has created a presentation to give to executives at A.B. O'Dair & Company, a New York City investment banking firm, and has asked you to finalize it by doing the following:

1. Open the file Infotech in the Tutorial.01 Cases folder on your Student Disk and save the file as InfoTech Capital.

2. Use the What's This? Help feature to learn how to increase the size of the title of slide 1 from 44 to 48 points, and then do so. *Hint*: Click Help on the menu bar, click What's This? and then click the pointer on the Increase Font Size button on the Formatting toolbar.

3. Delete "and Objective" from the title of slide 2.

4. Add the following speaker notes to the notes page of slide 3: "Remind audience that we are a customer-centered company."

5. Delete the first item of the main text of slide 4.

6. In slide 4, promote the four items that are double-indented to single-indented, so that all items in the main text are at the same level.

7. In slide 5, move the second item of the main text to become the third (last) item.

8. In slide 7, use cut and paste to move the text and make other changes so that the first item becomes "Initial venture capital of $2.5 million."

9. Spell check the presentation by using the Spelling button on the Standard toolbar or by clicking Tools, and then clicking Spelling. *Hint:* See Tutorial Assignment 10 for more details on spell checking the presentation.

10. Use Slide Show View to view the entire presentation.

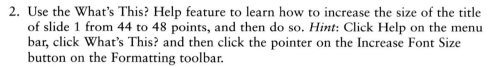

11. You decide to switch slides 5 and 6. Switch to Slide Sorter View, click on slide 6, press and hold the left mouse button, then drag it to the left. When a line appears to the left of slide 5, release the mouse button.

12. Save the file using the current filename.

13. Preview the slides in black and white to make sure they are all legible. If any text isn't legible, delete the background graphics from the design template.

14. Print the slides as handouts (6 slides per page).

15. Close the file.

3. Team One Facilities Management Virgil Pino works for Team One Facilities Management, an international company that manages municipal waste disposal facilities. Virgil asks you to help him to communicate the unfortunate news that escalating travel costs threaten Team One's profitability. Do the following:

1. Close any presentation that might be in the PowerPoint presentation window.

 2. Begin a new presentation by clicking File, then clicking New on the menu bar. In the New Presentation dialog box, click the Presentation Designs tab, click the Whirlpool icon, and then click the OK button.

3. In the New Slide dialog box, select the Title Slide layout button, and then click the OK button.

4. In Slide View replace the slide placeholders with the presentation title, "Rescuing Our Road Warriors," and the name of the author, "Virgil Pino."

 5. Virgil has already created some of the text for other slides, so insert the file Teamone into the current presentation.
   a. Click Insert and then click Slides from File to open the Slide Finder dialog box.
   b. Make sure the Find Presentation tab is selected, and then click the Browse button to locate and select the Teamone file in the Tutorial.01 Cases folder on your Student Disk.
   c. Click the Open button in the Insert Slides From File dialog box, click the Display button in the Slide Finder dialog box, click the Insert All button, and then click the Close button.

6. In slide 3, add a new bulleted item between the last and the next-to-the-last items. Type the text of the item, "Cost per trip increased by 30%."

7. Insert a new slide 4 in the Bulleted List layout (located on the first row, second column of the AutoLayout dialog box), and then click the OK button. Make the title of the slide "Alternatives Considered." Type the following four items in the main text of the slide:
   a. Decrease amount of travel
   b. Decrease travel costs
   c. Increase other means of networking
   d. Increase efficiency of each trip

8. In slide 5, delete the item, "Coordinate trips to visit more clients per trip."

9. Switch to Outline View and promote the item "Managers' Vision for the Future" so that it becomes the title of a new slide (slide 6).

10. In slide 6, move the first item in the main text so it becomes the last item.

11. In Outline View, add a new slide 7 in the Bulleted List layout, with the title "Summary" and with the bulleted items "Change to meet growth," "Overcome efficiency gap," "Manage travel time and money better," and "Rescue our road warriors."

 12. Create a new slide 8 while still in Outline View. Then go into Slide View, and change the Slide Layout to Blank. *Hint:* To change a slide layout, click Format, click Slide Layout, select the Blank layout, then click the Apply button.

 13. Spell check the presentation by using the Spelling button on the Standard toolbar or by clicking Tools, then clicking Spelling. *Hint:* See Tutorial Assignment 10 for more details on spell checking the presentation.

14. Save the presentation using the filename Rescuing Our Road Warriors.

15. Preview the slides in black and white, then print them as handouts (6 slides per page).

16. Close the file.

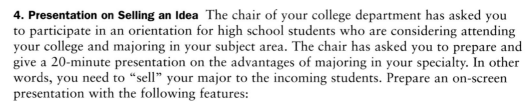

4. Presentation on Selling an Idea The chair of your college department has asked you to participate in an orientation for high school students who are considering attending your college and majoring in your subject area. The chair has asked you to prepare and give a 20-minute presentation on the advantages of majoring in your specialty. In other words, you need to "sell" your major to the incoming students. Prepare an on-screen presentation with the following features:

1. Use the AutoContent Wizard to begin developing an outline on "Project Overview." *Hint*: To start the AutoContent Wizard while PowerPoint is already running, click File, then click New. Don't use the New button on the Standard toolbar. In the New Presentation dialog box, click the Presentations tab, then double-click the AutoContent Wizard icon.

2. Make the title of your presentation (that is, what you're going to talk about) "Majoring in..." (with the name of your major). If you haven't selected a major, use one that you're considering.

3. Change the design template to Notebook, or to another template of your choice if Notebook is not available on your system.

4. Use the Help Contents to find out how to change the color of slide 1's title from brown to red, and then do so. *Hint:* Click Help on the menu bar, click Contents and Index, make sure the Contents tab is selected, click Adding and Formatting Text, click the Open button, click Change text color, and then click the Display button. Close the Help window after you finish reading it.

5. In slide 2, change the title to "Objective" and the main text placeholders to objectives of your presentation. For example you might want to use bulleted items such as "To show that ... is a good major," "To give overview of requirements," and "To list future jobs for ... majors." Include at least three objectives.

6. In slide 3, "Description," change the main text placeholders to list the requirements of your major.

7. In slide 4, change the title to "Meeting Your Needs," and then list in the main text several ways in which your major meets students' needs.

8. Delete slides 5 ("Competitive Analysis, cont.") and 6 ("Technology").

9. In the new slide 5, "Team/Resources," change the title to "Our Strengths" and list some of the resources of your department, such as "Friendly faculty," "Moderate course load," and "Opportunities for research."

10. Delete the remaining slides.

11. Add a new slide 6, "Summary," in which you summarize key points of your presentation.

12. Spell check the presentation by using the Spelling button on the Standard toolbar or by clicking Tools, and then clicking Spelling. *Hint:* See Tutorial Assignment 10 for more details on spell checking the presentation.

13. Preview the presentation in Slide Show View and Black and White View.

14. Save the presentation as "Majoring in ..." (with the name of your major).

15. Print the outline of your presentation.

16. Close the file.

Creating Graphics for Your Slides

Creating a Sales Presentation for Inca Imports

OBJECTIVES

In this tutorial you will:

- Resize and move text boxes and graphics boxes

- Remove background graphics

- Change the layouts of existing slides

- Insert pictures and clip-art images

- Create an organization chart

- Draw and manipulate a simple graphic using AutoShapes

CASE

Inca Imports Sales Presentation

Using the information gathered about Inca Imports' customers, Enrique Hoffmann, Director of Marketing, and his staff have identified other businesses in the southern California area that fit the profile of potential new customers. Enrique and his staff will focus their marketing efforts on these retail customers, who would benefit from having a wide range of fresh produce, year-round availability, and responsive customer service. Enrique and his staff are ready to prepare a presentation for these prospective clients.

In this tutorial you'll revise Enrique's current version of his PowerPoint presentation by reformatting and adding graphics to some of the slides. A **graphic** is a picture, clip art, graph, chart, or table that you can add to a slide.

In this session you will learn how to resize and move text boxes and graphics boxes, and to insert pictures and clip-art images.

Planning the Presentation

The marketing staff begins by planning their presentation:

- **Purpose of the presentation:** To convince potential new customers to start buying Inca Imports' products and services

- **Type of presentation:** A 45-minute sales presentation

- **Audience:** Retail buyers and other business representatives

- **Location of presentation:** A conference room at the offices of Inca Imports

- **Audience needs:** To recognize their need for Inca Imports' products and services and to understand how Inca Imports differs from other produce suppliers

- **Format:** One speaker presenting an electronic slide show consisting of five to seven slides

Resizing and Moving Text Boxes

After planning the presentation, Enrique and his staff created slides containing only text, knowing that they would later need to add graphics to make the presentation more interesting and effective.

DESIGN window	**USING GRAPHICS EFFECTIVELY**
	You should use graphics in the following situations: ■ To present information that words can't communicate effectively ■ To interest and motivate the reader ■ To communicate relationships quickly ■ To increase understanding and retention

Enrique has asked you to add a picture, clip art, organization chart, and graphic to his presentation. To begin you'll first need to start PowerPoint, open the current draft of Enrique's presentation, and then save it with a new filename.

To open an existing presentation and save it with a new name:

1. Start PowerPoint so the PowerPoint startup dialog box appears on the screen. You'll now retrieve the presentation that Enrique created using the AutoContent Wizard.

2. Make sure your Student Disk is in the disk drive, click the **Open an existing presentation** radio button in the PowerPoint startup dialog box, and then click the **OK** button (or press the **Enter** key). The Open dialog box appears on the screen.

TROUBLE? If the PowerPoint startup dialog box does not appear on your screen, click the Open button on the Standard toolbar to display the Open dialog box.

3. Open the Tutorial.02 folder on your Student Disk.

4. Click **Incasale** in the Names list box, then click the **Open** button. Slide 1 of the file Incasale, in Slide View, appears in the presentation window. Move the floating Common Tasks toolbar to the lower-right corner of the presentation window so it doesn't cover important parts of the slide. See Figure 2-1.

Figure 2-1 ◀
Slide 1 of the
presentation in
Slide View

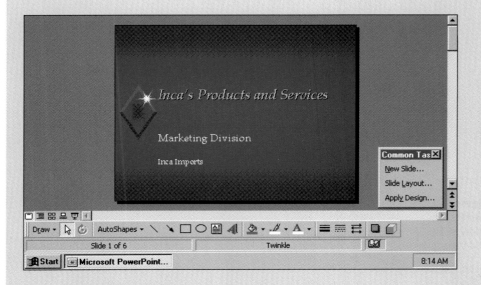

TROUBLE? If the presentation appears in a different view, click the Slide View button to get into Slide View.

TROUBLE? If the presentation window isn't maximized, click the Maximize button in the upper-right corner of the presentation window.

You're now ready to save the presentation using a different filename, just in case you need to revert to Enrique's original file.

5. Click **File**, then click **Save As** to open the Save As dialog box.

6. In the File name text box, type the new filename **Inca Sales Presentation**, and then click the **Save** button.

With the presentation open and saved with a new filename, you're ready to begin adding graphics to Enrique's presentation. To do this you'll work in Slide View, which allows you to view and modify the position, size, and alignment of text boxes and graphics (you can't do this in Outline View). **Text boxes** are the regions of the slide that contain text. On the title slide (slide 1) of Enrique's presentation, there are two text boxes: the first text box contains the presentation title ("Inca's Products and Services"), and the second text box contains the subtitle ("Marketing Division" with the company's name, "Inca Imports"). Text boxes and graphics are examples of objects. An **object** is any item (text box, clip art, graph, organization chart, or picture) on a slide that you can move, resize, rotate, or otherwise manipulate.

REFERENCE
window

RESIZING AND MOVING AN OBJECT

- Click anywhere on the object to select it. Resize handles appear around the object box.
- Drag a resize handle to change the size of the object.
- Drag the object (for a text box, use the edge of the box) to a new location to move the object.

On the title slide Enrique wants you to change the location of the text boxes for the title and subtitle, and then add the company's logo. A **logo** is a visual identification for a company. You'll need to make room for the logo on the left side of the slide by moving the two text boxes on the slide.

To resize and move text boxes on a slide:

1. Click I anywhere in the text of the title "Inca's Products and Services." A box appears around the text. See Figure 2-2. Notice that resize handles appear in the corners and on the edges of the text box. **Resize handles** are small squares, which, when dragged with the pointer, change the size of the box.

Figure 2-2 ◄
Presentation
window with
selected object

selected text box ——

resize handle ——

2. Position the pointer over the resize handle in the lower-left corner of the text box, so the pointer changes to ↗.

3. Press and hold the mouse button, then drag the resize handle down and to the right to make the text box the approximate dimensions shown in Figure 2-3. Notice that a dotted outline of the text box follows the pointer movements. Don't worry about making the text box exactly like that shown in the figure. Just resize it as closely as you can.

Figure 2-3 ◄
Resizing the
text box

pointer

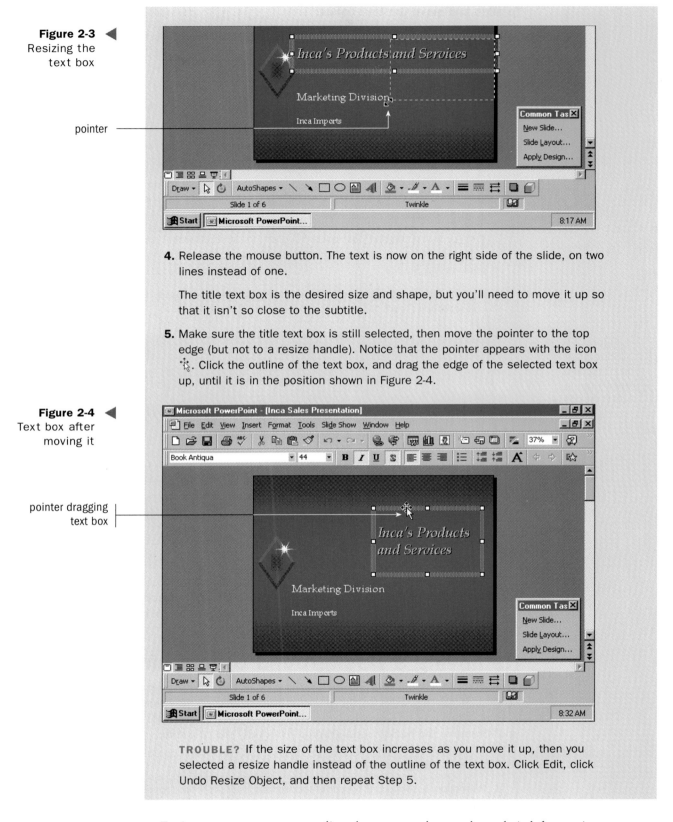

4. Release the mouse button. The text is now on the right side of the slide, on two lines instead of one.

The title text box is the desired size and shape, but you'll need to move it up so that it isn't so close to the subtitle.

5. Make sure the title text box is still selected, then move the pointer to the top edge (but not to a resize handle). Notice that the pointer appears with the icon ⁺⁺⁺. Click the outline of the text box, and drag the edge of the selected text box up, until it is in the position shown in Figure 2-4.

Figure 2-4 ◄
Text box after
moving it

pointer dragging
text box

TROUBLE? If the size of the text box increases as you move it up, then you selected a resize handle instead of the outline of the text box. Click Edit, click Undo Resize Object, and then repeat Step 5.

Enrique now wants you to align the two text boxes along their left margins.

To align and move the text boxes:

1. Make sure the "Inca's Products and Services" text box is still selected, press and hold down the **Shift** key, click the text box with the subtitle "Marketing Division," and then release the **Shift** key. Now both the title text box and the subtitle text box are selected, and you can modify all of the selected text at once.

Next you'll align the left edges of the two text boxes and then move the text boxes to the right.

2. Click the **Draw** list arrow on the Drawing toolbar, point to **Align or Distribute**, and then click **Align Left**. The text boxes are aligned along their left edges.

3. With the two text boxes still selected, position the pointer ⚛ on one of the text box edges, then drag the boxes to the right until the right edge of the lower box is at the right edge of the slide.

TROUBLE? If the text box resize handles disappeared when you clicked the mouse button, you clicked outside the text boxes. Select the text boxes again, then repeat Step 3.

4. Click anywhere outside the text to deselect the two text boxes. Your slide should now look like Figure 2-5.

Figure 2-5 ◀
Slide after resizing and repositioning text boxes

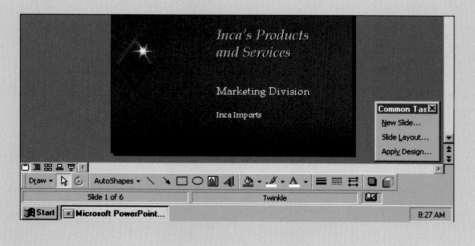

By resizing, moving, and aligning the text boxes, you have created space to insert the company's logo on the left side of the slide. One further obstacle remains: the twinkling diamond-shaped graphic is in the way. Your next task is to remove the background graphic from this slide only.

Removing a Background Graphic from a Slide

A **background graphic** is a graphic that is part of the slide master; it appears in the background of all the slides in the presentation. You can, however, remove a background graphic from any one or all of the slides in a presentation. For Enrique's presentation, you'll remove the background graphic from only the title slide.

To remove a background graphic:

1. With slide 1 still in the presentation window in Slide View, click **Format**, then click **Background**. The Background dialog box opens. See Figure 2-6.

PowerPoint

Figure 2-6 ◀
Background
dialog box

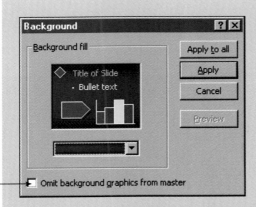

click to remove
background graphics

2. Click the **Omit background graphics from master** check box to select it. This tells PowerPoint that you don't want the background graphic on the selected slide.

3. Click the **Apply** button (*not* the Apply to all button). The graphic disappears from the slide background.

   TROUBLE? If you accidentally click the Apply to all button, PowerPoint removes the background graphic from all of the slides. You'll have to restore it to all of the slides by clicking Edit, then clicking Undo Background. Then repeat Steps 1–3.

Now that you have changed the size, position, and alignment of the text boxes and removed the background graphic from the title slide, you're ready to insert the company's logo into the slide.

Inserting a Picture into a Slide

Enrique wants you to insert the Inca Imports logo, a computer-generated image of fruit, to the left of the text boxes.

REFERENCE
window

INSERTING A PICTURE INTO A SLIDE

- Click Insert, point to Picture, then click From File to display the Insert Picture dialog box.
- Select the desired picture file from the disk, then click the Insert button.
- Move and resize the picture as desired.

To insert a picture into a slide:

1. With slide 1 showing in Slide View, click **Insert**, point to **Picture**, then click **From File**. The Insert Picture dialog box opens on the screen.

2. Change the Look in folder to Tutorial.02 on your Student Disk, click **Incalogo** in the list box to select the Inca Imports logo, and then click the **Insert** button. The picture appears in the middle of the slide.

   The picture remains selected, as you can see from the resize handles around the edge of the graphic. The Picture toolbar also appears as a floating box on the screen and will remain on the screen as long as the picture is selected.

3. With the logo still selected, drag the graphics box to the left of the text so that the top edge of the logo is aligned with the top of the title text. See Figure 2-7. Click anywhere outside the slide to deselect the picture and close the Picture toolbar.

Figure 2-7 ◄
Slide after inserting picture

Inca logo

Picture toolbar

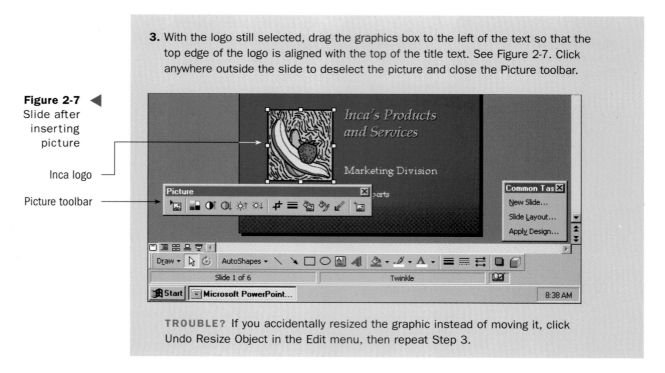

TROUBLE? If you accidentally resized the graphic instead of moving it, click Undo Resize Object in the Edit menu, then repeat Step 3.

You have completed editing slide 1 and are ready to work on slide 2 of Enrique's presentation.

Changing the Slide Layout

Enrique wants you to add an item to the bulleted list in slide 2, "Providing Quality Produce." He decides that with the addition of this item, the bulleted list will be too long to fit on the slide. The slide might look better with two columns. To make the change you could reformat the slide manually, but you decide to use the Slide Layout feature of PowerPoint. A **slide layout** is a predefined arrangement of placeholders on the slide for inserting the slide title, text, or graphics.

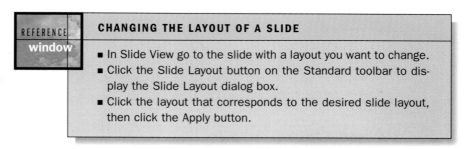

REFERENCE
window

CHANGING THE LAYOUT OF A SLIDE

- In Slide View go to the slide with a layout you want to change.
- Click the Slide Layout button on the Standard toolbar to display the Slide Layout dialog box.
- Click the layout that corresponds to the desired slide layout, then click the Apply button.

You'll now change the layout of slide 2 to accommodate a second column of text.

To change the layout of an existing slide:

1. Click the **Next Slide** button ⬇ at the bottom of the vertical scroll bar to move to slide 2.

2. Click the **Slide Layout** button 🖼 on the Standard toolbar to display the Slide Layout dialog box. See Figure 2-8.

Figure 2-8 ◄
Slide Layout
dialog box

current selected
layout

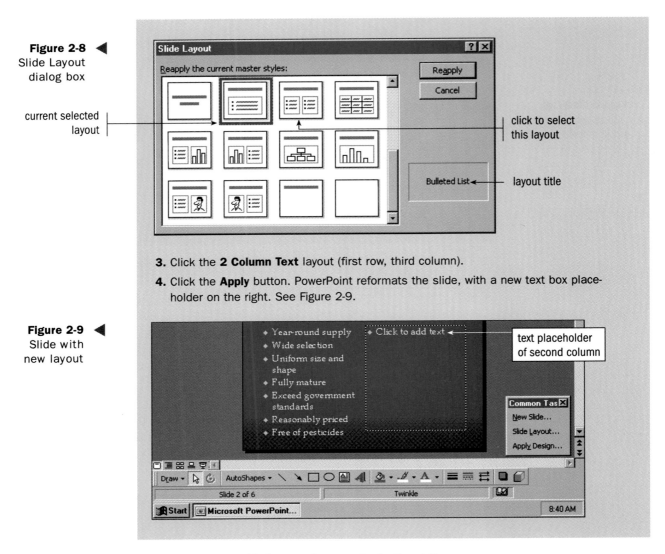

click to select
this layout

layout title

3. Click the **2 Column Text** layout (first row, third column).

4. Click the **Apply** button. PowerPoint reformats the slide, with a new text box placeholder on the right. See Figure 2-9.

Figure 2-9 ◄
Slide with
new layout

text placeholder
of second column

Now you can add the new item to the bulleted list.

To add new text to a text placeholder:

1. Click anywhere within the text placeholder that says "Click to add text." PowerPoint removes the message that was there, displays a black bullet, and positions the insertion point to the right of the bullet. The black bullet is a temporary marker. If you don't type text to the right of the bullet, it will not appear in your presentation.

2. Type **Hand-picked** and then press the **Enter** key. As you type notice that the black bullet changes color to cyan (blue-green). After you press the Enter key, a second bullet, black in color, appears to the left of the insertion point.

Now Enrique wants you to move the last three items in the first column to the end of the second column so the columns are balanced.

3. Click anywhere on the text in the first column. The text box becomes selected. Notice that the black bullet in the second column disappears.

4. Move I to the beginning of the phrase "Exceed government standards," then drag the pointer to the end of the phrase "Free of pesticides" to select all three items.

5. Click the **Cut** button 🔀 on the Standard toolbar. The text disappears from the screen and is moved to the Clipboard.

6. Click I below the existing text in the second column. The black bullet reappears. Now click the **Paste** button 📋 on the Standard toolbar. The three cut items appear in the second column. See Figure 2-10.

Figure 2-10 ◀
Slide after
moving text

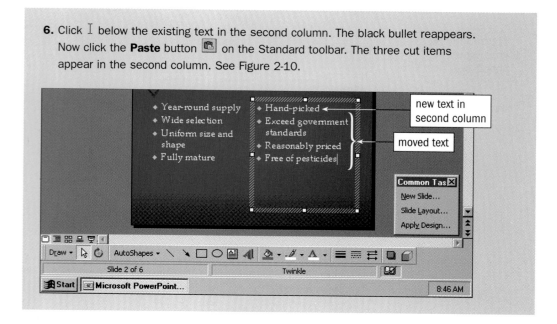

Slide 2 now contains the additional text that Enrique wanted and has a two-column design to accommodate the new text in an attractive way. You're ready to edit slide 3.

Inserting Clip Art

Slide 3, "Meeting Your Needs," has four items of information. Enrique wants to include some clip art to add interest to this slide. In PowerPoint **clip art** specifically refers to images in the Microsoft ClipArt Gallery, whereas a **picture** is any image from some other source, including clip-art libraries supplied by other companies.

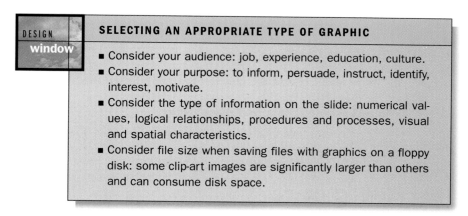

DESIGN window

SELECTING AN APPROPRIATE TYPE OF GRAPHIC

- Consider your audience: job, experience, education, culture.
- Consider your purpose: to inform, persuade, instruct, identify, interest, motivate.
- Consider the type of information on the slide: numerical values, logical relationships, procedures and processes, visual and spatial characteristics.
- Consider file size when saving files with graphics on a floppy disk: some clip-art images are significantly larger than others and can consume disk space.

You'll now change the layout of slide 3 and add clip art to it.

To change the layout of the slide and add clip art:

1. Click 🔽 to go to slide 3.

2. Click 🔳 to display the Slide Layout dialog box, click the layout with the description **Text & Clip Art** (third row, first column), then click the **Apply** button to change the layout of the slide. See Figure 2-11.

Figure 2-11 ◀
Slide with
new layout

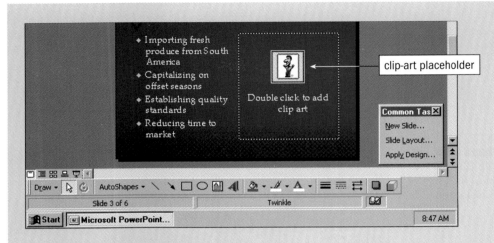

clip-art placeholder

3. Double-click the clip-art placeholder. PowerPoint displays the Microsoft Clip Gallery 3.0 dialog box. See Figure 2-12.

Figure 2-12 ◀
Microsoft Clip
Gallery 3.0
dialog box

current selected
image

sample clip art

scroll to see
additional categories

title of current image

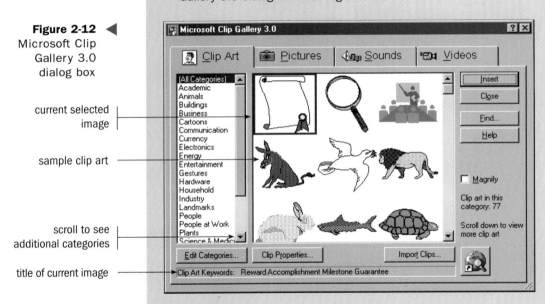

TROUBLE? If PowerPoint informs you that additional clips are available on the Microsoft Office 97 CD-ROM disc, insert the CD if you have it, then click the OK button. Otherwise, just click the OK button.

TROUBLE? If a Cannot Open Previews File dialog box appears, click the check box labeled "Don't attempt to open that file in the future," and then click the OK button.

TROUBLE? If the Microsoft Clip Gallery 3.0 dialog box doesn't appear, consult your instructor or technical support person.

4. Scroll the Categories list box as necessary, and then click **People at Work** to select that category.

TROUBLE? If you don't see a list of categories for the clip-art library, or if the clip art is missing altogether, consult your instructor or technical support person. If you do have clip art to choose from, but you don't have the People at Work category, choose any clip art you prefer to complete these steps.

5. If necessary scroll the clip-art images within the People at Work category, then click the image titled **Leadership** (a woman standing by a blackboard with a group of four people sitting in front of her). See Figure 2-13.

Figure 2-13 ◀
Clip Gallery
with new image
selected

click to select
this image

selected category

title of selected
image

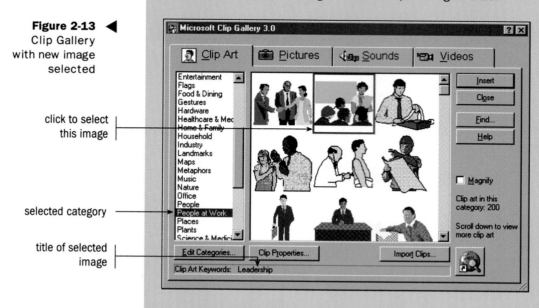

6. Click the **Insert** button. The clip art is inserted into the slide.

Looking at the slide Enrique thinks the clip-art image would look better without the blackboard. To remove the blackboard, you will need to ungroup the image into individual objects, then delete the blackboard object. To **ungroup** means to convert a single image into smaller, individual objects.

To ungroup and edit the clip-art image:

1. With the Leadership image still selected, click the **Draw** list arrow on the Drawing toolbar, then click **Ungroup**. PowerPoint displays a warning about discarding any embedded data or linking information.

2. Click the **Yes** button because this clip art has no special embedded data or linking information. (A graph from a spreadsheet, which might be modified if you change the spreadsheet data, would contain linking information that you wouldn't want to break.) Resize handles appear around the various objects in the picture.

3. Click in a blank area of the slide to deselect all objects, then click the blackboard behind the woman. The image of the blackboard is selected but not the people in the image.

TROUBLE? If you didn't use the Leadership clip-art image, your image may not be able to ungroup, or if it does ungroup, you may not be able to select one of the items individually. If this occurs, skip to Step 5.

4. Press the **Delete** key to delete the selected object. The blackboard disappears from the slide. See Figure 2-14.

Figure 2-14 ◄
Slide with
clip art

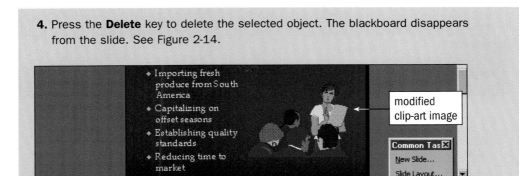

You have now completed slide 3 and made substantial progress on Enrique's presentation. It's time to save your work.

5. Click the **Save** button 🖫 on the Standard toolbar to save the current version of Inca Sales Presentation on your Student Disk.

Quick Check

1. List four situations in which you could use graphics effectively.

2. Explain the meaning of the following terms:
   a. text box
   b. object
   c. logo

3. Describe how to do the following:
   a. select a text box so that resize handles appear
   b. change the size of a text box
   c. move a text box on a slide
   d. change the alignment of two text boxes so they align along their left edges

4. How would you remove background graphics from all the slides in a presentation?

5. What's the difference between a clip-art image and a picture?

6. List three principles for selecting an appropriate type of graphic.

You've edited the first half of Enrique's presentation. In Session 2.2 you'll finalize the slides by creating an organization chart and graphic shape.

In this session you will learn how to create an organization chart and how to draw and manipulate graphic shapes.

Inserting an Organization Chart

Because Inca Imports is a fairly new company, Enrique and his staff feel that it's important for potential clients to understand its employees' high level of experience in the import and produce business. Enrique therefore asks you to create an organization chart to communicate this. An **organization chart** is a diagram of boxes, connected with lines, showing the hierarchy of positions within an organization.

REFERENCE window

INSERTING AN ORGANIZATION CHART

- Change the slide layout of the desired slide to Organization Chart.
- Double-click the organization chart placeholder.
- Type the personnel names, positions, and other information into the boxes of the organization chart.
- Add subordinate and co-worker boxes as desired.
- Click File, click Exit and Return to (presentation filename), then click the Yes button.

You'll create the organization chart now.

To create an organization chart:

1. If you took a break after the last session, make sure PowerPoint is running and the file Inca Sales Presentation is open.
2. Go to slide 4, click 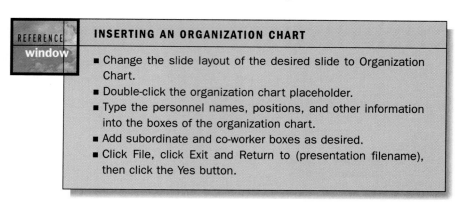, click the **Organization Chart** layout (second row, third column), and then click the **Apply** button.
3. Double-click the organization chart placeholder. After a short pause the Microsoft Organization Chart window appears on the screen with the Organization Chart toolbar across the top.
4. Click the **Maximize** button on the Microsoft Organization Chart window so that it fills the entire screen. See Figure 2-15. A chart with text placeholders appears in the window. The chart has two levels of organization. The first line in the box at the top of the chart is already selected, as you can tell from its dark background. When you start typing, the text will appear in that selected box.

Figure 2-15 ◀
Microsoft
Organization
Chart window

selected box,
first level

second-level boxes

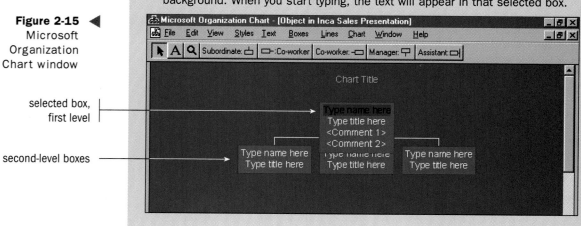

5. Type **Patricia Cuevas** on the first line, then press the **Tab** key (or the **Enter** key). The placeholder text "Type title here" becomes selected.

6. Type **President**, press the **Tab** key, and then type **13 years' experience**. This completes the first box. PowerPoint will automatically delete the fourth (extra) line for you if you don't use it.

7. Click the second-level box on the left side. The box becomes selected, as indicated by its black background.

8. Type **Angelena Cristenas**, press the **Tab** key, type **V.P. Operations**, press the **Tab** key, and then type **13 years' experience**. This completes the text of that text box in the organization chart.

9. Use the same procedure to complete the other two boxes of the organization chart so they contain the text shown in Figure 2-16, then click anywhere within the Microsoft Organization Chart window, but outside of any text or organization box, to take the chart out of editing mode.

Figure 2-16 ◀
First two levels
of organization
chart

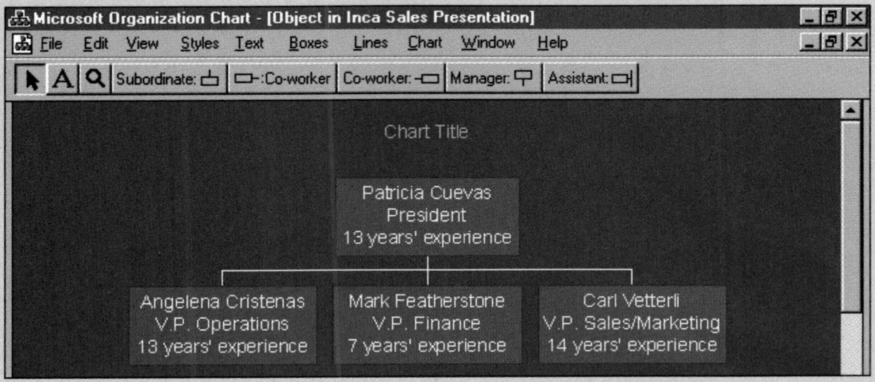

Microsoft Organization Chart - [Object in Inca Sales Presentation]

File   Edit   View   Styles   Text   Boxes   Lines   Chart   Window   Help

Subordinate: ⌐⌐   ⌐⌐:Co-worker   Co-worker: ⌐⌐   Manager: ⌐⌐   Assistant: ⌐⌐

Chart Title

Patricia Cuevas
President
13 years' experience

Angelena Cristenas
V.P. Operations
13 years' experience

Mark Featherstone
V.P. Finance
7 years' experience

Carl Vetterli
V.P. Sales/Marketing
14 years' experience

TROUBLE? If you made any typing errors, click the box containing the error, press the Tab key until the line containing the error is highlighted, then retype that line.

You have completed the first two levels of the organization chart. Enrique also wants to show the experience that personnel at Inca Imports have in handling produce and responding to customer delivery needs. The customer service employees work under Angelena Cristenas. You'll add the new levels of organization now.

To add subordinate levels to an organization chart:

1. Click the **Subordinate** button Subordinate: ⌐⌐ on the Organization Chart toolbar. The pointer changes to ⌐⌐.

2. Click anywhere within the box containing "Angelena Cristenas." A new organization level appears below Angelena's box.

3. Type **Carlos Becerra**. As soon as you begin to type, the other text placeholders appear in the box.

4. Press the **Tab** key, type **QA Manager**, press the **Tab** key, and then type **9 years' experience**. This completes the box for Carlos Becerra, QA (quality assurance) Manager.

5. Click Subordinate: ⌐⌐ and then click the box containing "Carlos Becerra" to add a subordinate box underneath Carlos.

6. Type **Norma Lopez**, press the **Tab** key, type **Customer Service**, press the **Tab** key, type **6 years' experience**, and then click anywhere in the Organization Chart window, but outside of any text or box. Your chart should now look like Figure 2-17.

Figure 2-17 ◀
Organization
chart after
adding
subordinate
box

new subordinate
boxes

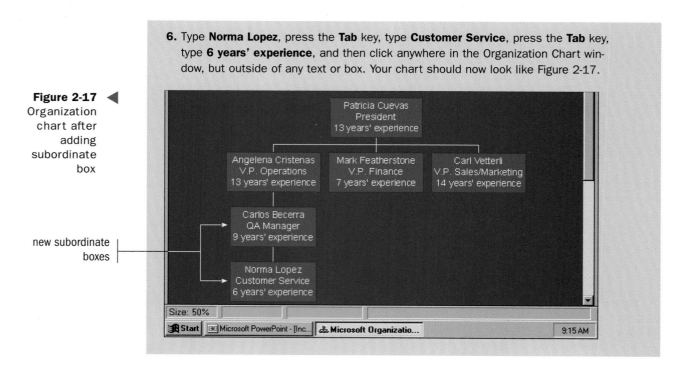

To complete the organization chart, Enrique asks you to add a co-worker to the chart.

To add a co-worker to an organization chart:

1. Click the **Right Co-worker** button Co-worker: ⊣□ on the Organization Chart toolbar. The mouse changes to ⊣□. This allows you to add a co-worker box to the right of an existing box.

2. Click the box containing "Norma Lopez" to add a new box to its right, type **Juanita Rojas**, press the **Tab** key, type **Manager, Quito Center**, press the **Tab** key, type **3 years' experience**, and then click anywhere in the window, but outside of any box or text, to take the chart out of editing mode.

You have completed the organization chart. To add it to slide 4, you simply need to exit the Organization Chart window.

To exit the Organization Chart window and add the chart to the slide:

1. Click **File**, then click **Exit and Return to Inca Sales Presentation**. A dialog box appears on the screen asking if you want to update the object. The object in this case is the new organization chart.

2. Click the **Yes** button. The Organization Chart window closes, and the chart is inserted in slide 4.

   After looking over the organization chart, Enrique asks you to enlarge it.

3. Drag the resize handle in the upper-left corner up and to the left, then drag the resize handle in the lower-right corner down and to the right until the organization chart is approximately the same size as the one shown in Figure 2-18.

Figure 2-18 ◀
Slide 4 with completed organization chart

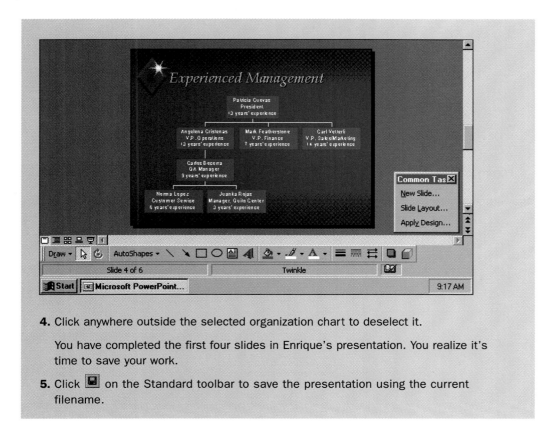

4. Click anywhere outside the selected organization chart to deselect it.

   You have completed the first four slides in Enrique's presentation. You realize it's time to save your work.

5. Click 🖫 on the Standard toolbar to save the presentation using the current filename.

Creating and Manipulating a Shape

As the last graphic to be added to his presentation, Enrique asks you to add an inverted triangle with text to slide 5 to demonstrate the three major benefits of the company. To create the triangle, you'll use PowerPoint's **AutoShapes** feature, which includes several categories of shapes that you can insert: lines, connectors, basic shapes (for example, rectangles, triangles), block arrows, flowcharts, stars and banners, callouts, and action buttons.

To insert a shape in a slide using AutoShapes:

1. Go to slide 5, click the **AutoShapes** list arrow on the Drawing toolbar, and then point to **Basic Shapes**. PowerPoint displays the Basic Shapes palette. See Figure 2-19.

Figure 2-19 ◀
AutoShapes palette

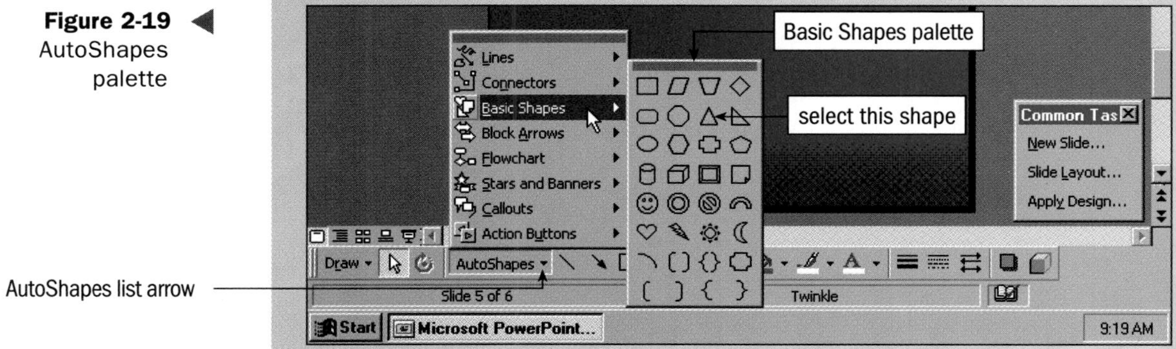

AutoShapes list arrow

2. Click the **Isosceles Triangle** button △ on the Basic Shapes palette. The pointer changes to +.

3. Position **+** approximately one inch below the first "n" in "International" (in the title of the slide), press and hold down the **Shift** key, and then click the mouse button and drag the pointer down and to the right. The outline of a triangle appears as you drag. (The Shift key makes the triangle equilateral, that is, with all three sides of equal length.)

4. Release the mouse button when your triangle is approximately the same size and shape as the one shown in Figure 2-20.

Figure 2-20 ◀
Slide with
drawn triangle

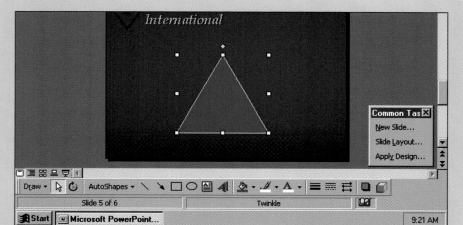

TROUBLE? If your triangle doesn't look like the one in Figure 2-20, you can move your triangle by dragging it to a new location; you can resize or change the shape of your triangle by dragging one or more of the resize handles; or you can press the Backspace key to delete your triangle and repeat Steps 1–4 to redraw the triangle.

Notice that the default color of the drawn object is magenta (a deep pink). You decide that magenta is too bright and want to change the color of the triangle to cyan (blue-green), which matches the color of the text on the slide.

5. With the triangle still selected, click the **Fill Color** list arrow 🔲 on the Drawing toolbar. A box with color tiles appears on the screen.

6. Click the cyan tile (the fourth tile from the left), which displays the ToolTip message "Follow Title Text Scheme Color" to let you know that this is the color of the title text in the current design template. The fill color of the triangle changes from magenta to cyan.

The triangle is the desired size and color, but you want to flip (invert) the triangle so it is pointing down instead of up.

To flip an object:

1. With the triangle still selected, click the **Draw** list arrow on the Drawing toolbar, point to **Rotate or Flip**, and then click **Flip Vertical**.

2. Click in a blank region of the slide to deselect the triangle. Your triangle should be positioned, colored, sized, and oriented like the one shown in Figure 2-21.

Figure 2-21
Slide with
completed
graphics object

triangle after change
of color and flip

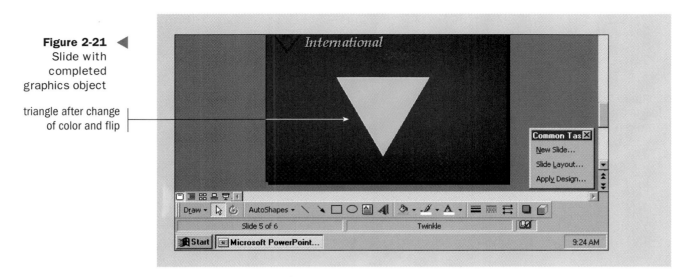

The shape is now in its final form. You're ready to add the text naming the three benefits of Inca Imports on each side of the triangle.

Adding a Text Box

Adding text boxes in PowerPoint is easy: You simply use the Text Box button 🔲 on the Drawing toolbar. You'll now add three text boxes around the triangle you just created.

To add a text box to the slide:

1. Click the **Text Box** button 🔲 on the Drawing toolbar. The pointer changes to ↓.

2. Move the pointer so it is above the upper edge of the triangle and below the "o" in "International," then click at that position. (The position doesn't have to be exact.) PowerPoint creates a small empty text box, with the insertion point inside.

3. Type **Quality Produce**.

4. Drag the edge of the text box until it is positioned just above and centered on the upper edge of the triangle, as shown in Figure 2-22.

Figure 2-22
First text box
on triangle

text box

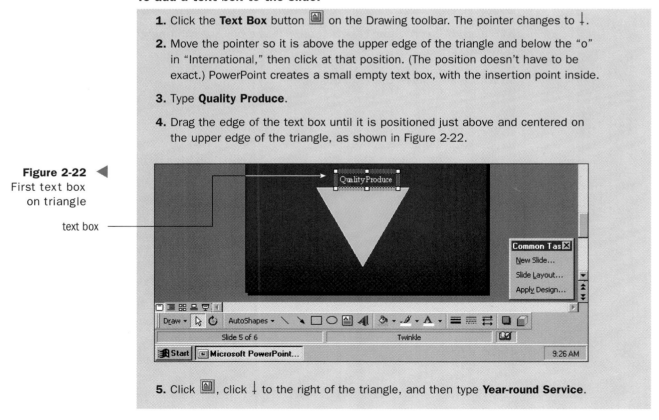

5. Click 🔲, click ↓ to the right of the triangle, and then type **Year-round Service**.

6. Click 🖼, click ↓ to the left of the triangle, and then type **Satisfied Customers**. Click in a blank area of the slide to deselect the text box. Your slide should now look like Figure 2-23.

Figure 2-23 ◀
Triangle with all three text boxes

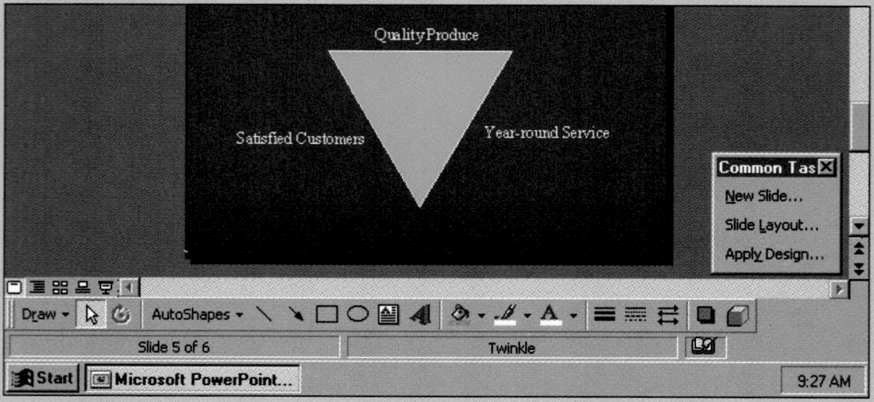

TROUBLE? If the text you added to the sides of the triangle is not in the same position as the text in the figure, don't worry. You'll move the text boxes in the next set of steps.

Next, you'll rotate the text boxes to make them parallel to the sides of the triangle.

Rotating Text Boxes

The method for rotating text is similar to the one for rotating graphics (or rotating any other object).

To rotate and move the text boxes:

1. Select the text box that contains "Year-round Service" by clicking anywhere within the text box. As usual the resize handles appear around the box.

2. Click the **Free Rotate** button 🔄 on the Drawing toolbar. The pointer changes to ⟲, and the corners of the selected box display rotate handles (small green circles) instead of resize handles.

3. Position ⟲ over one of the rotate handles (it doesn't matter which one). The arrow in the pointer disappears, so that the pointer looks like ↺.

4. Press and hold the **Shift** key, then press and hold the mouse button. Holding down the Shift key makes the rotation occur in 15-degree increments.

5. Rotate the handle counterclockwise until the top edge of the box is parallel to the lower-right edge of the triangle. See Figure 2-24.

Figure 2-24 ◄
Rotating a
text box

rotate pointer

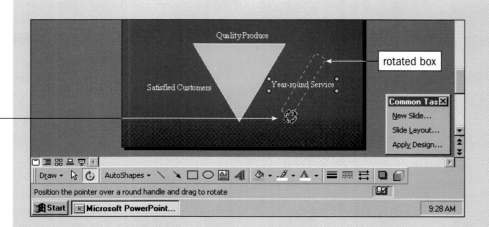

6. Move the pointer over the text "Year-round Service" and drag it until it's against and centered on the lower-right edge of the triangle.

   TROUBLE? If the edge of the text box isn't parallel to the edge of the triangle, you can repeat Steps 2–5 above to fix the rotation. If necessary, try not pressing the Shift key.

   TROUBLE? If the text box jumps from one location to another as you drag it so you can't position it exactly where you want it, hold down the Alt key as you drag the box.

7. Click the text box that contains "Satisfied Customers," then repeat Steps 2-6, except this time rotate the box counterclockwise until it is parallel to the lower-left edge of the triangle, then position the text box so it is close to and centered on the left edge of the triangle. Deselect the text box. Your slide should look like Figure 2-25.

Figure 2-25 ◄
Slide with
completed
diagram

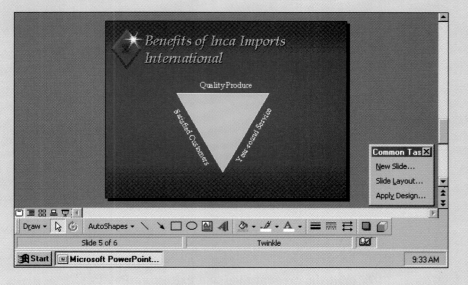

You have now completed the entire presentation, so you should save the final version to the disk. (The final slide, slide 6, is blank, so that when you make the presentation and advance from slide 5, you'll see a blank screen, indicating the end of the presentation.)

8. With your Student Disk still in the disk drive, click 🖫. PowerPoint saves the file using its current filename.

As a final check Enrique asks you to view the presentation.

Viewing and Printing the Completed Slide Show

You should always view a completed slide show before you print it. Furthermore, in this case, because Enrique has only a monochrome printer, he reminds you to make sure that all the slides will be legible in black and white before printing the presentation.

To view the completed presentation as a slide show:

1. Drag the scroll box to the top of the vertical scroll bar so slide 1 will appear first when you begin the slide show.

2. Click the **Slide Show** button 🖵 on the View toolbar to begin the slide show.

3. After you look at each slide, click the left mouse button (or press the spacebar) to advance to the next slide. Continue advancing until you've seen the entire slide show and PowerPoint returns to Slide View.

4. Click the **Slide Sorter View** button 🔡 to see all six slides at once. Your completed presentation should look like Figure 2-26.

Figure 2-26 ◀
Completed
slide
presentation

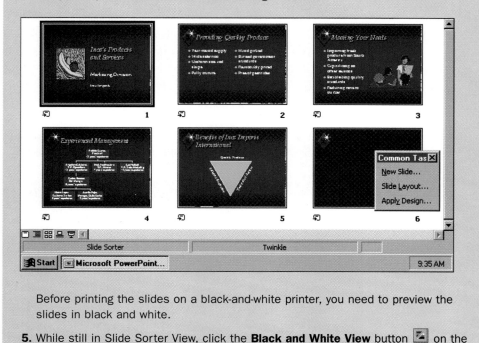

Before printing the slides on a black-and-white printer, you need to preview the slides in black and white.

5. While still in Slide Sorter View, click the **Black and White View** button 🖼 on the Formatting toolbar. The slides change from color to black and white.

As you can see, all the slides are legible in black and white. You're ready to print and then exit PowerPoint.

To print the presentation and exit PowerPoint:

1. Click **File**, click **Print**, select **Handouts (6 slides per page)** in the Print what list box, make sure the **Black & White** check box is selected, then click the **OK** button.

2. After printing is completed, click the **Close** button ⊠ in the PowerPoint window.

Quick Check

1. What is an organization chart?

2. How would you add an organization chart to a slide?

3. In the context of an organization chart, define the following:
   a. subordinate
   b. co-worker

4. How would you use AutoShapes to draw a shape, such as a rectangle or a circle?

5. How would you change the fill color of a shape?

6. How would you invert a triangle so it is pointed down instead of up?

7. How would you rotate an object (a text box or a graphics image)?

Enrique is pleased with the slides. He thinks the graphics you have added to the presentation (logo, clip art, organization chart, and triangle) will increase potential new customers' understanding of and interest in Inca Imports.

Tutorial Assignments

After Enrique presented his slides to potential new customers, he decided it would be helpful for his colleagues at Inca Imports to know about the success of these recent marketing efforts. He asks you to help him finalize this presentation by adding graphics. Complete the following for Enrique:

1. If necessary, start PowerPoint and make sure your Student Disk is in the disk drive.

2. Open the Report file in the Tutorial.02 TAssign folder on your Student Disk.

3. Save the file to your Student Disk as Marketing Report.

4. Make sure that slide 1 appears in the presentation window in Slide View.

5. Left-align the text in both text boxes, so that the text is flush with the left edge of the text boxes. *Hint*: Select the text, then click the Left Alignment button on the Formatting toolbar.

6. Decrease the size of each of the two text boxes so that they fit just around the text contained in each box. *Hint*: Drag one or more resize handles.

7. Move the two text boxes so that their right edges are near the right edge of the slide, and then align the left edges of the two text boxes.

8. Insert the picture file "Incalogo" from your Student Disk into slide 1, decrease the size of the logo by approximately 50%, then move the picture to the right of the globe, just below the colored line.

9. Change the layout of slide 2 to 2 Column Text, and then in the right column of slide 2, add the following three bulleted items: "Ad in food industry trade magazine," "Sample produce to interested businesses," and "Complimentary shipment to large companies."

10. In slide 3 change the layout to Clip Art & Text, so that the clip art is on the left and the text is on the right.

11. In the placeholder for the clip art in slide 3, add the image from the People at Work category titled "Consensus Cooperate Guarantee Synergy Agreeable," which pictures a man and a woman shaking hands with another man standing in the middle. If your copy of PowerPoint doesn't have that clip-art image, use another one of your choice and skip Step 12.

12. Ungroup the clip-art image and remove the man standing in the middle.

13. Add an organization chart to slide 4. Add Enrique Hoffmann, Director of Marketing, at the top of the chart. Add Melanie Zapatos and Samuel Clarke, both Marketing Managers, to the second level. Then, on the third level under Melanie Zapatos, add two Sales Representatives (as co-workers), Carlos Anderson and Ana Maria Prado; under Samuel Clarke add two Sales Representatives (as co-workers), Gina Parker and Jesus Calderon. Resize and move the completed organization chart as necessary so that it doesn't overlap the background graphic (globe). *Hint*: To delete an unwanted box in the organization chart, select the box, then press the Backspace or the Delete key.

14. Add a new slide 5. Choose Title Only as the slide layout. Make the title of the slide "Marketing Process." Add text and AutoShapes to create a slide that looks like Figure 2-27. You may have to move, resize, and align text and graphics boxes. *Hint*: To make the arrows the same size and shape, use AutoShapes to draw one of the arrows and then use the Copy and Paste buttons on the Standard toolbar to create the others. To align the centers of objects vertically (text boxes and graphics boxes), use the Draw, Align or Distribute, Align Center command sequence.

Figure 2-27 ◀

15. Spell check the presentation.

16. View the entire presentation in Slide Show View and in Black and White View.

17. Save the file with your changes, then print a copy of the slides (three slides per page) of the presentation. Print them using the Black & White option if you don't have a color printer. Remove background graphics if necessary to make the text legible.

18. Close the file.

Case Problems

1. Data Doctor—Enoch Norbert owns a computer-data-backup service in Framingham, Massachusetts. His company, Data Doctor, helps small businesses in the greater Boston area back up their disks and recover damaged data. Enoch asks you to use PowerPoint to help him create a presentation for potential customers. Complete the following for Enoch:

1. Open the presentation file Datadoc in the Tutorial.02 Cases folder on your Student Disk, and save it as Data Doctor.

2. To slide 1, add the picture Datalogo in the Cases folder on your Student Disk. Adjust the position and alignment of the text and the position of the picture to make the slide attractive and legible.

3. In slide 3, add the clip art titled "Stress Frustration Anger Chaos" (depicting a duck about to smash a PC) from the Cartoons category. If your copy of PowerPoint doesn't have this clip-art image or the ones that follow, use other clip art of your choice. *Hint*: You may need to reapply the Clip Art & Text layout.

4. In slide 4, add to the center of the slide (below the title) the clip art with the title "Future Forecast Listen Diagnose Incredible" (shows a fortune-teller) from the Cartoons category.

5. Also in slide 4, add a text box with the text "Data Doctor." Center the text box below the clip-art image.

6. In slide 5, increase the size of the font in the main text box (below the title) by selecting the text box, dragging the I-beam pointer over all the text, and then clicking the Increase Font Size button five or six times until the longest line of text just fills the width of the text box.

7. Use Slide Show View to view all the slides of the presentation, then save the file.

8. View all the slides of the presentation in black and white.

9. Print the slides of the presentation in black and white as six slides per page. Remove background graphics if necessary to make the text legible.

10. Close the file.

2. Business Plans Plus—Atu Hemuli helps minority entrepreneurs obtain funding by preparing business plans for them or by editing their existing plans. Atu asks you to help him create a seminar presentation for other professionals who are interested in becoming business-plan consultants. Complete the following for Atu:

1. Open the Busplans file in the Tutorial.02 Cases folder on your Student Disk, and save it as Business Plans Plus.

2. Insert a new slide 2 into the presentation. Use the Bulleted List slide layout. Add the title "What does a business-plan consultant do?" Then add the following bulleted items to the main text: "Guides clients in writing business plans," "Conducts market research," "Gathers financial information," "Projects growth," and "Projects sales potential."

3. Change the layout of slide 3 (formerly slide 2) to Text & Clip Art, then add any one of the clip-art images of a handshake from the Gestures category. If your copy of PowerPoint doesn't have this type of clip-art image (or the ones that follow), use other clip art of your choice.

4. Change the layout of slide 4 to Text & Clip Art, then add a different clip-art image of a handshake from the Gestures category.

5. Add a new slide 6 in the Title Only layout. Make the title "Networking Is the Key to Your Future." Create a drawing of an arrow pointed to the right with the words "The Future" inside the arrow. Change the color of the fill of the arrow and the color and the size of the text, as necessary, to make the arrow match the color scheme of the presentation and to make the text legible. *Hint*: Select the Right Arrow from the Block Arrows palette of the AutoShapes.

6. Use Slide Show View to review the entire presentation.

7. Save the file, then print the slides in black and white as six slides per page.

8. Close the file.

3. Porter and Coles Ad Agency—Sheri Porter and Sherone Coles are partners who founded the Porter and Coles Ad Agency. They decide to prepare a presentation to provide potential clients with the hourly rates for Porter and Coles's services and provide a graph on the costs of preparing a document as a function of the number of pages. Complete the following for Sheri and Sherone:

1. Open the presentation file Porter from the Tutorial.02 Cases folder on your Student Disk, save it as Porter and Coles, and then do the following:

2. In slide 1, increase the font size of the slide title by selecting the text box and clicking the Increase Font Size button twice.

3. In slide 2, to the right of the main text, without changing the slide layout, add the PowerPoint clip-art image "Ghost Man Anger Problem" (a cartoon character sitting at a computer) from the Cartoons category. If your copy of PowerPoint doesn't have this clip-art image or the ones that follow, use other clip art of your choice. *Hint*: Use the Insert Clip Art button on the Standard toolbar, then resize and move the graphic image so it fits neatly to the right of the text.

4. In slide 3, replace the clip-art placeholder with the "Information Communication Happy Newspaper" image from the Cartoons category. *Hint*: You may need to reapply the Text & Clip Art layout.

5. In slide 4 add a clip-art image to the right of the main text. From the Communication category, use "Information Telephone Communication."

6. In slide 5 insert the picture Artist.wmf if you can find it on your computer. Position the text and the clip-art image so they don't overlap. *Hint*: If your computer system has Microsoft Office installed on it, you can find the file by clicking the Start button in the lower-left corner of your screen, clicking Find, clicking Files or Folders, and then typing "Artist.wmf" and having the Find feature look on your hard disk for the file. When you find the file, note the directory it is in and close Find File. Then, when you insert the picture in PowerPoint, go back to that directory to select the file. If you can't find the file, use another clip-art image you think is appropriate.

7. Use Slide Show View to review the entire presentation.

8. Save the file, then print the slides in black and white as three slides per page.

9. Close the file.

4. Presentation on Past Employment or Service—Prepare a presentation dealing with one of your past employment or volunteer service experiences. Employment could include any paid or unpaid work you have done. Service could include work for your own family or volunteer work in your community, church, club, or school. In creating your presentation, do the following:

1. Select an appropriate design template.

2. Create a title slide with the title "My Work as a ..." or "Employment in the ... Industry." Use your name as the subtitle.

3. Include at least four slides. Slide topics might be "My Duties," "Work Conditions," "Working with Other Employees," "My Boss," "How to Be More Efficient," "Pay and Benefits," "Holidays and Other Days Off," and "Recommendations for Future Employees."

4. Include at least one object from the "Stars and Banners" category of AutoShapes. For example you could insert a banner, increase its size, and write a job title or description in it.

5. Include clip-art or other graphic images on at least three slides.

6. Spell check your presentation.

7. Save your presentation in the Tutorial.02 Cases folder using the filename My Job. If you get an error message that your Student Disk is full, then save the file to a new, blank disk.

8. Print your presentation slides, as three slides per page, making sure the slides are legible in black and white if you have a monochrome printer.

9. Close the file.

Answers to Quick Check Questions

SESSION 1.1

1   PowerPoint provides everything you need to produce a presentation that consists of black-and-white or color overheads, 35mm slides, or on-screen slides. The presentation components can consist of individual slides, speaker notes, an outline of the presentation, and audience handouts.

2   You should plan a presentation before you create it to improve the quality of your presentation, make your presentation more effective and enjoyable, and save time and effort. Some of the presentation elements that should be considered include the presentation's purpose, type, audience and its needs, location, and format.

3   The AutoContent Wizard automatically creates a general outline for you to follow based on the category and length of your presentation.

4   a. A slide master is a slide that contains the text and graphics that will appear on every slide of a particular kind in the presentation.
b. A placeholder is a region of a slide or a location in an outline reserved for inserting text or graphics.
c. The title of a slide is its main heading.
d. The main text of a slide is indented and bulleted under the title.

5   The 6 × 6 rule is to use six or fewer items per screen and incomplete sentences of six or fewer words.

6   A red, wavy line indicates that you have typed a word that isn't in PowerPoint's built-in dictionary and that therefore may be misspelled.

7   It's important to save your work frequently so that you won't lose all your work if, for example, a power failure occurs.

SESSION 1.2

1   a. Select the text of an outline item, then click the Move Up button on the Outline toolbar.
b. Click the slide icon to the left of the slide title, click Edit, then click Delete Slide, or press the Backspace key or the Delete key.
c. Select the text, then type new text.
d. Drag the I-beam pointer to select the text, then delete or retype it.

2   Promote means to increase the level of an outline item; demote means to decrease the level of an outline item.

3   In Outline View you can see the text of several slides at once, which makes it easier to work with text. In Slide View you can see the design and layout of the slide.

4   a. Select the text, click the Cut button, move the insertion point to a new location, and then click the Paste button.
b. Click New Slide on the Common Tasks toolbar, or click the New Slide button on the Standard toolbar.

5   A design template is a file that specifies the colors and format of the background and the type style of the titles, accents, and other text in a presentation. To change the template, click the Apply Design button on the Standard toolbar (or click Apply Design on the Common Tasks toolbar), select a new design template, and then click the Apply button.

6   The Office Assistant provides help by looking through the Help system to find an answer to your question.

7   Speaker notes are printed pages that contain a picture of and notes about each slide to help the speaker remember what to say while a particular slide is displayed during the presentation. To create speaker notes, click the Notes Page View button, click the Zoom list arrow and click 100% so that you can view the speaker notes at full size, click the placeholder, and then type the speaker notes.

8   You should preview a presentation before printing it to not only make sure that the slides are satisfactory, but also that the presentation is legible in black and white if you have a monochrome printer.

SESSION 2.1

1   Situations to use graphics effectively: to present information that words can't communicate effectively; to interest and motive the reader; to communicate relationships quickly; to increase understanding and retention.

2   a. Text box: region of the slide that contains text.
    b. Object: any item (text box, clip art, graph, organization chart, picture) on a slide that you can move, resize, rotate, or otherwise manipulate.
    c. Logo: a visual identification for a company.

3   a. Click anywhere within the text.
    b. Select the text box, then position the pointer over a resize handle and drag the text box until it becomes the desired size.
    c. Select the text box, then place the pointer on the edge of the text box (but not on a resize handle) and drag the text box to the new location.
    d. Select both text boxes, click the Draw list arrow on the Drawing toolbar, point to Align or Distribute, and then click Align Left.

4   In Slide View, click Format, click Background, click the Omit background graphics from master check box, then click the Apply to all button.

5   Clip art specifically refers to images in the Microsoft ClipArt Gallery; a picture is any image from some other source, including clip-art libraries supplied by other companies.

6   To select an appropriate type of graphic you should consider your audience (job, experience, education, culture), your purpose (to inform, instruct, identify, motivate), and the type of information on the slide (numerical values, logical relationships, procedures and processes, visual and spatial characteristics).

SESSION 2.2

1   An organization chart is a diagram of boxes, connected with lines, showing the hierarchy of positions within an organization.

2   Change the slide layout to Organization Chart; double-click the organization chart placeholder; type the personnel names, positions, and other information into the boxes of the organization chart; add subordinate and co-worker boxes as desired; click File; click Exit and Return to (presentation filename); and then click the Yes button.

3   a. Subordinate: a box that goes beneath another box in an organization chart.
    b. Co-worker: a box that goes on the left or right side of another box in an organization chart.

4   Click the AutoShapes list arrow on the Drawing toolbar, point to the appropriate tool (such as Basic Shapes), move the pointer into the slide area, and drag the pointer to draw the object.

5   With the object selected, click the Fill Color list arrow on the Drawing toolbar, then click the desired color tile.

6   Select the object, click the Draw list arrow on the Drawing toolbar, point to Rotate or Flip, and then click Flip Vertical.

7   Select the object to be rotated, click the Free Rotate button on the Drawing toolbar, position the pointer over one of the rotate handles, press and hold the Shift key, and then press and hold the mouse button.

Microsoft
PowerPoint 97

LEVEL II

TUTORIALS

TUTORIAL 3

Presenting a Slide Show
Annual Report of Inca Imports International

P 3.3

TUTORIAL 4

Integrating PowerPoint with Other Programs and with the World Wide Web
Presenting a Proposal to the Executive Officers

P 4.1

Read This **Before You Begin**

STUDENT DISKS

To complete the Level II tutorials and end-of-tutorial assignments in this book, you need 3 Student Disks. Your instructor will either provide you with Student Disks or ask you to make your own.

If you are supposed to make your own Student Disks, you will need 3 blank, formatted high-density disks. You will need to copy a set of folders from a file server or standalone computer onto your disks. Your instructor will tell you which computer, drive letter, and folders contain the files you need. The following table shows you which folders go on each of your disks, so that you will have enough disk space to complete all the tutorials, Tutorial Assignments, and Case Problems:

Student Disk	Write this on the disk label	Put these folders on the disk
1	Student Disk 1: PowerPoint 97 Tutorial 3	Tutorial.03
2	Student Disk 2: PowerPoint 97 Tutorial 4	
	Tutorial and Tutorial Assignments	Tutorial.04
3	Student Disk 3: PowerPoint 97 Tutorial 4	
	Case Problems	Tutorial.04

When you begin each tutorial, be sure you are using the correct Student Disk. See the inside front or inside back cover of this book for more information on Student Disk files, or ask your instructor or technical support person for assistance.

USING YOUR OWN COMPUTER

If you are going to work through this book using your own computer, you need:

■ **Computer System** Microsoft Windows 95 or Microsoft Windows NT Workstation 4.0 (or a later version) and Microsoft PowerPoint 97 must be installed on your computer. This book assumes a custom installation of PowerPoint 97 that includes the Web Page Authoring (HTML) feature. To install the video and sound clips used in Tutorial 4, students will need access to files in the ClipGallery on the Office 97 CD-ROM.

■ **Student Disks** Ask your instructor or lab manager for details on how to get the Student Disks. You will not be able to complete the tutorials or end-of-tutorial assignments in this book using your own computer until you have Student Disks. The Student Files may also be obtained electronically over the Internet. See the inside front or inside back cover of this book for more details.

To complete the Level II tutorials and end-of-tutorial assignments in this book, your students must use a set of files on 3 Student Disks. These files are included in the Instructor's Resource Kit, and they may also be obtained electronically over the Internet. See the inside front or inside back cover of this book for more details. Follow the instructions in the Readme file to copy the files to your server or standalone computer. You can view the Readme file using WordPad.

Once the files are copied, you can make Student Disks for the students yourself, or you can tell students where to find the files so they can make their own Student Disks. Make sure the files get correctly copied onto the Student Disks by following the instructions in the Student Disks section above, which will ensure that students have enough disk space to complete all the tutorials and end-of-tutorial assignments.

COURSE TECHNOLOGY STUDENT FILES

You are granted a license to copy the Student Files to any computer or computer network used by students who have purchased this book.

Presenting a Slide Show

Annual Report of Inca Imports International

In this tutorial you will:

- Insert slides from an existing presentation

- Apply a design template from another presentation and use the Slide Master to modify that design template

- Find and replace text

- Hide a slide and add a black final slide

- Build a graph and create a table

- Apply special effects to slides

- Create overhead transparencies and print a slide show in color

- Use the Style Checker to finalize a presentation

- Prepare 35mm slides and use the PowerPoint Viewer

Inca Imports International

A year after receiving a loan from Commercial Financial Bank of Southern California to expand Inca Imports International's business, Patricia Cuevas needs to present her first annual report on the company's progress. She will make two presentations: one to the company's board of directors and one to the company's stockholders. Patricia decides that she can create one slide show for both audiences. In her presentation, Patricia also plans to include previously created slides about Inca Imports' successful marketing campaign. Patricia asks you to help her prepare the presentation.

SESSION

3.1

In this session, you will learn how to add slides and apply a design template from another presentation, and then use the Slide Master to customize the overall appearance of your slide show. Using the Slide Master, you will change the slide color scheme, text alignment, and the bullet and font styles. You will then use the Title Master to add a scanned picture to the title slide in the presentation. Finally, you will also find and replace text, rearrange and hide a slide, and add a black final slide.

DESIGN window

PREPARING FOR A PRESENTATION MEETING

- Prepare an agenda. Include the date, time, place, discussion topics, presenter names, and, if it's a small meeting, the attendees. List any materials needed for the meeting.
- Prepare your presentation. Request help from others, as necessary, and then follow up.
- Have a backup copy of your presentation in case you run into any equipment failures.
- Check the physical arrangements, including the size of the room, chairs, tables, podium, and thermostat setting.
- Check the needed equipment, including the microphone, chalkboard or white board with chalk or markers, computer with projection system (if you're giving an on-screen presentation), slide projector, overhead projector, and VCR and TV (if you're using video).
- Prepare other items, as needed, including handouts, beverages, refreshments, pads, pencils, name cards, and reference materials.

Planning the Presentation

Before you begin to create her slide show, Patricia discusses with you the purpose of and audience for her presentation:

- **Purpose of the presentation:** To present an overview of the progress that Inca Imports has made during the past year

- **Type of presentation:** General presentation

- **Audience for the presentation:** Inca Imports' board of directors; Inca Imports' stockholders at their annual meeting

- **Audience needs:** A quick overview of Inca Imports' performance over the past year

- **Location of the presentation:** Small boardroom for the board of directors; large conference room at the meeting site for the stockholders

- **Format:** Oral presentation; on-screen slide show for the board of directors; 35mm slide show for the stockholders; both presentations to consist of five to seven slides

Inserting Slides from Another Presentation

Because Patricia's presentation will consist of a combination of previously created slides with new slides, you'll begin by opening a blank presentation (instead of using the AutoContent Wizard) and creating a title slide. You'll then insert the slides on Inca Imports' marketing campaign that Enrique Hoffmann has already developed.

To open a blank presentation:

1. Start PowerPoint, and in the PowerPoint startup dialog box, click the **Blank presentation** option button, and then click the **OK** button. The New Slide dialog box opens with the AutoLayout selections.

    TROUBLE? If you've already started PowerPoint, close all other presentations and then click the New button on the Standard toolbar.

2. If necessary, click the **Title Slide** layout to select it, and then click the **OK** button. The placeholders for a title slide appear on the screen in Slide View.

    TROUBLE? If the presentation window isn't maximized, click the Maximize button on the presentation window.

3. Click the title placeholder, and then type **Annual Report**.

4. Click the subtitle placeholder, type **Inca Imports International**, press the **Enter** key, and then type **1999**.

5. Click anywhere outside of any text boxes to deselect them. Your screen should look like Figure 3-1.

Figure 3-1 ◀
Title slide of
blank
presentation

title ——————

subtitle (two lines) ——————

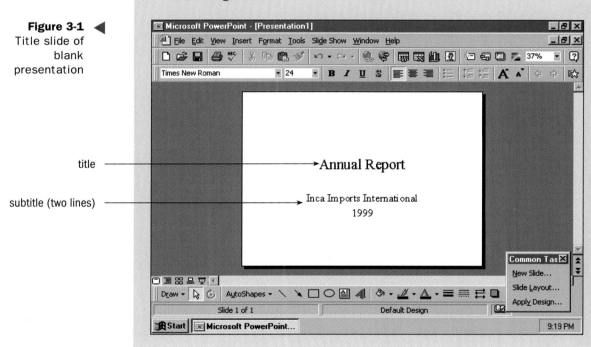

Now that you've created the title slide of the annual report presentation, you're ready to insert the previously created marketing campaign slides.

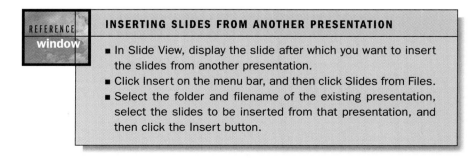

REFERENCE
window

INSERTING SLIDES FROM ANOTHER PRESENTATION

■ In Slide View, display the slide after which you want to insert the slides from another presentation.
■ Click Insert on the menu bar, and then click Slides from Files.
■ Select the folder and filename of the existing presentation, select the slides to be inserted from that presentation, and then click the Insert button.

You'll insert selected slides from Enrique's presentation now.

To insert slides from another presentation:

1. Make sure the title slide of the annual report presentation is still in Slide View, click **Insert** on the menu bar, and then click **Slides from Files**. PowerPoint displays the Slide Finder dialog box. This dialog box allows you to find slides from a presentation on disk and insert any or all of the slides from that presentation.

2. If necessary, click the **Find Presentation** tab to select it, click the **Browse** button, change the Look in list box to **Tutorial.03** on your Student Disk, click **Products** in the list of filenames, click the **Open** button in the Insert Slides from Files dialog box, and then click the **Display** button in the Slide Finder dialog box to display the slides from the existing presentation.

3. Click slide **1** to select it, and then click the **Display Slide Titles** button 🔳 in the dialog box. See Figure 3-2.

Figure 3-2 ◀
Slide Finder
dialog box

path to presentation
file ⎯⎯⎯⎯⎯⎯

currently selected
slide ⎯⎯⎯⎯⎯⎯

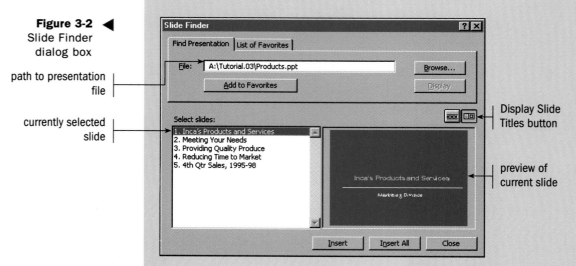

Display Slide
Titles button

preview of
current slide

Patricia asks you to insert only slides 2 through 4 from Enrique's presentation.

4. To select slides 2 through 4, click **2. Meeting Your Needs** in the Select slides list box, and then press and hold down the **Shift** key while you click **4. Reducing Time to Market**.

5. Click the **Insert** button, and then click the **Close** button to return to the presentation window. Slide 4 of Enrique's presentation ("Reducing Time to Market") appears in the presentation window as slide 4 in your new presentation.

6. Click the **Previous Slide** button 🔲 to see slide 3, and then click it again to see slide 2.

The three selected slides from Enrique's existing presentation are now included in your new slide show using the current design template, which is blank. (When you open a new blank presentation, the default design template is blank, with a white background, black text, black round bullets, and Times New Roman font.) Patricia asks you to apply the same design template that Enrique used in his presentation.

Applying a Design Template from Another Presentation

Although you can apply a design from one of the many design templates that PowerPoint provides, you can also apply a template from another presentation. The advantage of this is that, if you've created your own design or modified a PowerPoint design template to fit your own tastes or needs, you can use that modified design in other presentations. For example, Enrique's Products presentation, from which you just inserted some slides, has a customized design. You'll apply the design to the new presentation now.

To apply a design template from another presentation:

1. Click the **Apply Design** button on the Common Tasks toolbar to display the Apply Design dialog box.

2. Change the Look in list box to **Tutorial.03** on your Student Disk, click the **Files of type** list arrow, click **Presentations and Shows**, and then click **Products** if necessary in the list of filenames. You have selected the presentation file with the design template you want to apply to your current presentation.

3. Click the **Apply** button, and then display slide 2. See Figure 3-3. The slide has the design from Enrique's Products presentation.

Figure 3-3 ◀
New slide 2
after inserting
slides and
applying design
template

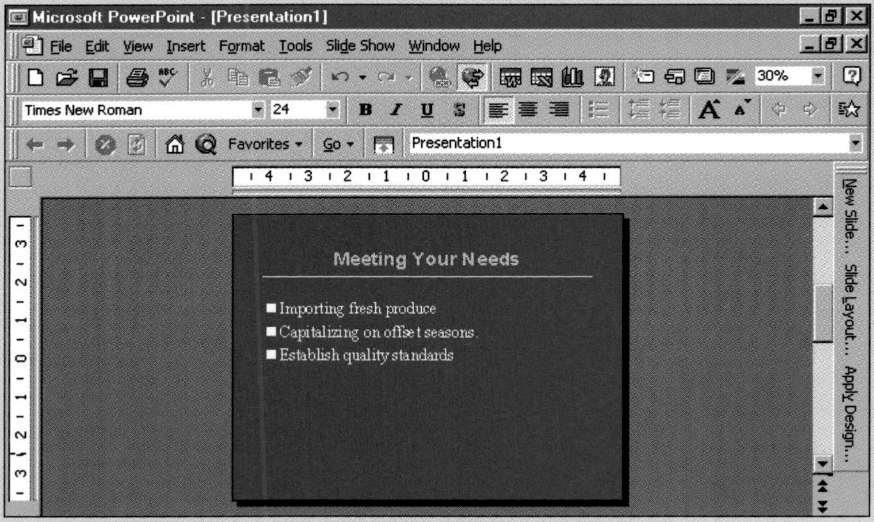

4. Save the presentation to the Tutorial.03 folder on your Student Disk using the filename **Annual Report**.

After studying the design of the presentation, Patricia and you agree that you should change some of the design elements. Specifically, you decide to change the color scheme, modify the font and bullets, change the text alignment, and, on the Title Master, add a scanned image. An easy way to make all these changes is to use the Slide Master.

Using the Slide Master

The **Slide Master** is a slide that contains the text, symbols, and graphics that appear on all the slides (except the title slide) in the presentation, as well as controls the format and color of the text, bullets, and background on all the slides. You can make changes to individual slides without using the Slide Master, but certain changes—like changing the color scheme or inserting a picture—should be made on the Slide Master to take effect on all the slides and promote overall consistency in the presentation.

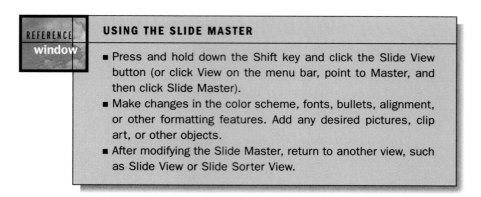

REFERENCE
window

USING THE SLIDE MASTER

- Press and hold down the Shift key and click the Slide View button (or click View on the menu bar, point to Master, and then click Slide Master).
- Make changes in the color scheme, fonts, bullets, alignment, or other formatting features. Add any desired pictures, clip art, or other objects.
- After modifying the Slide Master, return to another view, such as Slide View or Slide Sorter View.

To use the Slide Master, you first have to display it. You'll do that now.

To display the Slide Master:

1. Press and hold down the **Shift** key and position the pointer over the **Slide View** button. The ScreenTip now reads "Slide Master." See Figure 3-4.

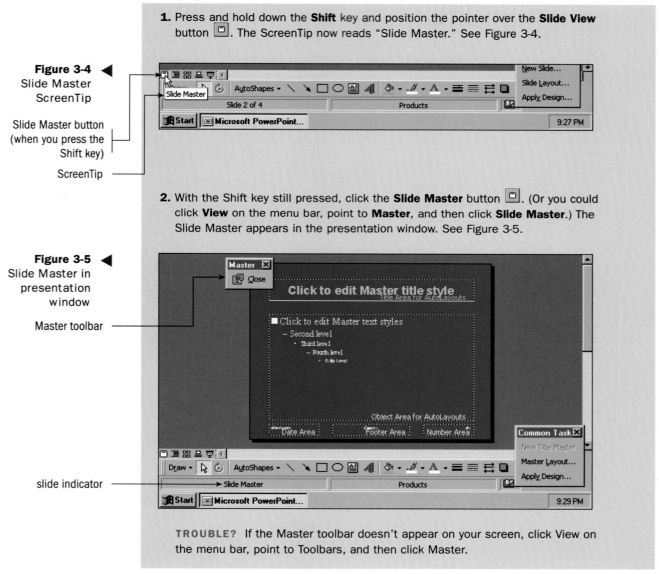

Figure 3-4 ◄
Slide Master
ScreenTip

Slide Master button
(when you press the
Shift key)

ScreenTip

2. With the Shift key still pressed, click the **Slide Master** button. (Or you could click **View** on the menu bar, point to **Master**, and then click **Slide Master**.) The Slide Master appears in the presentation window. See Figure 3-5.

Figure 3-5 ◄
Slide Master in
presentation
window

Master toolbar

slide indicator

TROUBLE? If the Master toolbar doesn't appear on your screen, click View on the menu bar, point to Toolbars, and then click Master.

With the Slide Master displayed in the presentation window, you're ready to change the color scheme.

Changing the Slide Color Scheme

The **color scheme** is the set of colors used for the color of the title text, bulleted text, background, lines, and so forth. You can choose one of PowerPoint's default color schemes, or you can customize your own. For her presentation, Patricia asks you to create a custom color scheme.

To change the slide color scheme:

1. Click **Format** on the menu bar, click **Slide Color Scheme** to display the Color Scheme dialog box, and then click the **Custom** tab in the dialog box. See Figure 3-6.

Figure 3-6 ◀
Color Scheme
dialog box

color of background
(selected)

click to change color

preview of current
color scheme

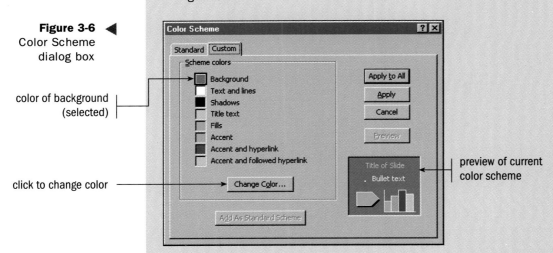

Patricia asks you to select a light tan background color, black text and lines, red title text, gray shadows, dark tan fills, and dark blue accent.

2. If necessary, click the **Background** color tile, click the **Change Color** button to display the Background Color dialog box, and then, if necessary, click the **Standard** tab. See Figure 3-7. You can now select any color from the palette of standard colors.

Figure 3-7 ◀
Standard color
palette

current background
color

background

fills

shadows

accent

title

text and lines

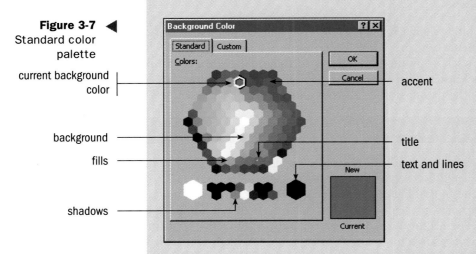

3. Click the light tan hexagonal tile (labeled "background" in Figure 3-7), and then click the **OK** button. The Background Color dialog box closes, and the Background color tile in the Color Scheme dialog box becomes light tan.

4. Click the **Text and lines** color tile, click the **Change Color** button, and then, if necessary, click the **Standard** tab.

5. Click the black hexagonal tile (labeled "text and lines" in Figure 3-7), and then click the **OK** button.

6. Using the same procedure and Figure 3-7 as a guide, change the Shadows color to gray, the Title text color to red, the Fills color to dark tan, and the Accent color to dark blue. The Color Scheme dialog box should now look like Figure 3-8.

Figure 3-8 ◀
Color Scheme
dialog box with
new scheme

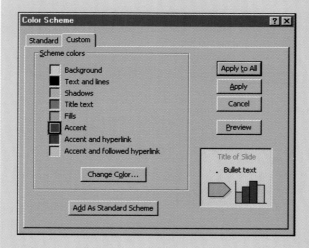

7. Click the **Apply to All** button. (You could also click the **Apply** button; because you're working on the Slide Master, any change to this slide will apply to all slides.)

   Notice that the background of the Master Slide doesn't change to tan because Enrique had manually changed it in his Products presentation file to dark blue. You'll change it now to the desired color.

8. Click **Format** on the menu bar, click **Background** to display the Background dialog box, click the **Background fill** list arrow, click the **Follow Background Scheme Color** tile (the tan tile at the far left), and then click the **Apply to All** button.

The color scheme is now set to how Patricia wants it. You could have changed the color scheme for the entire presentation without using the Slide Master, but other changes, such as modifying bullets and fonts, take effect on all the slides only if you use the Slide Master. Therefore, it's a good idea to always use the Slide Master when you're changing the design so that all your slides will be consistent.

Modifying Fonts and Bullets

Patricia likes the color scheme, and now asks you to change the font and the bullet style in the bulleted lists. A **font** is a set of characters (letters, digits, and other characters such as !, @, and $) that have a certain design and appearance. The current font in the bulleted list of Patricia's presentation, listed on the left of the Formatting toolbar, is Times New Roman. The height of the font, listed to the right of the Font list box on the Formatting toolbar, is measured in points. A **point** is $\frac{1}{72}$ of an inch. Therefore, a 24-point font is $\frac{24}{72}$ or $\frac{1}{3}$ of an inch.

Patricia wants you to change the font in the first-level text of the bulleted list from 30-point Times New Roman to 28-point Century Schoolbook.

PowerPoint

To change the text font:

1. On the Slide Master, click anywhere in the phrase "Click to edit Master text styles" at the beginning of the bulleted list.

2. Click the **Font** list arrow on the Formatting toolbar, and then scroll down and click **Century Schoolbook**.

TROUBLE? If your computer system doesn't have Century Schoolbook, look for New Century Schoolbook. If that font isn't on your system, use another font, such as Baskerville Old Face, Book Antiqua, or Garamond.

3. Click the **Font Size** list arrow, and then scroll down and click **28**.

You have now changed the font of the first-level text in a bulleted list. Patricia also asks you to change the bullet style.

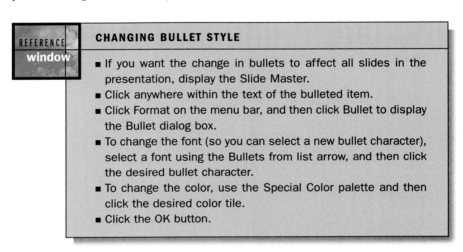

REFERENCE window

CHANGING BULLET STYLE

■ If you want the change in bullets to affect all slides in the presentation, display the Slide Master.
■ Click anywhere within the text of the bulleted item.
■ Click Format on the menu bar, and then click Bullet to display the Bullet dialog box.
■ To change the font (so you can select a new bullet character), select a font using the Bullets from list arrow, and then click the desired bullet character.
■ To change the color, use the Special Color palette and then click the desired color tile.
■ Click the OK button.

You'll change the bullet character to a diamond and its color to red.

To change the character and color of bullets:

1. With the Slide Master still in the presentation window, make sure the insertion point is still in the phrase "Click to edit Master text styles."

2. Click **Format** on the menu bar, and then click **Bullet** to open the Bullet dialog box. See Figure 3-9. The current selection of symbols appears in the grid in the middle of the dialog box.

Figure 3-9 ◀
Bullet dialog
box

current font

select small diamond
shape

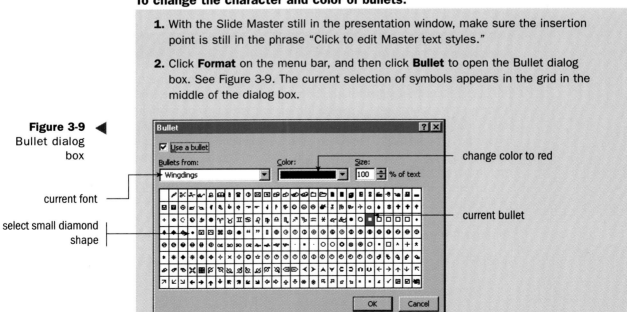

change color to red

current bullet

3. Click the **Bullets from** list arrow, and then scroll down and click **Wingdings** (if necessary).

   TROUBLE? If your system doesn't have a symbols font (such as Wingdings, Symbols, Dingbats, or Monotype Sorts) available in the Bullets from list box, skip to the next section, "Changing Text Alignment."

4. Click the symbol for a small diamond, as shown in Figure 3-10, which is appropriate for a presentation to stockholders (rather than an informal bullet, like a smiling face or a pointing hand). When you click the shape, the size of the selected shape doubles so you can see it more clearly.

   Next, you'll change the bullet color.

5. Click the **Color** list arrow, and then click the red **Follow Title Text Scheme Color** tile. You have now created a new bullet style. See Figure 3-10.

Figure 3-10 ◀
Completed
Bullet dialog
box

font

bullet character
(small diamond)

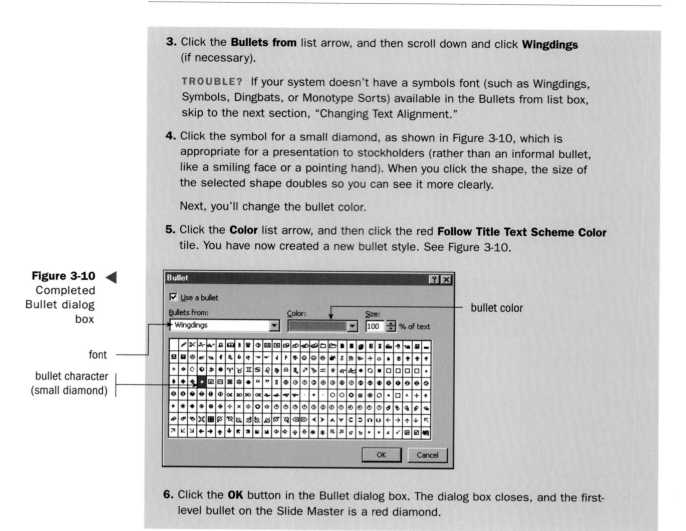

6. Click the **OK** button in the Bullet dialog box. The dialog box closes, and the first-level bullet on the Slide Master is a red diamond.

Having changed the font and bullet style on the Slide Master, you're now ready to make your next design change: modifying the text alignment of the title text.

Changing Text Alignment

The **alignment** of text in a text box refers to how the text lines up horizontally between the margins. **Left alignment** is the alignment of text along the left margin of the text box. If the text box contained a paragraph of text with two or more lines, the left edges of the lines would all be aligned vertically but the right edges would be **ragged**, that is, uneven along the right side of the text box. With **right alignment**, the text is aligned along the right margin but ragged along the left edge of the text box. With **center alignment**, the lines of text are centered between the two edges of the text box.

Currently, the title text in the Slide Master is centered. Patricia wants you to change it to left-aligned, so that it is flush with the left edge of the text box.

To align the text in a text box:

1. Click an edge of the title text box at the top of the Slide Master. When you select the box, a thick, gray line appears around the text box, and resize handles appear at the corners and at the center of each edge of the box.

2. Click the **Left Alignment** button 🖳 on the Formatting toolbar. The text in the box moves to the left edge. See Figure 3-11.

Figure 3-11
Setting text to
left alignment

Left Alignment button
(selected)

left-aligned text

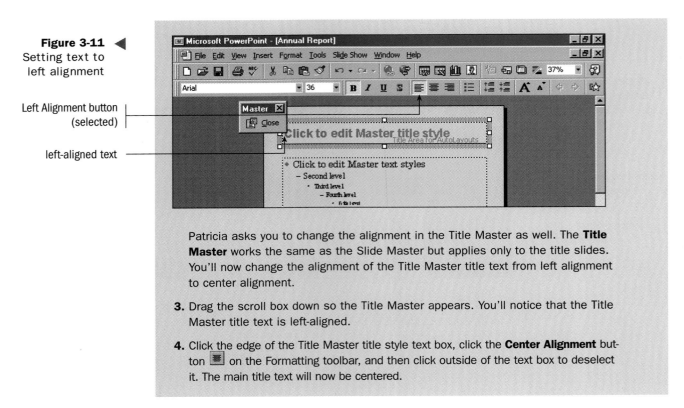

Patricia asks you to change the alignment in the Title Master as well. The **Title Master** works the same as the Slide Master but applies only to the title slides. You'll now change the alignment of the Title Master title text from left alignment to center alignment.

3. Drag the scroll box down so the Title Master appears. You'll notice that the Title Master title text is left-aligned.

4. Click the edge of the Title Master title style text box, click the **Center Alignment** button ▤ on the Formatting toolbar, and then click outside of the text box to deselect it. The main title text will now be centered.

You have changed the color scheme, modified the font and bullet style, and changed the text alignment. Your last design change is to add a scanned image to the Title Master.

Adding a Scanned Image to the Title Master

Patricia wants you to add a scanned (and edited) image of Machu Picchu, the ruins of the Lost City of the Incas, to the Title Master. This image serves as a second logo for Inca Imports. Because you are adding the scanned image to the Title Master, it will appear only on the title slide. If you were to add more than one title slide to the presentation, it would appear on all the title slides. To add a picture (whether it's a scanned image or a piece of art) to the Title Master, you follow the same procedure as adding a picture to a regular slide.

To add a scanned image to a Title Master:

1. With the Title Master still in the presentation window, click **Insert** on the menu bar, point to **Picture**, and then click **From File** to open the Insert Picture dialog box.

2. If necessary, change the Look in folder to **Tutorial.03** on your Student Disk, and then click the file **MachPicc**, a scanned picture of Machu Picchu, the Lost City of the Incas.

3. Click the **Insert** button to insert the picture into the middle of the Title Master. The Picture toolbar also appears on the screen while the scanned image is selected. You'll now change the size and position of the picture.

4. Click the **Format Picture** button 🖼 on the Picture toolbar to open the Format Picture dialog box, and then click the **Size** tab.

5. In the Scale section of the dialog box, make sure the **Lock aspect ratio** check box is checked, so that when you change the height, the width will also change automatically (so the picture dimensions don't become distorted), change the scale Height to **50%**, and then click the **OK** button.

6. Drag the picture so it rests centered above the title text box, and then deselect the picture. See Figure 3-12.

Figure 3-12 ◀
SlideMaster in
presentation
window

scanned image, sized
and positioned

centered Master
title text

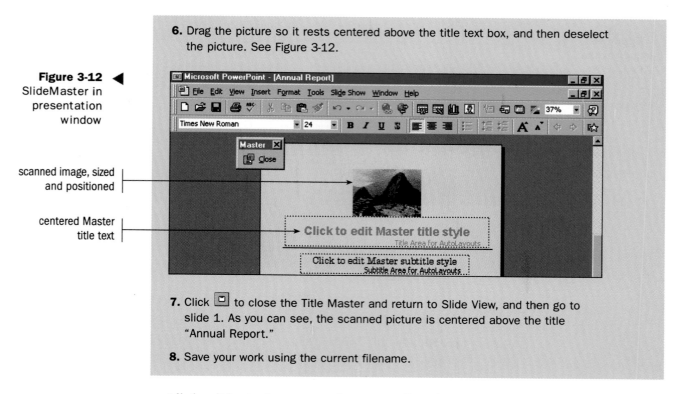

7. Click ⬜ to close the Title Master and return to Slide View, and then go to slide 1. As you can see, the scanned picture is centered above the title "Annual Report."

8. Save your work using the current filename.

All the slides in the presentation now reflect the changes you have made to the Slide Master and Title Master.

Patricia reviews your progress on the presentation and is pleased with your changes. However, she remembers two errors in the text of the presentation and asks you to correct them. First, the phrase "Establish quality standards" needs to be "Establishing quality standards." Second, the phrase "Year around" should be "Year-round" wherever it occurs in the document. To find and correct these phrases in the document, you'll use the Find and the Replace features of PowerPoint.

Finding and Replacing Text

The **Find** command locates a specified sequence of characters in the presentation. (In this short presentation, you could probably find the phrases just as fast by reading each slide one at a time, but in a presentation with many slides, you can find text much faster by using the Find feature.) The **Replace** command searches through a presentation for a sequence of characters and then substitutes one or more occurrences of this sequence with a specified replacement sequence.

You'll first use the Find command to find the phrase "Establish quality standards."

To find text in the presentation:

1. Click **Edit** on the menu bar, and then click **Find**. The Find dialog box opens. See Figure 3-13.

Figure 3-13 ◀
Find dialog box

click these
check boxes

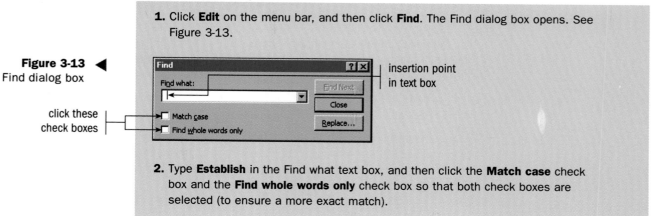

insertion point
in text box

2. Type **Establish** in the Find what text box, and then click the **Match case** check box and the **Find whole words only** check box so that both check boxes are selected (to ensure a more exact match).

3. Click the **Find Next** button. PowerPoint searches the presentation until it locates the words "Establish quality standards" in the third bulleted item on slide 2, displays that slide in the presentation window, and selects the phrase.

4. Because this is the phrase you're trying to find, you can now click the **Close** button in the Find dialog box. Click I immediately to the right of the selected word "Establish" to deselect the word.

   You're now ready to add "ing" so that the word becomes "Establishing."

   TROUBLE? If the insertion point is after the space to the right of the word, move the insertion point back one space so it's immediately to the right of the word.

5. Type **ing**. The phrase "Establishing quality standards" now uses the same verb tense as the other two bulleted items on the slide.

Having used the Find command to correct the first error, you're now ready to use the Replace command to correct the second error: replacing "Year around" with "Year-round."

To replace a phrase in the presentation:

1. With the insertion point still in slide 2 (actually, the insertion point could be anywhere in the presentation), click **Edit** on the menu bar, and then click **Replace**. The Replace dialog box opens.

2. Type **Year around** into the Find what text box, press the **Tab** key to move the insertion point to the Replace with text box, and then type **Year-round**. Make sure the **Match case** and **Find whole words only** check boxes are selected. See Figure 3-14.

Figure 3-14 ◀
Replace dialog
box

search phrase ⎯⎯⎯

replacement phrase ⎯⎯⎯

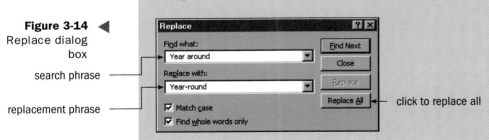

click to replace all

3. Click the **Replace All** button in the dialog box. PowerPoint searches for all occurrences of "Year around" and replaces them with "Year-round." When the Replace operation is completed, PowerPoint displays a dialog box to inform you that it has finished searching. In this case, PowerPoint replaced only one occurrence of "Year around" with "Year-round."

4. Click the **OK** button in the message dialog box, and then click the **Close** button in the Replace dialog box.

5. Go to slide 3 to see the phrase "Year-round supply," the first bulleted item on the slide.

Patricia thanks you for correcting these two errors so quickly. After reviewing the presentation again, she decides that one of the slides should be hidden, and that the presentation should end with a black (blank) slide. You'll make these changes next.

Hiding Slides and Adding a Black Final Slide

Patricia asks you to hide a slide, not delete it, because she might want to use it in a later presentation. It's easy to hide slides in PowerPoint using Slide Sorter View.

To hide a slide and add a black slide:

1. Click ⊞ to display the slides of the presentation in Slide Sorter View. Notice that the Slide Sorter toolbar appears below the Standard toolbar.

2. Click slide **4** to make it the current slide, and then click the **Hide Slide** button 🔲 on the Slide Sorter toolbar. The slide number for slide 4 now has a slash through it, indicating that it won't appear when you run the slide show. See Figure 3-15.

Figure 3-15 ◀
Presentation in
Slide Sorter
View

selected slide

hidden

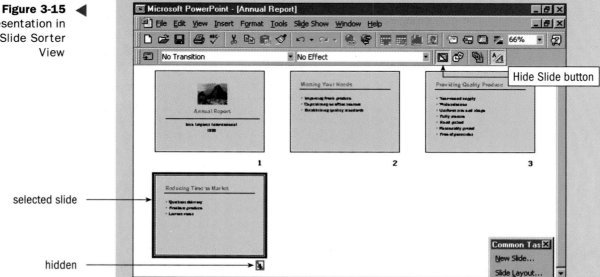

With slide 4 hidden, you're now ready to add a black slide to the end of Patricia's presentation.

3. Click **Tools** on the menu bar, click **Options**, click the **View** tab (if necessary), click the **End with black slide** check box (if necessary), and then click the **OK** button.

To make sure you've successfully hidden the slide and added a black slide, you'll review the presentation in Slide Show View.

4. Click slide **1**, and then click the **Slide Show** button 🖳. The slide show begins.

5. Go through the entire slide show. If you find a problem, return to Slide View and fix it.

Now Patricia decides that she wants slide 4 in the slide show after all.

6. Switch to Slide Sorter View, click slide **4**, and then click the **Hide Slide** button 🔲 to deselect it. Now when you run the slide show the next time, slide 4 will also appear.

7. Save your work using the current filename.

Quick Check

1. List the major items that you should include in your preparation for a presentation meeting.

2. Describe how you would insert slides from an existing presentation into a new one.

3. Why would you apply a design template from another presentation?

4. Describe the purpose of the Slide Master and when you would use it.

5. How would you do the following?
   a. display the Slide Master
   b. change the color scheme of a slide
   c. modify the text alignment
   d. modify a bullet style

6. How do you insert a scanned image into a slide?

7. What is the Replace command and when would you use it?

8. Why would you hide a slide in a presentation?

You have made good progress on Patricia's presentation: You have inserted slides from another presentation, used the Slide Master and Title Master to change the format and appearance of all the slides in the presentation, used the Find and Replace commands to edit the text, hidden (and unhidden) a slide, and added a black slide. In Session 3.2, you'll complete the presentation by building a graph, creating a table, adding special effects, and using the Style Checker. You'll then prepare the materials Patricia will need, such as overheads, for her presentation.

SESSION

3.2

In this session, you will learn how to build a graph and create a table, as well as add transition and animation effects to a slide show. You will also learn how to use the Style Checker, create 35mm slides, prepare overheads, and print the slide show in color. Finally, you will learn about the PowerPoint Viewer and the Pack and Go Wizard.

Building a Graph (Chart)

On slide 4 of the presentation, Patricia asks you to add a column chart that compares Inca Imports' time to market (that is, the time from picking to customer delivery, in hours) during the past four quarters with those of its two major competitors in southern California.

REFERENCE window	**INSERTING A CHART**
	■ Display the desired slide in Slide View.
	■ If necessary, change the slide layout to Text & Chart or Chart & Text.
	■ Double-click the chart placeholder. PowerPoint displays a datasheet.
	■ Edit the information in the datasheet for the data that you want to plot.
	■ Click anywhere outside the datasheet, and then click anywhere outside the chart box.

You'll now create a chart that compares the time-to-market information. You'll begin by adding a chart to slide 4.

To add a chart to the slide:

1. If you took a break after the last session, make sure PowerPoint is running and the file Annual Report is open in Slide View, and then go to slide 4, "Reducing Time to Market."

2. Click the **Slide Layout** button 🖼 on the Standard toolbar, click the **Text & Chart** layout (second row, first column), and then click the **Apply** button. The text on the slide becomes formatted into a smaller text box on the left side of the slide, and a chart placeholder appears on the right side.

3. Double-click the chart placeholder. After few moments, PowerPoint inserts a sample graph and displays a **datasheet**, or a grid of cells, similar to a Microsoft Excel worksheet, in which you can add data and labels.

   TROUBLE? If the colors on the slide become distorted, don't worry. They'll return to normal once you close the datasheet window.

To create the chart for Patricia's presentation, you simply change the information in the sample datasheet on the screen. The information on the datasheet is stored in **cells**, which are the boxes that are organized into rows and columns. The rows are numbered 1, 2, 3, ... and the columns are labeled A, B, C.... Next, you'll edit the information in the datasheet to reflect the three companies' times to market.

To edit the information in the datasheet:

1. Position the pointer over the cell that contains the word "East." The pointer changes to ✛.

2. Click in the cell that contains the word "East," and then type **Inca** (short for "Inca Imports International").

3. Press the **down arrow** key to select the cell labeled "West," and then type **SCP** (which stands for "Southern California Produce," one of Inca Imports' major competitors).

4. Press the **down arrow** key to select the cell labeled "North," and then type **CCF** (which stands for "Central City Foods," Inca Imports' other major competitor). See Figure 3-16.

Figure 3-16 ◄
Creating a chart

datasheet ——

new labels in column ——

sample chart ——

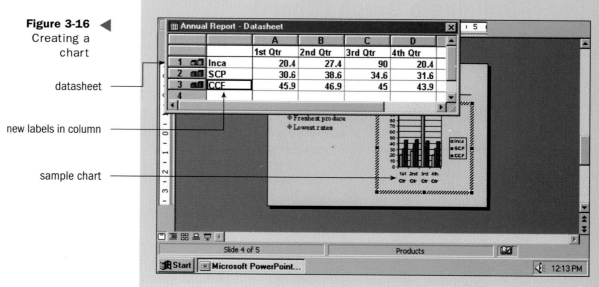

Now you're ready to change the actual numbers in the datasheet.

5. Click in cell **A1**, the cell at which column A and row 1 intersect, and then type **16**. This is Inca Imports' average time to market in hours during the first quarter of the year.

6. Click in cell **B1**, type **18**, press the **Tab** key, type **17**, press the **Tab** key, and then type **16**. This completes the data for Inca Imports.

7. Use the same procedure to replace the current data for SCP and CCF with the data shown in Figure 3-17. Carefully check your datasheet to make sure it matches Figure 3-17. Make any necessary corrections.

Figure 3-17 ◀
Completed
datasheet

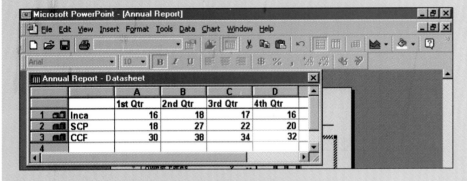

8. Click the **Close** button ⊠ in the datasheet window to remove the datasheet from the screen. The completed chart appears in slide 4.

Patricia reviews the chart and suggests that you insert a title to label the vertical axis of the chart.

To add an axis title to a chart:

1. Make sure the chart is still selected, click **Chart** on the menu bar, and then click **Chart Options** to open the Chart Options dialog box.

2. Click in the **Value (Z) axis** text box, type **Hours**, and then click the **OK** button. The label "Hours" appears to the left of the vertical axis

3. With the Value (Z) axis title still selected, click **Format** on the menu bar, click **Selected Axis Title** to display the Format Axis Title dialog box, and then click the **Alignment** tab.

4. In the Orientation section, change the Rotation to **90** degrees, and then click the **OK** button to return to the chart on the slide. The "Hours" on the vertical axis is now rotated so it reads bottom to top.

5. Click anywhere in a blank area of the chart box to deselect "Hours."

6. Position the pointer over the left center resize handle of the chart box, so that the pointer changes to ↔, and then drag the handle to the left until the left edge of the graph box is near the right edge of the text of the slide. See Figure 3-18.

Figure 3-18
Completed and resized chart

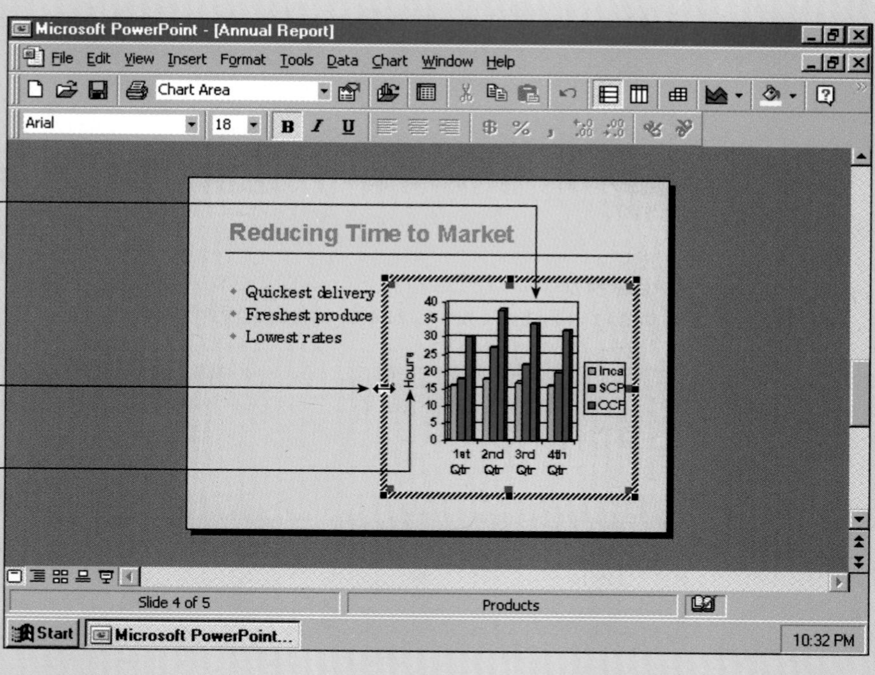
Microsoft PowerPoint - [Annual Report]
File Edit View Insert Format Tools Data Chart Window Help
Chart Area
Arial
18
Reducing Time to Market
Quickest delivery
Freshest produce
Lowest rates
Hours
40
35
30
25
20
15
10
5
0
1st Qtr
2nd Qtr
3rd Qtr
4th Qtr
Inca
SCP
OCP
Slide 4 of 5
Products
Start
Microsoft PowerPoint...
10:32 PM
completed chart
making chart wider
axis title (rotated)

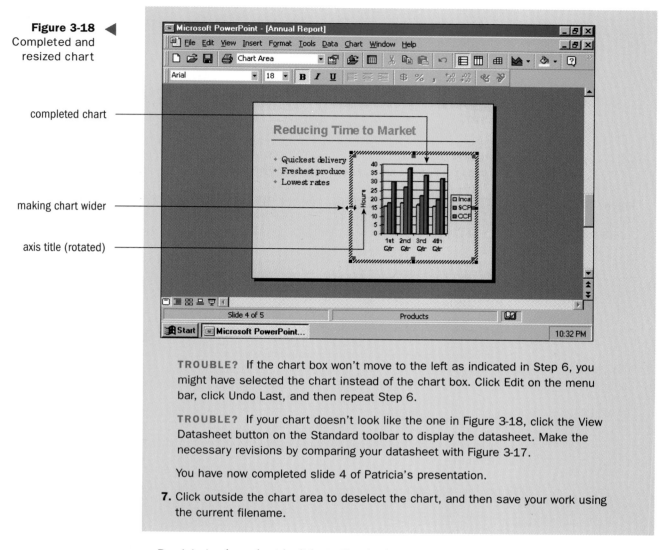

TROUBLE? If the chart box won't move to the left as indicated in Step 6, you might have selected the chart instead of the chart box. Click Edit on the menu bar, click Undo Last, and then repeat Step 6.

TROUBLE? If your chart doesn't look like the one in Figure 3-18, click the View Datasheet button on the Standard toolbar to display the datasheet. Make the necessary revisions by comparing your datasheet with Figure 3-17.

You have now completed slide 4 of Patricia's presentation.

7. Click outside the chart area to deselect the chart, and then save your work using the current filename.

Patricia is pleased with slide 4. She thinks just two more slides are needed to complete her presentation: a new slide 5 that summarizes Inca Imports' performance and a new slide 6 that shows Inca Imports' sales and profits. You'll add slide 5 first.

Adding a New Slide

Slide 5 will be a simple bulleted list that summarizes the performance of Inca Imports.

To add new slides:

1. Make sure slide 4, in Slide View, appears in the presentation window.
2. Click on the Standard toolbar to insert a new slide into the presentation and open the New Slide dialog box.
3. Click the **Bulleted List** layout, and then click the **OK** button.
4. Click the title placeholder, and type **Inca's Solid Performance**.
5. Click the main text (bulleted list) text box, and type three bulleted items: **Improved products and services**, **Implemented new marketing plan**, and **Increased profitability**.
6. Click outside the text boxes to see the completed slide. See Figure 3-19.

PowerPoint

Figure 3-19 ◄
New slide 5

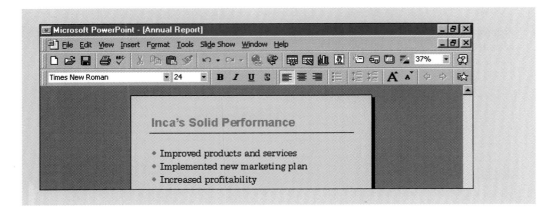

That completes the new slide 5. You're ready to add the last slide to Patricia's presentation.

Creating a Table

Patricia wants her presentation to end with strong evidence of the fiscal health of Inca Imports. She asks you, therefore, to add a new slide 6 with a table of data that shows Inca Imports' sales and profits during the previous four years. A **table** is information arranged in horizontal rows and vertical columns. Each rectangular area where a row and column intersect is called a cell. You should use a table instead of a chart if you have to present extensive data or if you want to stress the actual numbers rather than the trend. In this presentation, Patricia wants to stress the numbers for sales and profits, so she selects a table as the means for presenting the information.

When you create a table in PowerPoint, you actually use the Table feature from Microsoft Word. If you're familiar with Word, you're probably already familiar with many of the features of creating a table in PowerPoint.

Entering Information into the Table

In the new slide 6, you'll create a table that includes a title, three columns (labeled "Year," "Sales," and "Profits"), and five rows (one row with the headings and four rows of data).

To create a table:

1. Click 🖼 on the Standard toolbar to open the New Slide dialog box, click the **Table** layout (first row, fourth column), and then click the **OK** button.

2. Click the title placeholder and type the title **Four Years of Profitability**.

3. Double-click the table placeholder. The Insert Word Table dialog box opens.

4. Set the number of columns to **3** and the number of rows to **5**, and then click the **OK** button. After a moment, a blank, 3×5 table appears on the slide. See Figure 3-20.

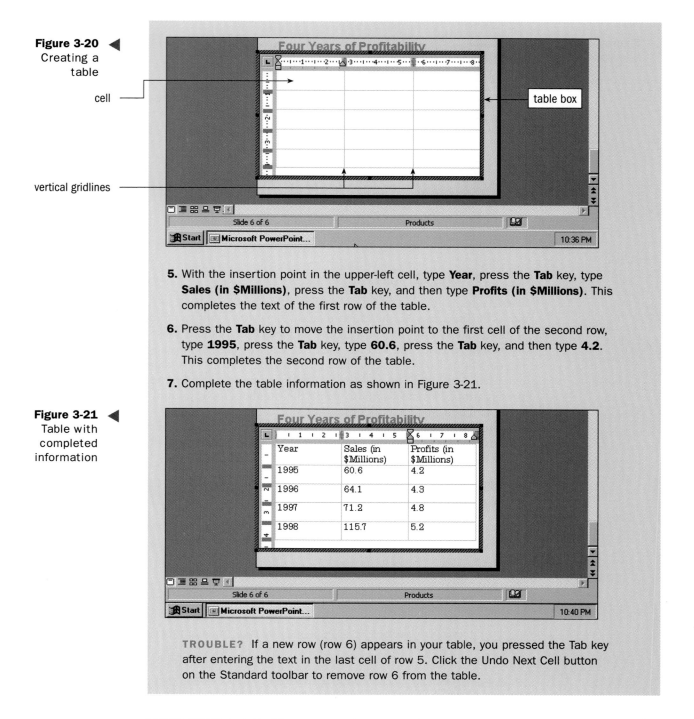

Figure 3-20 ◀
Creating a
table

cell

table box

vertical gridlines

5. With the insertion point in the upper-left cell, type **Year**, press the **Tab** key, type **Sales (in $Millions)**, press the **Tab** key, and then type **Profits (in $Millions)**. This completes the text of the first row of the table.

6. Press the **Tab** key to move the insertion point to the first cell of the second row, type **1995**, press the **Tab** key, type **60.6**, press the **Tab** key, and then type **4.2**. This completes the second row of the table.

7. Complete the table information as shown in Figure 3-21.

Figure 3-21 ◀
Table with
completed
information

Year	Sales (in $Millions)	Profits (in $Millions)
1995	60.6	4.2
1996	64.1	4.3
1997	71.2	4.8
1998	115.7	5.2

Slide 6 of 6   Products

Start | Microsoft PowerPoint...   10:40 PM

TROUBLE? If a new row (row 6) appears in your table, you pressed the Tab key after entering the text in the last cell of row 5. Click the Undo Next Cell button on the Standard toolbar to remove row 6 from the table.

Formatting the Table

If you were to run the slide show now, you would see that the table has the necessary information, but it has not been formatted to improve its appearance and readability. For example, the current table has no **rules**, which are the horizontal or vertical lines that divide rows, columns, or cells. The lines that you currently see in the presentation window are **gridlines**, the lines showing the cell boundaries. The gridlines themselves do not appear in the slide show or in the printed presentation. You'll now draw rules along certain gridlines to make the table more attractive and readable.

PowerPoint

To add rules to the table:

1. Click the **Tables and Borders** button 🗗 on the Standard toolbar. The Tables and Borders toolbar opens. See Figure 3-22. Note that the Tables and Borders toolbar may already be displayed, as well as anchored, on your computer screen.

Figure 3-22 ◀
Tables and Borders toolbar

Draw Table button
(selected)

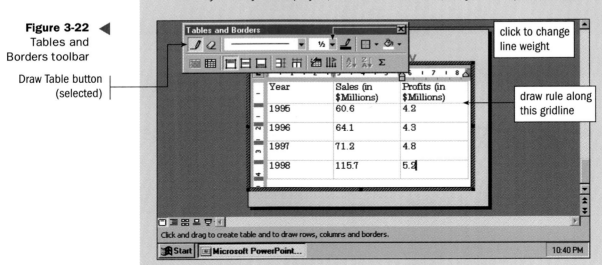

2. If necessary, click the **Draw Table** button 🖉 on the Tables and Borders toolbar to select it (the button should be pressed). The pointer becomes ⌀ as you move it onto the table.

3. Click the **Line Weight** list arrow on the Tables and Borders toolbar, and then click **3 pt**. This changes the line weight (thickness) from ½ point to 3 points, so that when you draw a rule along a gridline, the rule will be 3 points thick.

4. Move ⌀ to the left edge of the horizontal gridline below the first row of the table. Click the left mouse button, drag the pointer along the gridline to the right edge of the table, and then release the mouse button. A thick line appears below the heading row of the table.

5. Using this same method, draw a 3-point rule along the bottom horizontal gridline of the table. See Figure 3-23.

Figure 3-23 ◀
Rules
(horizontal
lines) on table

line weight

new rules

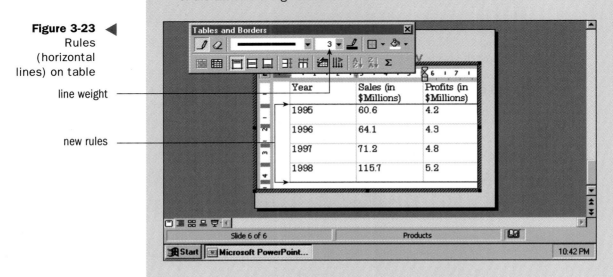

TROUBLE? If you misdraw a line, click Edit on the menu bar, click Undo Borders and Shading, and then redraw the line.

6. Click 🗗 on the Standard toolbar to close the Tables and Borders toolbars.

Now you'll select the first row of the table, change the text to boldface, and center the text within each cell of the first row.

7. Move the pointer to the left edge of the first row, so that the pointer becomes ⬁, and then double-click. This selects the entire first row of the table.

8. Click the **Bold** button [B] on the Formatting toolbar, click the **Center** button [≡], and then click in any cell other than one in the top row. The text of the heading row is now boldfaced and centered.

9. Click below the table in the blank area of the slide to deselect the table. Your slide 6 should look like Figure 3-24.

Figure 3-24 ◄
Slide 6 with
completed
table

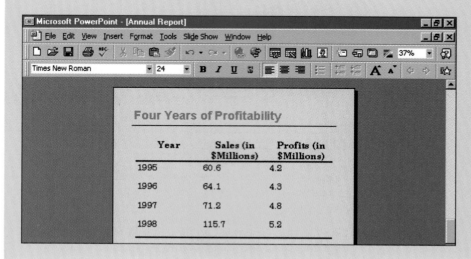

When you show the table to Patricia, you suggest that you align the sales and profitability numbers along the right edge of each cell, rather than along the left edge. This would make the column of numbers more readable. Similarly, you think the dates below the "Year" heading should be centered. Patricia agrees with your suggestions and asks you to edit the table accordingly.

Editing the Table

Editing a table requires that you return to the Word Table feature. You do this by double-clicking the table.

To edit the table:

1. Double-click anywhere in the table of slide 6.

2. Move the point to the left edge of the second cell in the second row (the cell that contains "60.6") so that the pointer becomes ⬁.

3. Click the left mouse button, and then drag the pointer to the right and down until all the cells with sales and profits numbers are selected.

4. Click the **Align Right** button [≡] on the Formatting toolbar.

5. Select the four cells below the "Year" heading, click [≡] on the Formatting toolbar, and then click below the table in the blank space of the slide. See Figure 3-25.

Figure 3-25 ◄
Table with
right-aligned
numbers and
centered years

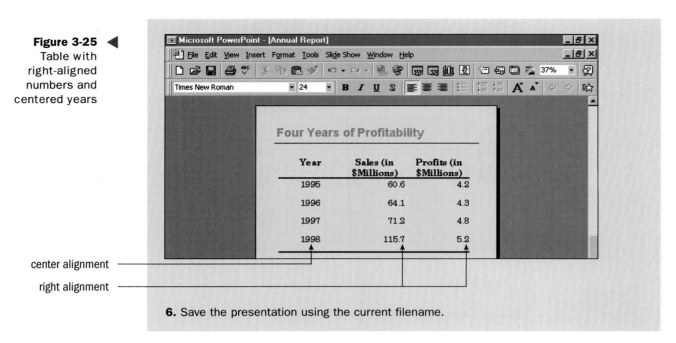

center alignment ———

right alignment ———

6. Save the presentation using the current filename.

This completes the table on slide 6, the last slide that Patricia wants to include in her presentation. To make her presentation more interesting, Patricia now asks you to add special effects to the slide show.

Adding Special Effects

Special effects—such as fading out of one slide as another appears, animated (moving) text, and sound effects—can liven up your presentation, help hold your audience's attention, and emphasize key points. On the other hand, special effects can also distract or even annoy your audience. Your goal is to apply special effects conservatively and tastefully so that, rather than making your presentation look gawky and amateurish, they add a professional look and feel to your slide show.

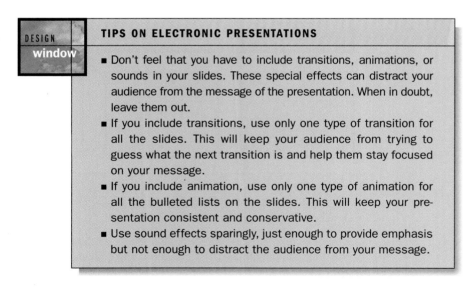

DESIGN
window

TIPS ON ELECTRONIC PRESENTATIONS

- Don't feel that you have to include transitions, animations, or sounds in your slides. These special effects can distract your audience from the message of the presentation. When in doubt, leave them out.
- If you include transitions, use only one type of transition for all the slides. This will keep your audience from trying to guess what the next transition is and help them stay focused on your message.
- If you include animation, use only one type of animation for all the bulleted lists on the slides. This will keep your presentation consistent and conservative.
- Use sound effects sparingly, just enough to provide emphasis but not enough to distract the audience from your message.

Adding Slide Transitions

The first special effect that Patricia wants you to add is a transition effect. A **transition effect** is a method of moving one slide off the screen and bringing another slide onto the screen during a slide show. You must be in Slide Sorter View to add transitions.

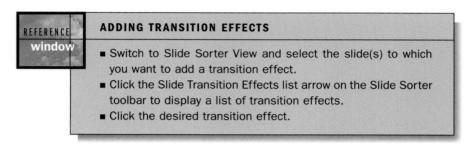

REFERENCE window

ADDING TRANSITION EFFECTS

- Switch to Slide Sorter View and select the slide(s) to which you want to add a transition effect.
- Click the Slide Transition Effects list arrow on the Slide Sorter toolbar to display a list of transition effects.
- Click the desired transition effect.

You'll add a transition to all the slides in the presentation.

To add a transition effect:

1. Click ⊞ to switch to Slide Sorter View.

2. Click **Edit** on the menu bar, and then click **Select All** to select all the slides in the presentation. Now when you apply a slide transition, all the slides will have that transition. Currently, the Slide Sorter toolbar shows "No Transition" in the Slide Transition Effects list box. See Figure 3-26.

Figure 3-26 ◄
Slide Sorter
View with all
slides selected

click to set
transition effect

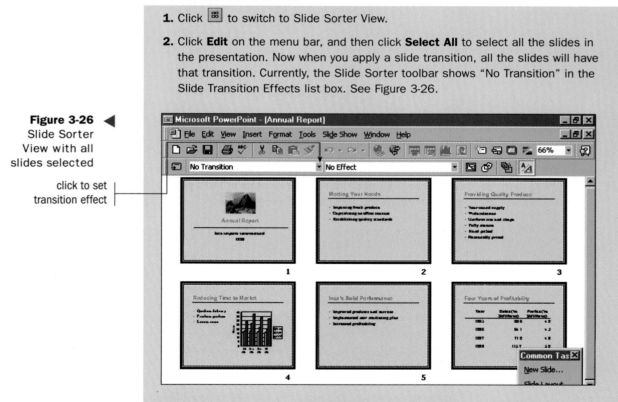

3. Click the **Slide Transition Effects** list arrow on the Slide Sorter toolbar to display the list of transitions.

4. Scroll down the list and then click **Dissolve**. If you watched carefully, you saw PowerPoint demonstrate the dissolve transition on the first slide.

5. Click anywhere outside of a slide to deselect the slides. A transition icon appears below the lower-left corner of each slide.

   You can test the transition of any slide now by clicking on the transition icon.

6. Click the transition icon below slide 6. As you can see, PowerPoint momentarily displays slide 5 at that location, and then performs the transition to slide 6. Click any of the transition icons to see how the transition looks for that slide.

Having added transitions to the slides, you're ready to add more special effects: animation and sound.

Adding Animation and Sound

Animation is the special visual or sound effect of an object (such as graphics or bulleted text). For example, Patricia asks you to add an animation effect that allows you to progressively display individual bulleted items, one item at a time. In addition, she asks you to include sound with the animation effect. As a result, on the slides that have several bulleted items, you will add the animation effect so that when you first display the slide in your slide show, only the slide title appears, without any of the bulleted items. Then when you click the left mouse button (or press the spacebar), the first bulleted item appears, with a "whooshing" sound. When you click the left mouse button again, the second bulleted item appears with a "whoosh," and so on. You will also tell PowerPoint to dim the previous bulleted item as a new one is added. The advantage of this type of animation effect is that you can focus your audience's attention on one item at a time, without the distractions of other items on the screen.

REFERENCE window	**ADDING ANIMATION**
	■ In Slide Sorter View, select the slide(s) to which you want to add an animation effect.
	■ Click the Text Preset Animation list arrow on the Slide Sorter toolbar to display a list of animation effects.
	■ Click the desired animation effect.
	■ To dim previous items in a bulleted list and add sound effects, display the desired slide in Slide View, click Slide Show on the menu bar, click Custom Animation, click the Effects tab, click the desired Animation Order item, click the After Animation list arrow, click the tile of the desired color, click the Sound list arrow, click the desired sound, and then click the OK button.

You'll now add an animation effect and sound to the bulleted lists in Patricia's presentation.

To add an animation effect and sound:

1. Click slide **2**, press and hold down the **Shift** key, and then click slides **3** through **5** to select the four slides that have bulleted lists. Release the **Shift** key.

2. Click the **Text Preset Animation** list arrow on the Slide Sorter toolbar to display the list of preset animations. These are called "preset" because they are built into PowerPoint. You can also create custom animations.

3. Click **Fly From Right**. This specifies the type of animation effect you want. In this case, the text in each bulleted item will fly from the right edge of the slide to its position on the left edge of the slide. Notice that a slide animation icon appears next to the transition icon below the lower-left corner of each slide with an animation effect.

   You're now ready to add sound to the animation effect.

4. Click anywhere other than within the selected slides to deselect them, click slide **2** to select it, and then click ⊡ to display slide 2 in Slide View.

5. Click **Slide Show** on the menu bar, click **Custom Animation**, click **1. Text 2** in the Animation order list box, and then click the **Effects** tab (if necessary). See Figure 3-27. Notice that the Entry animation is already set to "Fly From Right."

Figure 3-27 ◄
Custom
Animation
dialog box

selected region
of slide

current animation
effect

change to Whoosh

click to set
"dimmed" color

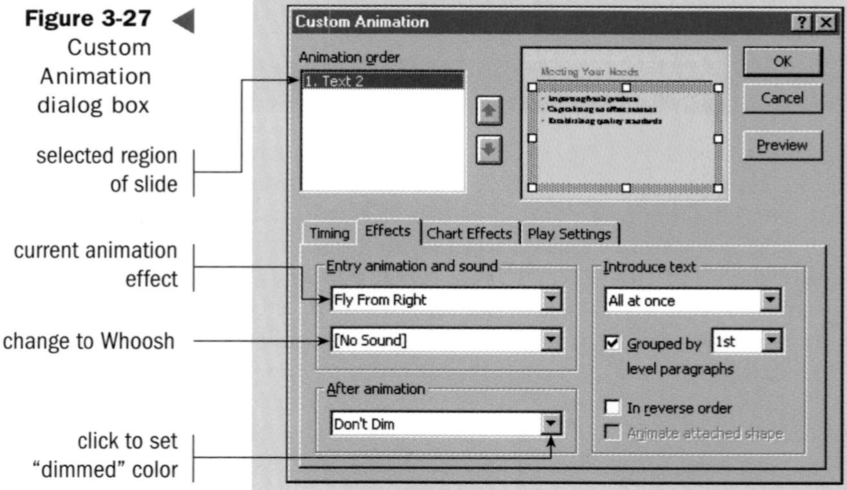

6. Click the **Sound** list arrow in the Entry animation and sound section in the dialog box, and then scroll down and click **Whoosh**. As each bulleted item flies into view during a slide show, PowerPoint will make a whooshing sound.

   Your last task to complete the animation effect is to dim the previous bulleted items when a new one appears on the screen.

7. Click the **After animation** list arrow, and then click the dark tan tile (labeled "Follow Fills Scheme Color"). As a new bulleted item appears in a slide show, the previous bulleted items will be dark tan.

8. Click the **Preview** button in the Custom Animation dialog box to see how the animation will look and sound, and then click the **OK** button to apply these animation effects to slide 2.

   TROUBLE? If you don't hear anything, you might not have a sound card in your computer system. If you know you have a sound card, you might have to turn up the volume. If you don't know how to do this, consult your instructor or technical support person.

9. Repeat this same method of applying animation effects to slides 3 through 5, and then save your work using the current filename.

You'll now view the slides with animation effects in Slide Show View so you can see the transitions and the "Fly From Right" animations and hear the sound effects.

Starting the Slide Show in the Middle

Because you're interested in viewing only the animation effects, which you applied to slides 2 through 5, you'll view the presentation beginning with slide 2.

To view the completed presentation:

1. Go to slide 2 in Slide View. When you begin a slide show, whichever slide appears in the presentation window in Slide View will be the slide where the slide show begins.

2. Click ▣ to begin the slide presentation. Slide 2, "Meeting Your Needs," appears on the screen.

3. Click the left mouse button (or press the spacebar) to display the first bulleted item, "Importing fresh produce." As you can see, the bulleted item flies from the

right edge of the screen to its final position at left. If your computer has a sound card, you can also hear the "whoosh" during the animation.

4. Click the left mouse button to display the second bulleted item and dim the first one. See Figure 3-28.

Figure 3-28 ◄
Slide 2 in Slide
Show View

dimmed bulleted
item

current bulleted
item

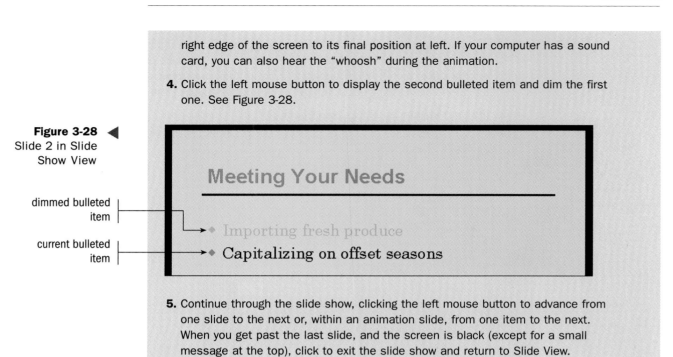

5. Continue through the slide show, clicking the left mouse button to advance from one slide to the next or, within an animation slide, from one item to the next. When you get past the last slide, and the screen is black (except for a small message at the top), click to exit the slide show and return to Slide View.

Patricia is pleased with the presentation. To finalize her slide show, Patricia asks you to use the Style Checker.

Checking the Presentation Style

PowerPoint provides a useful function called the **Style Checker**, which checks your presentation for correct spelling, visual clarity, case, end punctuation, and consistency in other stylistic elements. Patricia wants you to check the presentation to make sure its style is accurate and consistent.

To check the presentation style:

1. With any slide in the presentation window in Slide View, click **Tools** on the menu bar, and then click **Style Checker**. The Style Checker dialog box opens.

2. Make sure all three check boxes in the dialog box are selected, and then click the **Options** button to open the Style Checker Options dialog box. If necessary, click the **Case and End Punctuation** tab. See Figure 3-29.

Figure 3-29 ◄
Style Checker
Options dialog
box

checked check boxes

selected option
buttons

selected
case styles

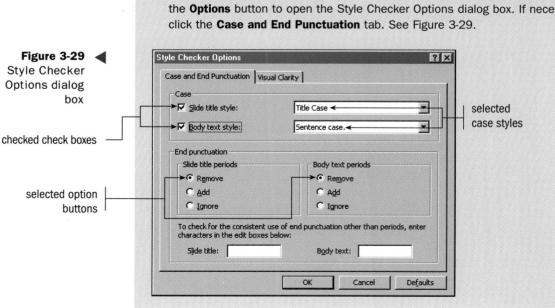

3. Make sure the various options in your dialog box are set like those in Figure 3-29. Namely, in the Case section, make sure the Slide title style is set to **Title Case**, and the Body text style is set to **Sentence case**. Also make sure the End Punctuation is set to remove slide title periods and body text periods.

4. Click the **Visual Clarity** tab. See Figure 3-30.

Figure 3-30 ◄
Style Checker
Options dialog
box with
default settings

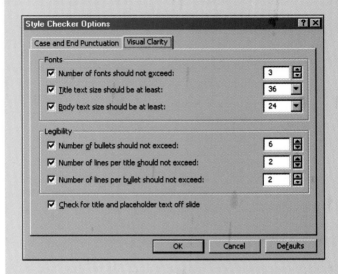

5. Make sure all the options on the Visual Clarity tab are set to those shown in Figure 3-30, which are PowerPoint's default options.

6. Click the **OK** button in the Style Checker Options dialog box, and then click the **Start** button in the Style Checker dialog box. PowerPoint begins checking through each slide. When it gets to slide 2, the Style Checker issues a style inconsistency warning: "Paragraph 2 of placeholder 2 of slide 2 has end punctuation." See Figure 3-31.

Figure 3-31 ◄
Style Checker
message

click to fix problem ——————

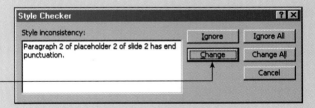

This tells you that one of the items on the slide has a period, which you want to remove.

7. Click the **Change** button. The Style Checker removes the period and continues checking the other slides.

Next, you get the warning that slide 3 has too many bulleted items and that the presentation has too many fonts. If you carefully go through the current slides, you'll find only two fonts, Arial and Century Schoolbook. PowerPoint thinks there are more fonts because other fonts were part of the original design template. The problem with too many bullets on slide 3, however, is real, so you decide to delete the last bullet, an item that Patricia feels isn't important anyway.

8. Click the **OK** button in the warning message dialog box, go to slide 3, and delete the final bulleted item, "Free of pesticides."

You should always look through the presentation after completing a style check because the Style Checker might introduce new errors. In this case, the first letter of the second two words in the company name on slide 1 have been changed to lowercase. You'll have to fix this problem.

9. Move to slide 1 and correct the subtitle, so that the company's name reads "Inca Imports International," and then save the presentation using the current filename.

As you can see from this example, the Style Checker has some strengths and limitations. The strengths are that if you accidentally misspell words, make bulleted lists too long, improperly punctuate some of the bulleted items or titles, or make some other stylistic mistake, PowerPoint can find the problems. The weaknesses are that sometimes the Style Checker changes the case of phrases that should stay as you originally typed them, or warn you of conditions that aren't really problems. The strengths, however, greatly outweigh the weaknesses. You should always run the Style Checker as part of your final polishing of a PowerPoint presentation.

Now that you've completed Patricia's slide show, your final tasks are to help her produce the materials she'll need for her presentation.

Preparing Presentation Materials

Patricia will present the electronic slide show to the board of directors in a suitably equipped conference room at Inca Imports. The conference room at the stockholders meeting, however, doesn't have the equipment necessary to run an electronic slide show, so Patricia plans to use 35mm slides.

Preparing 35mm Slides

Inca Imports, like most small businesses, lacks the facilities to make 35mm slides or print color output from computer files, but most U.S. cities have service bureaus that can convert computer files into 35mm slides. PowerPoint also supports the services of Genigraphics Corporation, a service bureau that handles 35mm slides, color overheads, and posters. PowerPoint contains the software necessary to prepare and deliver a file to Genigraphics. If you send the file to a Genigraphics facility, the company will create 35mm slides of the presentation and mail them back to you.

REFERENCE window	USING GENIGRAPHICS TO PREPARE 35MM SLIDES
	■ Click File on the menu bar, click Page Setup to open the Page Setup dialog box, click the Slides sized for list arrow, click 35mm Slides, and then click the OK button.
	■ Click File, point to Send To, and then click Genigraphics to start the Genigraphics Wizard.
	■ Continue through the Genigraphics Wizard, answering each question appropriately and filling in the necessary information.
	■ When you have completed the Genigraphics Wizard, click the Finish button, and then save the Genigraphics file.

Patricia uses PowerPoint to prepare and deliver a file to Genigraphics, and within a few days, receives her 35mm slides from them. Because her presentation to the stockholders is so important, Patricia decides to be safe and asks you to create color overheads of the presentation as well, in case the 35mm slide projector doesn't work.

Preparing Overheads

With PowerPoint, you can prepare overhead transparency masters quickly and easily. You simply have to change the slide design to Overhead. However, some designs that work well for slides don't work as well for overheads, so you may need to change the design template. Patricia asks you to change the slide design to one that is more appropriate for overheads.

To change the presentation design to overheads:

1. Click **File** on the menu bar, and then click **Page Setup** to open the Page Setup dialog box.

2. Click the **Slides sized for** list arrow, and then select **Overhead**.

   Patricia wants to change the orientation of the printing from landscape, which is wider than it is tall, to portrait, which is taller than it is wide. Overheads fit the projector better if they are in portrait orientation.

3. Click the **Portrait** option button in the Slides Orientation section, click the **OK** button, and then switch to Slide Sorter View. The slides are displayed in portrait orientation. See Figure 3-32.

Figure 3-32 ◀
Presentation in
Overhead
format

distorted scanned image

distorted chart

illegible table

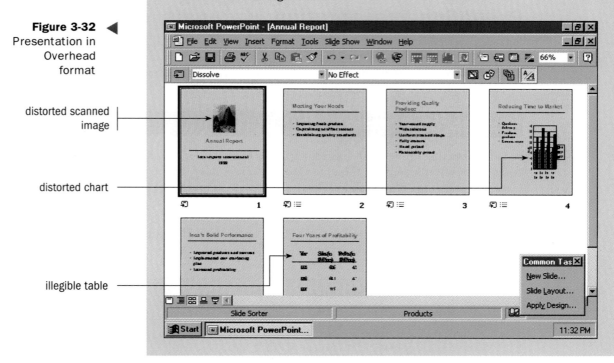

As you can see in Figure 3-32, most of the slides are readable, but the scanned image on slide 1, the chart on slide 4, and the table on slide 6 have become distorted. You'll fix these problems now.

To fix the image and the table in the slide show:

1. Click slide **1**, and then press and hold the **Shift** key and click 🖳 to display the Title Master.

2. Right-click the picture of Machu Picchu, and then click **Format Picture** to open the Format Picture dialog box.

3. Click the **Size** tab, click the **Lock aspect ratio** check box to deselect it, change the scale Height and Width to **66%**, and then click the **OK** button.

PowerPoint

4. Drag the picture so it's centered above the Master Title text box.

5. Switch to Slide View, go to slide 4, drag the appropriate resize handles to make the chart wider and shorter, so it's no longer stretched out.

6. Go to slide 6. As you can see, the spacing between the characters in the table has become distorted to fit the table onto the slide in portrait orientation.

7. Double-click anywhere on the table to edit it, select all the cells in the table, click the **Font Size** list arrow on the Formatting toolbar, click **26** to change the font size from 28 to 26, and then deselect the table.

Your final tasks are to change the background color to white (which Patricia believes will work better for overheads), save the file, and then print the presentation on a color printer.

Printing the Slide Show in Color

To modify, save, and print the presentation on a color printer:

1. Click ⊞ to return to Slide Sorter View, click **Format** on the menu bar, click **Background** to open the Background dialog box, click the **Background fill** list arrow, click **More Colors**, click the white hexagonal tile, click the **OK** button, and then click the **Apply to all** button. The background of all the slides becomes white. See Figure 3-33.

Figure 3-33 ◀
Completed
presentation
in Overhead
format

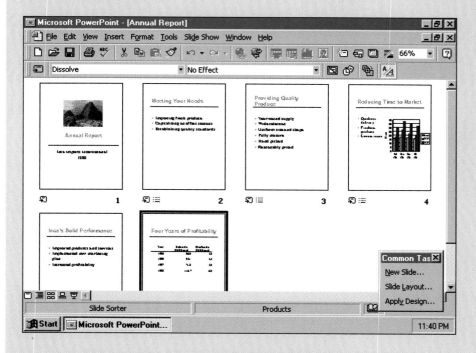

2. Click **File** on the menu bar, click **Save As**, and then save the presentation to the Tutorial.03 folder of your Student Disk using the filename **Annual Report Overheads**.

3. If necessary, take your disk to a computer on which PowerPoint is installed and a color printer (that supports overhead transparencies) is attached.

   TROUBLE? If you don't have access to a color printer, or if your instructor tells you to print the overheads as black-and-white masters, you may use your regular black-and-white printer.

4. Click **File**, and then click **Print** to open the Print dialog box.

5. Make sure that **Slides (without animations)** is selected in the Print what list box and that the **Black & white** option is *not* selected if you're printing to a color printer (or *is* selected if you're printing to a black-and-white printer).

6. Click the **Frame slides** check box so that PowerPoint will draw a box around each slide.

7. If you're using a color printer, make sure the printer has transparency sheets (or regular paper, if your instructor wants you to use regular paper) in its page feed, and then click the **OK** button to print the overhead presentation.

8. Save your changes and then exit PowerPoint.

Patricia is now ready for almost any problem that might arise as she gives her presentation. She has her PowerPoint presentation on disk as well as on 35mm slides and overheads. She has, however, one last, important step in getting ready: making sure her presentation will run even if PowerPoint isn't installed on the computer in the boardroom where she will give her presentation. She knows that she doesn't need PowerPoint installed because she can use the PowerPoint Viewer.

Preparing the Presentation to Run on Another Computer

The PowerPoint **Viewer** is a separate program that you can use to give your slide show on any Windows 95 or Windows NT computer. The Microsoft PowerPoint license allows you to create a Viewer disk and to install the Viewer program on other computers without additional charge.

Patricia will use the **Pack and Go Wizard** to create a Viewer disk that contains the PowerPoint Viewer files and a copy of her presentation. In a sense, the Pack and Go Wizard makes PowerPoint a portable program. Patricia can use the Pack and Go disk to install the Viewer and run the presentation file on any computer. Although Patricia can't change any of the slides using the PowerPoint Viewer, she is able to review the entire slide show, including special effects.

 REFERENCE window

PREPARING A PACK AND GO DISK AND RUNNING THE VIEWER

- Place a blank, formatted disk in one of the disk drives.
- Click File on the menu bar, and then click Pack and Go to start the Pack and Go Wizard.
- Continue through the Pack and Go Wizard, answering each question appropriately and filling in the necessary information.
- When you have completed the Pack and Go Wizard, click the Finish button. PowerPoint saves the Viewer and all other necessary files to the Pack and Go disk.
- To run the Viewer, put the Pack and Go disk in the disk drive, click the Windows 95 Start button, click Run, type a:\pngsetup in the Open text box, and then click the OK button.
- Fill in the necessary information in the Pack and Go Setup dialog box, click the OK button, and then answer further questions, including Yes when you're asked if you want to run the presentation.

GIVING EFFECTIVE SLIDE SHOW PRESENTATIONS

- Dress appropriately for the meeting.
- Maintain a professional demeanor at all times.
- Introduce yourself and briefly explain what you'll be showing your audience.
- Look at your audience. Make adequate eye contact.
- Speak clearly and audibly.
- If you're using a microphone, adjust it to your height so you won't have to lean down or stretch up to speak into it.
- Keep your language appropriate for the audience and situation. Avoid jargon and slang.
- Summarize your presentation, come to a logical conclusion, and field questions courteously.

Quick Check

1 How do you edit the datasheet of a chart?

2 What are the gridlines in a table? Why would it be useful to draw rules along certain gridlines?

3 Define the following terms:
   a. transition effect
   b. animation effect
   c. sound effect

4 Describe in general terms (not in specific steps) how you would do the following:
   a. add a transition effect to a slide
   b. add sound to an animation effect on a slide

5 Using the Style Checker has both its advantages and disadvantages: name one of each. Why do the advantages outweigh the disadvantages?

6 Describe what you would need to do to create overheads from your PowerPoint slide presentation.

7 What is the purpose of the Genigraphics Wizard?

8 What is the PowerPoint Viewer? When would you use it?

Using PowerPoint, the on-screen slides, 35mm slides, and overheads have been completed in an attractive and readable format. Further, Patricia believes that the special effects for the on-screen slide show will help her audience stay focused on her presentation. She thanks you for your help.

Tutorial Assignments

After Angelena Cristenas, Vice President of Operations at Inca Imports, reviews Patricia's presentation (using the Viewer disk), she asks you to create a similar presentation that will describe Inca Imports' benefits to new employees. Complete the following for Angelena:

1. If necessary, start PowerPoint and make sure your Student Disk is in the appropriate disk drive.

2. Create a new blank presentation with a title slide. Title the slide "Employee Benefits" and subtitle it "Inca Imports International."

3. Using the Slide Master, change the color scheme as follows: background color, dark green; text and lines color, light blue; shadow color, black; and title text color, white. Leave the other items in their default color.

4. Change the background shade style to From corner, and the variant with the lightest color in the lower-left corner and the darkest in the upper-right corner. *Hint*: Click the Background fill list arrow in the Background dialog box, and then click Fill Effects to change the shade style and variant.

5. Change the Slide Master title font to Arial, and the text alignment to left alignment.

6. Insert the MachPicc scanned image (from the Tutorial.03 folder on your Student Disk) into the Slide Master. Resize it to a height of 1.5 inches, with the aspect ratio preserved. Position the logo in the lower-right corner of the text box of the Slide Master slide text style, near the text "Object Area for AutoLayouts."

7. Add a new slide with the Bulleted List layout. Make the title of the new slide "Basic Benefits." Type the following first-level bulleted list items: "Medical and Dental Insurance," "Group Term Life Insurance," "Disability Insurance," "Occupational Accidental Death & Dismemberment Insurance," and "Master Retirement Plan."

8. Insert all the slides from the existing presentation file Benefits from the Tutorial.03 TAssign folder on your Student Disk into the current presentation, following slide 2.

9. Use the Replace command to replace all occurrences of ampersands (&) to the word "and."

10. To all the slides, add the transition effect called "Random Bars Vertical."

11. To slides 2 through 5, add the preset animation effect called "Fly From Bottom Left." In each of these slides, set the animation effect to dim the previous items to a gray color. Set the sound effect in the animation to Laser.

12. Move slide 5 so it becomes slide 4.

13. In slide 6, remove the bullets that appear to the left of the address of the benefits office. *Hint:* Using the Slide Master, highlight the Second level text, display the Bullet dialog box, and then deselect the Use a bullet check box.

14. Set the options so that a black slide appears at the end of the slide show.

15. Check the style of the presentation for consistency, with the Slide title style set to Title Case and the Body text style set to Sentence case. Fix any problems with punctuation. Manually fix any case (capitalization) problems the Style Checker may have introduced (namely, in the company name and in the benefits office address).

16. Use the Handouts Master to set the layout of the printed handouts so that they will automatically reflect the date they were printed in the upper-right corner. *Hint:* Press the Shift key and the Outline View button, click View on the menu bar, click Header and Footer, and then make sure the Notes and Handouts tab is selected.

17. Save the presentation as Supplemental Benefits in the Tutorial.03 TAssign folder on your Student Disk, print the presentation in black and white as handouts (six slides per page), and then close the file.

Case Problems

1. Training on Sexual Harassment Katherine Jaidar is the Director of Human Resources Development for McNeil Manufacturing Company, a large manufacturer of gardening supplies—rakes, hoes, shovels, hoses, sprinkling systems, and tillers. One of her responsibilities is to provide training to McNeil employees on sexual harassment in the workplace. Katherine asks you to prepare a PowerPoint presentation for her training classes. Do the following:

1. Create a new presentation with a title slide. Make the title "Sexual Harassment in the Workplace"; make the first line of the subtitle "Training for employees of," and the second line of the subtitle "McNeil Manufacturing Company."

2. Add a new slide with the Bulleted List layout. Make the title "Definition of Sexual Harassment," and type the following bulleted items: "Promise of career advancement for sexual favors," "Threats of career jeopardy if sexual demands are rejected," and "Deliberate, repeated, unsolicited comments, gestures, or physical actions of a sexual nature."

3. Insert a new slide 3 using the Table layout. Type the title "Cases of Sexual Harassment at McNeil."

4. Insert a table into slide 3. Add information and format the table similar to that shown in Figure 3-34.

Figure 3-34 ◄

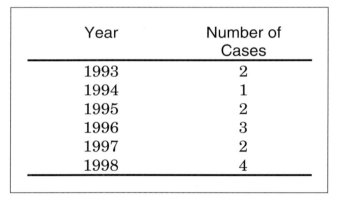

Year	Number of Cases
1993	2
1994	1
1995	2
1996	3
1997	2
1998	4

5. Insert all the slides from the file Harass in the Tutorial.03 Cases folder on your Student Disk after slide 3 of the current presentation.

6. Apply the design template from Harass to the current presentation.

7. Set the title text style on the Slide Master to center alignment, and change the color of the first-level master text style to a dark green.

8. Because slide 7 will only be shown to managers, hide the slide in the presentation.

9. Add the "Fly From Bottom" animation effects to all the slides that have bulleted lists. Include the feature to dim previous points to gray. Add the sound effect Typewriter.

10. To all the slides, add the transition effect called "Checkerboard Across" with a slow speed. *Hint*: You can set the transition speed in the Transition dialog box, which opens when you click the Slide Transition button on the Slide Sorter toolbar.

11. Check the style (including spelling) of your presentation. Make sure none of the lines of text ends with a period and that the case (capitalization) is consistent.

12. Run the slide show to ensure that the transitions work properly, save the presentation as Harassment Policy, and then print all the slides of the presentation as a handout, six slides per page, in black and white.

13. Convert the page setup to Overheads, with a page orientation of portrait. Make any adjustments in the text or table of the presentation so that everything is readable.

14. Save the presentation as Harassment Policy Overheads in the Tutorial.03 Cases folder on your Student Disk.

15. Print the overheads as black-and-white handouts (two slides per page), making any necessary adjustments to ensure readable handouts, and then close the file.

2. Posthaste Inc. Dennis Pham owns a highly successful mail center that provides shipping and photocopying services. He has just decided to offer two computers for use on the premises and wants to create an eye-catching PowerPoint presentation that will inform customers about the services that Posthaste provides. Dennis has created a rough draft of this presentation, and asks you to finalize it by doing the following:

1. Open the presentation file Pham from the Tutorial.03 Cases folder on your Student Disk.

2. Apply the Zesty design template, and then change the first-level bullet style to purple, filled squares.

3. Animate the clip-art image of the courier in slide 1 so that it flies in from the left. *Hint:* In Slide View, select the clip-art image and then use the Custom Animation feature.

4. Add appropriate clip-art images to slides 2 and 5.

5. In slide 6, convert the information into a pie chart. Use "Customer Survey Results" as the chart title and show the percents next to the pie sections. Edit and format the chart as necessary to make it readable and attractive. *Hint:* Delete the current bulleted item before applying the Chart layout. To create a pie chart, click the Chart Type list arrow on the Formatting toolbar. To show the percentage next to the pie section, click the Data Labels tab in the Chart Options dialog box.

6. Add "Dissolve" animation effects to all of the slides that have bulleted lists. Have the animation effect dim previous points, and include an appropriate sound effect.

7. To all the slides, add the transition effect called "Uncover Right-Down" with a slow speed. *Hint:* You can set the transition speed in the Transition dialog box.

8. Check the style of your presentation using the Style Checker.

9. Save the presentation as Posthaste in the Tutorial.03 Cases folder on your Student Disk, print all the slides of the presentation as handouts (in color, if possible), with three slides per page, and then close the file.

3. Skytower Records Regina Khan is the director of marketing for Skytower Records. She will present the results of the past year's marketing efforts to the company's board of directors. Regina is excited about the results, and wants to create a presentation that will highlight the good news. She asks you to help her complete the presentation by doing the following:

1. Open the presentation file Records from the Tutorial.03 Cases folder on your Student Disk.

2. Add an appropriate clip-art image to the Title Master.

PowerPoint

3. In slide 3, add a chart that compares the market share of the top music stores over the past three years, as follows: Raging Records (Raging): 67% in 1996, 54% in 1997, and 40% in 1998; Skytower Records (Skytower): 21% in 1996, 28% in 1997, and 33% in 1998; and Cutting Edge CDs (Cutting), 12% in 1996, 18% in 1997, and 27% in 1998. *Hint:* Change the A through C labels to 1996, 1997, and 1998, respectively, and delete the information in the D column.

4. In slide 4, format the table so that it's more readable and attractive by changing the alignment and adding rules.

5. Add an appropriate clip-art image to slide 5, and then move the slide so that it appears before the current slide 3.

6. Select the option to display a black slide to signal the end of the presentation.

7. Add transition effects for all slides, and add animation effects (with sound and dimming of previous points) for all slides with bulleted lists.

8. Include speaker notes on slides 2 through 5. Remember to zoom the page to 100% in Notes Page View to type your notes.

9. Customize the speaker notes printouts by decreasing the notes area to half its default size and increasing the slide area to use up the remaining space. *Hint:* Use the Notes Master by holding down the Shift key and then clicking the Notes Page View button.

10. Run the Style Checker to ensure that your slide is consistent and the spelling is correct.

11. Save the presentation as Skytower in the Tutorial.03 Cases folder on your Student Disk, print the speaker notes in black and white, and then close the file.

4. Presentation on Your College As a community service, you have been asked to present information about your college to area high-school students. Prepare a presentation that includes information about the advantages of enrolling at your school.

Create a new presentation that includes at least six slides. Choose an appropriate and attractive color scheme, background shading, and fonts. Your slides should include clip art, a graph and/or table, and interesting transition and animation effects. Make sure your presentation includes the principles of good design discussed in this tutorial, and remember to keep your audience in mind. When you're done with your slides, view the slide show, print handouts (as two slides per page) of the presentation, save the presentation in the Tutorial.03 Cases folder using the filename My College, and then close the file.

Integrating PowerPoint with Other Programs and with the World Wide Web

Presenting a Proposal to the Executive Officers

Inca Imports International

Two years ago, Inca Imports International established a permanent distribution facility in Quito, Ecuador, and began an aggressive marketing campaign to attract new clients. Both of these moves proved highly successful: Inca Imports expanded to a company of 80 employees and has become the leading supplier of imported fruits and vegetables in southern California. Patricia Cuevas, President and CEO, and Angelena Cristenas, Vice President of Operations, are pleased with the progress of their company and now want to expand further. They want Inca Imports' executive officers to consider establishing an office in the northeastern United States, with headquarters in New York City. Patricia has asked Angelena to coordinate, prepare, and deliver the main parts of the presentation to the company's executive officers.

Angelena decides to create the presentation using PowerPoint and asks for your assistance. To maximize the impact of her PowerPoint presentation, Angelena asks you to integrate information from other programs, including an outline created in Microsoft Word, clip art from Microsoft Clip Gallery, a sound clip, a video clip, and a Microsoft Excel chart.

After completing her slide show, you'll then help Angelena rehearse her presentation, showing her how to move quickly between slides, add meeting notes and action items, and create hyperlinks to other slides. Finally, so that Angelena's slide show can be seen by those not able to attend her presentation, you'll help Angelena learn how to run a presentation conference and then publish her presentation on the World Wide Web.

OBJECTIVES

In this tutorial you will:

▪ Import an outline from Word into a PowerPoint presentation, modify it, and then export it back to Word

▪ Embed a clip-art image, video clip, and sound clip

▪ Link and modify an Excel chart

▪ Add a tab stop

▪ Use the Slide Navigator and Meeting Minder

▪ Create and edit hyperlinks

▪ Set up a self-running presentation

▪ Learn how to run a conference presentation

▪ Convert a presentation to an HTML document and display the HTML document on a Web browser

SESSION

4.1

In this session, you will learn the definitions of three key words: importing, linking, and embedding, and then begin to use these techniques as you create a presentation. Specifically, you will learn how to import a Word outline into your slide presentation, modify the outline in PowerPoint, and then export it as a Word document. You will also embed (and then modify) a clip-art image, as well as a video clip and a sound clip.

Planning the Presentation

Before you begin to help create Angelena's slide show, she discusses with you her plans for the presentation:

Purpose of the presentation: To propose a major expansion, present advantages and disadvantages of the expansion, and elicit further discussion from Inca Imports' executive officers

Type of presentation: Proposal of a new idea

Audience: Executive officers of Inca Imports: Mark Featherstone, Vice President of Finance; Carl Vetterli, Vice President of Sales and Marketing; Enrique Hoffmann, Director of Marketing; Montgomery Lender, Director of Sales; Carlos Becera, Quality Assurance Manager; and Norma Lopez, Customer Service Manager

Audience needs: To understand the advantages and disadvantages of the expansion to help the executive officers make an informed decision

Location of presentation: Company boardroom, with computer projection system

Format: Electronic slide show, with imported, embedded, and linked graphics, sound, and spreadsheets

With the presentation carefully planned, you're ready to begin creating Angelena's slide show. Before you create the PowerPoint presentation that will integrate other program files (for example, from Word 97 and Excel 97), however, you need to understand about importing, embedding, and linking objects.

Using Integration Techniques: Importing, Embedding, and Linking

In PowerPoint, an **object** is a word-processing file, spreadsheet chart, graphic, organization chart, or some other type of data or information from another program that appears within a presentation. You have already worked with objects, such as clip art from Microsoft Clip Gallery and a scanned picture. PowerPoint supports importing, embedding, and linking objects. Each of these terms is described and defined as follows:

Importing an object means inserting a file that was created using one program into another program's file. For example, for Angelena's presentation, you'll import an outline that was created in Word. When you insert the Word outline, PowerPoint automatically reformats the outline so that it becomes part of the PowerPoint presentation. When you use an imported file, the **source program** (in this case, Word) and the **destination program** (in this case, PowerPoint) don't communicate with each other in any way, as illustrated in Figure 4-1. For example, if you want to modify the Word outline after importing it to PowerPoint, you edit it in PowerPoint, not in Word, by using PowerPoint commands.

Figure 4-1
Integration
techniques

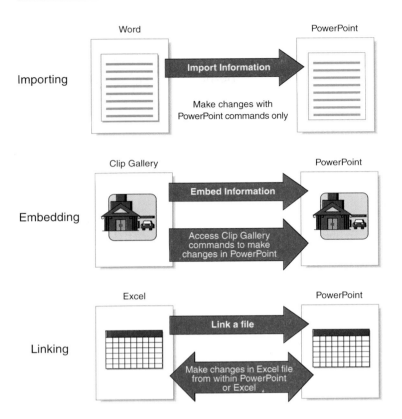

Although similar to importing an object, **embedding** allows a one-way connection to be maintained with the source program. For example, if you embed an Excel chart in a PowerPoint presentation and then double-click on the chart, you could use Excel commands to edit the chart while still in PowerPoint. (Note that to edit the embedded Excel chart while in PowerPoint, Excel must be installed on the same computer that you're using to create the PowerPoint presentation.) However, when you finish editing the embedded chart and return to PowerPoint, the changes you made to the chart will appear in PowerPoint only, not in the original Excel file that you used to create the chart. This is because the embedded object is a copy of the original Excel file, not the Excel file itself. Therefore, if you make subsequent changes to the original Excel file while using Excel, the changes will not be reflected in the embedded chart in PowerPoint.

Linking an object is similar to embedding, except that linking an object creates a two-way connection. When an object is linked, you can open the source program from within the destination program, make changes, and the changes are reflected in both the source program and the destination program. For example, if you link an Excel spreadsheet, PowerPoint uses the original Excel file, not just a copy of it, so that whether you modify the file from within Excel or from within PowerPoint, the original file gets modified.

You should be aware that embedding and linking on some machines, especially those with limited memory, can be slow. Furthermore, not all software allows you to embed or link objects. Only those programs that support **Object Linking and Embedding** (**OLE**, pronounced oh-LAY) let you embed or link objects from one program to another. Fortunately, sophisticated programs like PowerPoint, Word, and Excel are all OLE-enabled programs and fully support object linking and embedding. In this tutorial, you'll import, embed, and link objects as you help Angelena create an effective PowerPoint presentation.

Importing an Outline from Word

Angelena has already created an outline of her presentation in Word. You'll begin preparing her presentation by importing her outline into PowerPoint.

IMPORTING A WORD OUTLINE

- Create and save the outline in Word by clicking the Outline View button and typing the headings.
- Start PowerPoint, start a blank presentation, and switch to Slide View.
- Click Insert on the menu bar, and then click Slides from Outline.
- Type the name of the Word file that you want to import, and then click the Insert button.

Before importing her Word outline, however, Angelena asks you to create a PowerPoint title slide to begin the presentation.

To create a title slide:

1. Start PowerPoint, click the **Blank presentation** option button on the PowerPoint startup dialog box, and then click the **OK** button. The New Slide dialog box opens.

2. Click the **Title Slide** layout if necessary to select it, and then click the **OK** button. A blank title slide appears in the presentation window.

3. If necessary, click the **Slide View** button 🔲 and the **Maximize** button 🔲 of the presentation window to make sure the presentation is in Slide View and the window is maximized.

4. Click the **Title** text box, type **Proposal to Expand into the Northeast**.

5. Click the **Subtitle** text box, type **Patricia Cuevas**, press the **Enter** key, type **Angelena Cristenas**, and then deselect the text box.

Now that you've created the title slide for Angelena's presentation, you're ready to import the Word outline.

To import the outline into PowerPoint and view the presentation:

1. With the title slide in the presentation window, click **Insert** on the menu bar, and then click **Slides from Outline**. The Insert Outline dialog box opens.

2. Change the Look in list box to **Tutorial.04** on your Student Disk, click **Outline** (the Word document that Angelena created), and then click the **Insert** button.

   PowerPoint opens the Word outline and converts it to PowerPoint slides. The presentation now consists of seven slides: the title slide and the six first-level headings from the outline. To see this, switch to Slide Sorter View.

3. Click the **Slide Sorter View** button 🔳 to display the slides in miniature. See Figure 4-2.

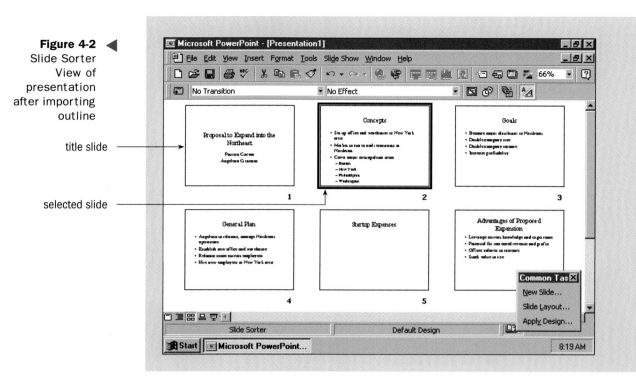

Figure 4-2 ◀
Slide Sorter
View of
presentation
after importing
outline

title slide

selected slide

The outline that you have imported no longer has any connection to the original Word file (Outline) nor to Word. You have created a completely new copy of the outline. If you were to move or delete the file in Word, or if your computer no longer had Word installed, the outline you imported into PowerPoint would remain unaffected. To edit the outline, you would use PowerPoint commands, because the text no longer has access to Word.

Angelena reviews the PowerPoint outline and notices two problems: The "Goals" slide should precede the "Concepts" slide, and the second-level bulleted items on the "Concepts" slide, that is, the names of northeastern cities, are neither necessary nor desirable for Angelena's purposes. She asks you to correct these two problems and then export the outline back to a Word document. Angelena can then use the outline to create a more detailed document about the proposed expansion.

Modifying and Exporting the Outline

To **export** means to save a document, outline, or other object in a file format different from the current one. In PowerPoint, you'll use the Send To command to send (export) the PowerPoint outline to a Word document window. First you'll edit the outline, apply a design template, and save the modified PowerPoint outline, and then you'll export the outline to a Word document.

To edit the outline and apply a design template:

1. While still in Slide Sorter View, move slide 3 ("Goals") to the left of the current slide 2 ("Concepts"), so that "Goals" becomes slide 2.

2. Select the current slide 3 ("Concepts"), and then switch to Slide View.

3. Select and then delete the names (and their bullets) of the four cities at the bottom of the slide.

   You're now ready to apply a design template to the presentation and save it to your Student Disk.

4. Click **Apply Design** on the Common Tasks toolbar, select the design named **Notebook** from the Presentation Designs folder (in the Microsoft Office\Templates folder), and then click the **Apply** button.

5. Switch to Slide Sorter View to check that the design template was applied correctly. If you look closely, you'll notice that the slides with bulleted lists have a black title font instead of a brown title font, which is the default title color for this design template.

   When you apply a design template, you often need to also update the layout. You'll do that now.

6. Click **Edit** on the menu bar, click **Select All** to select all the slides, press and hold down the **Shift** key, and then click slide **1** to deselect it. Now all the slides in the bulleted list format are selected.

7. Click **Slide Layout** on the Common Tasks toolbar to display the Slide Layout dialog box, and then click the **Reapply** button. The slide titles are now brown. See Figure 4-3.

Figure 4-3 ◄
Presentation after applying design

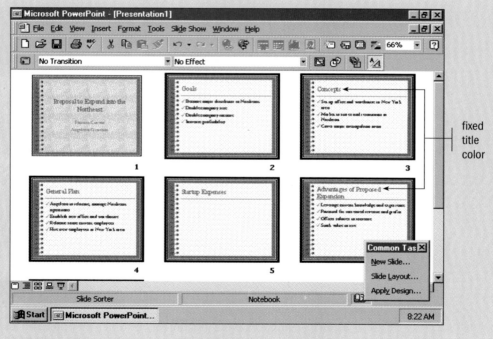

8. Select slide **1**, return to Slide View, and then save the presentation to the Tutorial.04 folder on your Student Disk using the filename **Inca Proposal**.

Having edited and formatted the outline, you're ready to export it.

To export an outline to Word:

1. Click **File** on the menu bar, point to **Send To**, and then click **Microsoft Word**. The Write-Up dialog box opens. You can now choose how you want to send the presentation to Word. Angelena wants you to export the presentation as an outline only.

   TROUBLE? If you don't have Word 97 installed on your computer, simply read the steps in this section without completing them.

2. Click the **Outline only** option button, and then click the **OK** button. After a few moments, Word opens and the outline of the presentation appears in the document window. If necessary, maximize the Word window. See Figure 4-4.

Figure 4-4
Exported
outline in Word

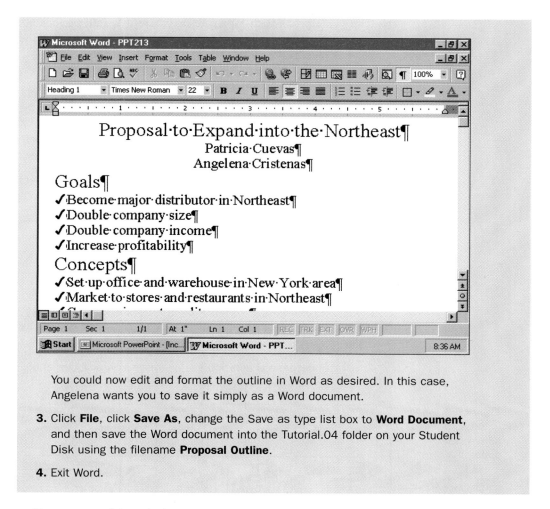

You could now edit and format the outline in Word as desired. In this case, Angelena wants you to save it simply as a Word document.

3. Click **File**, click **Save As**, change the Save as type list box to **Word Document**, and then save the Word document into the Tutorial.04 folder on your Student Disk using the filename **Proposal Outline**.

4. Exit Word.

You can use this technique to export any PowerPoint presentation to Microsoft Word. This is beneficial, as in Angelena's case, for creating a Word document that explains or expands on the points of a presentation.

Angelena is pleased with the PowerPoint outline. She now asks you to enhance the presentation by embedding and linking objects in it. Specifically, you'll embed a clip-art image, video clip, and sound clip, and link an Excel chart and worksheet. You'll begin by embedding a clip-art image.

Embedding and Modifying Clip-Art Images

If you've inserted a clip-art image using Microsoft Clip Gallery, you have already embedded an object. As an embedded object, the clip-art image stays connected to the Clip Gallery. Because the image is connected to the Clip Gallery, you can double-click the image to return to the Clip Gallery to replace the image with a different picture. If the image were imported rather than embedded and you wanted to change the clip-art picture, you would need to delete the current picture and then import another one.

Your first step in enhancing Angelena's presentation is to locate and embed a clip-art image into slide 3 and then modify it. You'll then learn more powerful applications of embedding objects by embedding a video clip and a sound clip.

Searching for a Clip-Art Image

Because of the proposed location of the new office and warehouse, Angelena decides that she wants a clip-art image that evokes the feeling of the New York City area embedded into slide 3. She therefore asks you to use an image of skyscrapers, but you're not sure if the Clip Gallery has such a picture or where it would be located. To solve this problem, you can use the Clip Gallery's Find feature. You'll now search the Clip Gallery to find an image of skyscrapers.

To search for a clip-art image:

1. In Slide View, display slide 3 in the presentation window, and then click the **Insert Clip Art** button 🖼 on the Standard toolbar to open Microsoft Clip Gallery 3.0. The **Clip Gallery** is a collection of objects—clip art, pictures, sound clips, and video clips—that allows you to add, remove, find, and insert these objects into programs.

   TROUBLE? If PowerPoint displays a message that additional objects appear on the Office 97 CD, just click the OK button. You won't need the additional objects from the Office 97 CD.

   Now you're ready to use the Clip Gallery's Find feature to locate an image of a skyscraper.

2. Make sure the **Clip Art** tab is displayed, and then click the **Find** button in the Microsoft ClipArt Gallery 3.0 dialog box. The Find Clip dialog box opens.

3. With "[All Keywords]" selected in the Keywords list box, type **skyscraper**, and then click the **Find Now** button. The Clip Gallery finds one or more clip-art images and displays them as miniatures in the Clip Gallery dialog box.

4. Scroll (if necessary) until you see an image with a cluster of brightly colored buildings, and then click that image. See Figure 4-5.

Figure 4-5 ◀
Microsoft Clip
Gallery 3.0
dialog box

Clip Art tab ⎯

selected clip-art
image

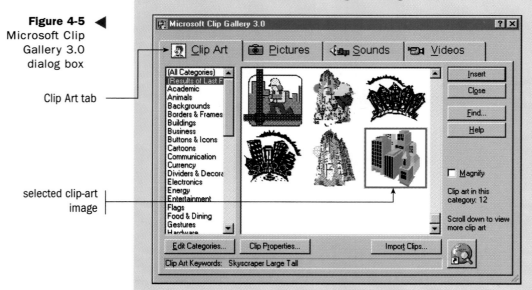

TROUBLE? If you can't find the skyscrapers image, try searching for other words that describe a skyscraper, like large or tall. If you still can't find a similar clip-art image, ask your instructor or your technical support person for assistance.

5. With the proper skyscrapers image selected, click the **Insert** button. The Clip Gallery inserts and centers the image into slide 3 of the presentation. PowerPoint also displays the Picture toolbar, which allows you to modify the embedded picture.

The image is now embedded in the presentation. Unless you try to ungroup the image from within PowerPoint, the image and its source program, Microsoft Clip Gallery, will remain connected. As long as the programs stay connected, you can double-click the image to return to the Clip Gallery. You can then select another clip-art image to embed, which will replace the current image.

Looking at slide 3, you notice that the clip-art image, which is centered on the slide, is too bright and obscures some of the bulleted text. Angelena agrees that a more attractive and readable format would be to move the clip-art image to the right, recolor the image, and then change the stacking order so that the slide text will be visible. You begin by repositioning the clip-art image using guides.

Positioning the Image Using Guides

You're already familiar with positioning an image by dragging and dropping. Under most circumstances, you can estimate the location that you want, but sometimes you'll need to position the image with greater precision. For example, if you have clip-art images on two or more related slides and want their positions to be the same on both slides, you can use guides to help you. **Guides** consist of two visible lines, one vertical and one horizontal. When you turn on the Guides feature, you drag each guide to the location on the slide where you want to position the image. To help you align guides and other objects accurately on each slide, you can use the Snap to Grid feature.

The **grid** is an *invisible* patchwork of lines that crosses the presentation window at intervals of about one-twelfth of an inch. When Snap to Grid is turned on (which it is by default when you start PowerPoint), objects that you drag will automatically "snap" to the closest invisible grid line, as if pulled there by a magnet.

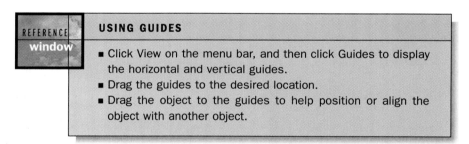

REFERENCE
window

USING GUIDES

- Click View on the menu bar, and then click Guides to display the horizontal and vertical guides.
- Drag the guides to the desired location.
- Drag the object to the guides to help position or align the object with another object.

You'll use the Snap to Grid feature to position the guides, and then you'll use the guides to reposition the skyscraper clip art on slide 3.

To position an image using guides:

1. Make sure the Snap to Grid option is turned on by clicking the **Draw** list arrow on the Drawing toolbar, and then pointing to **Snap**. If To Grid is selected, it is already turned on and you can simply close the Draw menu by clicking on the image in the presentation window, otherwise, click **To Grid** to turn on the Snap to Grid feature.

2. Click **View** on the menu bar, and then click **Guides**. The guides appear on the screen. See Figure 4-6.

Figure 4-6 ◄
Presentation
window with
guides

vertical guide

clip-art image

horizontal guide

Picture toolbar

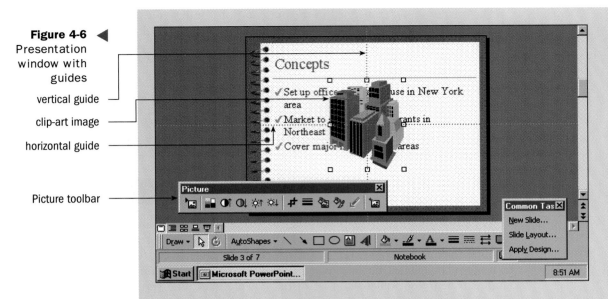

As you can see, the guides cross at the center of the slide. You'll now change the location of the guides by dragging them.

3. Move the mouse pointer over the horizontal guide at a location outside the slide itself, and then drag the guide up until the position label on the guide reads **1.50** (or close to it), which means that the guide is 1.5 inches above the center of the slide. See Figure 4-7.

Figure 4-7 ◄
Moving the
horizontal guide

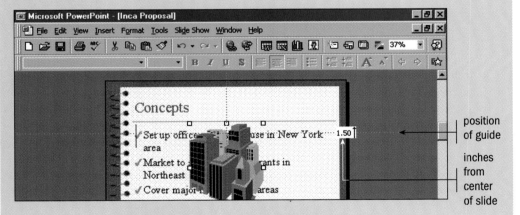

position
of guide

inches
from
center
of slide

TROUBLE? If you try to drag the guide and accidentally drag something else, release it, click the Undo Move Object button on the Standard toolbar, and then try dragging the horizontal guide again.

4. In a similar manner, drag the vertical guide to the right until the position label reads **0.75** (or close to it), which is 0.75 inch to the right of the center of the slide.

The guides are now positioned where Angelena wants to place the clip-art image.

5. Drag the skyscrapers image so that its left edge is flush with the vertical guide and its top edge is flush with the horizontal guide. See Figure 4-8.

Figure 4-8 ◄
Clip-art image
positioned on
guides

Recolor Picture
button

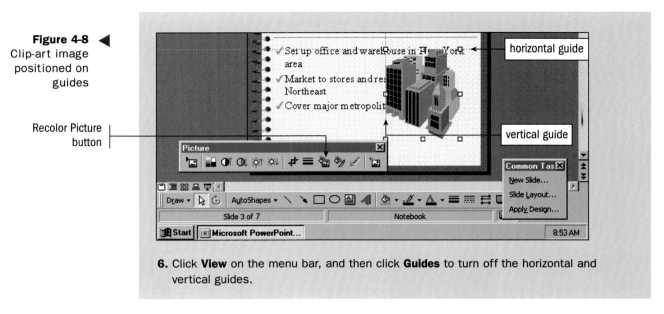

6. Click **View** on the menu bar, and then click **Guides** to turn off the horizontal and vertical guides.

The clip-art image is now positioned precisely where Angelena wants it. You're now ready to recolor the image.

Recoloring the Image

Angelena likes the image of the skyscrapers but thinks that their bright colors don't complement the slide design colors. Fortunately, PowerPoint allows you to recolor the clip-art image.

To recolor the picture:

1. With the image still selected and the Picture toolbar still on the screen, click the **Recolor Picture** button 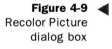 to display the Recolor Picture dialog box. See Figure 4-9.

Figure 4-9 ◄
Recolor Picture
dialog box

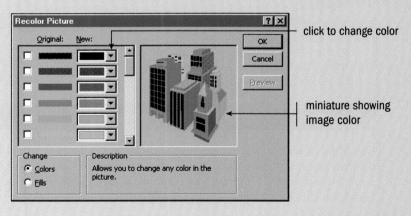

2. Make sure the **Colors** option button is selected in the Change section, and then click the **New** list arrow for the first tile color (currently black). A menu opens with the earth-tone colors of the current color scheme. Click the off-white **Follows Background Scheme Color**, the leftmost tile. The black color changes to an off-white color.

3. Click the **New** list arrow for the second tile (currently a navy blue). Click the third tile from the left, the **Follow Shadows Scheme Color**. The navy blue color changes to taupe.

4. Using the same method, change the third color tile (currently a medium blue) to the **Follow Accent and Hyperlink Scheme Color**, the next-to-the-last tile on the color palette.

5. Continue changing all the original colors (except the last one, which is white) to the earth tones shown on the color palette. Don't use the off-white, black, or red colors. In general, if the original color is dark, change it to one of the darker rust colors; if the original color is light, change it to one of the lighter tan colors. The exact recolor scheme you use doesn't matter, as long as you include a good mix of colors. Make sure that you scroll through and change the entire list of colors, not just the ones currently shown in the Original and New windows of the Recolor Picture dialog box.

6. When you have changed all the original colors to new ones, click the **OK** button in the Recolor Picture dialog box. The cluster of buildings now might have a color scheme similar to what you see in Figure 4-10.

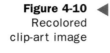
Figure 4-10
Recolored
clip-art image

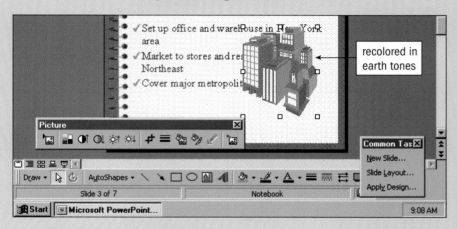

TROUBLE? If your buildings don't have the same colors as those in Figure 4-10, don't worry. If you don't like your colors, you can change them using the method given above.

Angelena likes the new colors that you have chosen for the skyscrapers image. Your last task in completing this slide is to change the stacking order of the objects so that all of the slide text is visible.

Changing the Stacking Order of Objects

All objects (text or graphics) on a slide are stacked in a certain order, so that if two or more objects occupy the same space, the one in front hides some or all of the ones behind it. You can change the stacking order by bringing an object forward or sending it backward. You'll send the clip-art image behind the text so that all of the slide text will be visible.

To order an object behind another:

1. With the skyscrapers image still selected, click the **Draw** list arrow on the Drawing toolbar, point to **Order**, and then click **Send to Back**. The image becomes the back object on the slide, and the text now appears in front of the clip-art image.

   The only problem now is that the some of the colors of the buildings might be so dark that the black text of the bulleted list is hard to read. You can solve the problem by increasing the brightness of the image.

2. With the image still selected and the Picture toolbar still on the screen, click the **More Brightness** button until the text is readable, and then deselect the image. See Figure 4-11.

Figure 4-11 ◄
Slide 3 with
clip-art image
sent to back
and brightened

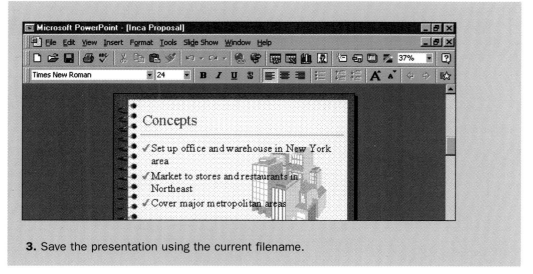

3. Save the presentation using the current filename.

Angelena is pleased with how the clip-art image you have embedded has enhanced her slide show. However, she thinks that her presentation still needs more pizzazz, something that will catch the attention of her audience, like animation and sound. To add the desired pizzazz, you decide to embed a video clip in slide 2 and embed a sound clip in slide 4.

Embedding a Video Clip

A **video clip** is an animated picture file, usually with the filename extension .AVI. In Angelena's presentation, you'll embed the file Basket.avi, a video clip of a basketball going into a basket. This clip includes both picture and sound, whereas other video clips might only include picture.

To embed a video clip into the slide show:

1. Display slide 2 in Slide View, click [icon] on the Standard toolbar to display the **Microsoft Clip Gallery 3.0** dialog box, and then click the **Videos** tab.

TROUBLE? If PowerPoint displays a message that additional objects appear on the Office 97 CD, just click the OK button. The video clip should be installed on your system. If it isn't, consult your instructor or technical support person.

2. Click the image of the basketball basket, titled "Basketball Through Hoop Digital Video Victory Trump Success," a three-second video clip with sound, and then click the **Insert** button. PowerPoint inserts the video clip into the slide.

TROUBLE? If you can't find this video clip, consult your instructor or technical support person. You might need to just read through the steps without completing them.

3. Drag the picture so it is positioned at about the location shown in Figure 4-12.

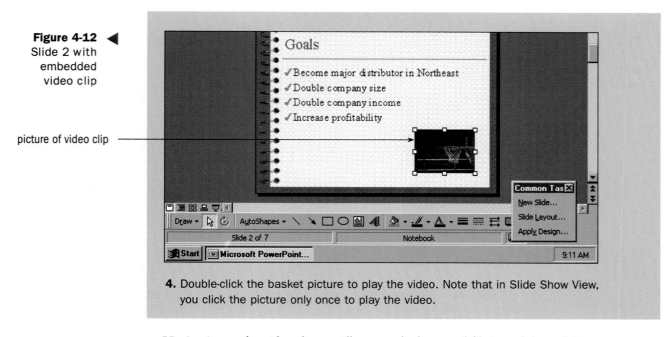

Figure 4-12 ◀
Slide 2 with
embedded
video clip

picture of video clip ——

4. Double-click the basket picture to play the video. Note that in Slide Show View, you click the picture only once to play the video.

Having inserted a video clip, you'll now embed a sound file into slide 4 of the presentation.

Embedding a Sound File

To use sound effects in PowerPoint, the computer system used for the presentation must have a sound card and speakers that are loud enough for your audience to hear the sounds clearly. The sound card responds to data from specific types of files.

The two most popular types of files are wave (.WAV) files and MIDI (.MID) files. Microsoft Windows supports both types of sound files. Wave files have the advantage of producing sound without disturbing the appearance of a PowerPoint on-screen slide. The disadvantage is that they are rather large in size and require significant disk space. MIDI files, on the other hand, take up less disk space. If you have a MIDI editor, you can easily produce musical sound clips. The disadvantage of MIDI files is that the MIDI dialog box appears on the screen when the sound is audible, and then, after the sound ends, disappears from the screen. This causes the screen to blink, which can be distracting during a PowerPoint presentation.

To use a wave or MIDI file, it must be embedded into a PowerPoint presentation so that it stays connected to the wave or MIDI driver that allows it to play.

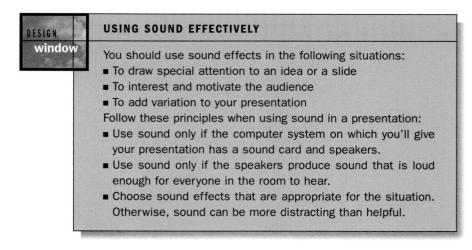

DESIGN window

USING SOUND EFFECTIVELY

You should use sound effects in the following situations:
- To draw special attention to an idea or a slide
- To interest and motivate the audience
- To add variation to your presentation

Follow these principles when using sound in a presentation:
- Use sound only if the computer system on which you'll give your presentation has a sound card and speakers.
- Use sound only if the speakers produce sound that is loud enough for everyone in the room to hear.
- Choose sound effects that are appropriate for the situation. Otherwise, sound can be more distracting than helpful.

Angelena decides that embedding a sound clip in slide 4 will help emphasize the importance of the slide. You could insert a sound clip from Microsoft Clip Gallery 3.0 in the same way you inserted a clip-art image and a video clip. Or you could include sound as part of the slide animation, as you might have done in a previous tutorial. However, because Angelena wants to be able to play the sound clip at any time while displaying slide 4, she asks you to use a wave file.

To embed the sound clip in slide 4:

1. Display slide 4, "General Plan," in Slide View in the presentation window.

2. Click **Insert** on the menu bar, point to **Movies and Sounds**, and then click **Sound from File**. The Insert Sound dialog box opens.

3. If necessary, change the Look in list box to **Tutorial.04** on your Student Disk, click **Victory**, and then click the **OK** button.

   PowerPoint inserts the sound wave icon in the slide and embeds the sound file in the presentation.

   TROUBLE? If an error message appears, your computer might have insufficient memory. Ask your instructor or your technical support person for assistance.

4. Drag the sound wave icon to the lower-right corner of the slide. Because the icon will appear on the screen when you give your presentation, you want the icon out of the way of any text.

   With the sound wave icon on the screen, you can click the icon at any time during the slide show to play the sound. You'll test it now.

5. Double-click the sound icon to play the sound. Note that while giving the slide show, you would click the sound icon only once to play the sound.

6. Save your document using the current filename.

Quick Check

1. Define the following terms:
   a. object
   b. import (an object)
   c. embed (an object)
   d. link (an object)
   e. OLE

2. Once you import a Word outline into PowerPoint and you make changes in the text of the outline, how is the original Word outline affected?

3. How do you export a PowerPoint presentation as a Word outline?

4. What are guides? How do they differ from the grid?

5. If you wanted a certain type of clip art but weren't sure if it existed in Microsoft Clip Gallery, how would you search for it?

6. If you wanted a clip-art image or other picture to go behind the text on a slide, what would you do?

7. How do you embed a video clip into a slide? How do you play the video clip in Slide View? In Slide Show View?

8. Give an advantage and a disadvantage of using a wave (.WAV) file rather than a MIDI (.MID) file for sound effects in PowerPoint.

Angelena's PowerPoint presentation now includes an imported outline from Word, an embedded clip-art image, an embedded video clip, and embedded sound. In the next session, you'll continue to use OLE techniques to enhance Angelena's presentation by linking an Excel chart and worksheet, and then finalize her presentation by adding a new slide. You'll then help Angelena ensure that her presentation will run smoothly and be available to all of her intended audience.

SESSION

4.2

In this session, you will learn how to link an Excel chart and worksheet, add a tab stop, use the Slide Navigator to jump from one slide to another, use the Meeting Minder to generate meeting notes and action items, and add hyperlinks to other presentations. You will also learn how to set up a self-running presentation, run a presentation conference, and publish the presentation on the World Wide Web.

Linking an Excel Chart

For her presentation, Angelena decides to include a three-dimensional (3-D) line graph of the projected month-by-month expenses for starting up the company's expansion. She divides the expenses into four categories: Planning, Property, Personnel, and Totals. Angelena chooses a 3-D line graph because it's effective for visualizing changes.

The 3-D line graph has been created by Mark Featherstone, Vice President of Finance, and his staff. They have used some of the powerful charting features of Excel 97 to create a separate Chart tab within an Excel workbook.

Angelena anticipates that she might have to modify Mark's worksheet after she creates the PowerPoint presentation. For example, the estimates for planning and personnel might increase or decrease as airfares change over time. Therefore, because Angelena and Mark want any changes made to the worksheet to be reflected in both the Excel file and the PowerPoint file, Angelena will link the PowerPoint presentation with the Excel worksheet. As a result, Angelena will have access to Excel from within PowerPoint and will be able to change the worksheet in both files.

REFERENCE window	**LINKING AN OBJECT**
	■ In Slide View, click Insert on the menu bar, and then click Object.
	■ In the Insert Object dialog box, click the Link check box.
	■ Click the Create from File option button, type the filename of the object, and then click the OK button.

You'll link Mark's Excel graph to slide 5 in Angelena's presentation now.

To insert the chart and link the Excel worksheet:

1. If you took a break after the last session, make sure PowerPoint is running and that Inca Proposal is open in the presentation window in Slide View.

2. Go to slide 5, "Startup Expenses," click the **Slide Layout** button on the Common Tasks toolbar to open the Slide Layout dialog box, click the layout titled **Object** (fourth column, fourth row), and then click the **Apply** button. The slide now contains the title and an object placeholder.

3. Double-click the object placeholder. The Insert Object dialog box opens.

4. Click the **Create from file** option button, and then click the **Browse** button to open the Browse dialog box.

   Usually you would now simply select the Excel file you want to link, however, in this instance you'll first make a copy of it, in case you make a mistake or if you or others want to go through the tutorial again.

5. From the Tutorial.04 folder on your Student Disk, right-click on the filename **Expenses** to display the shortcut menu, click **Copy** on the shortcut menu, right-click in a blank area of the filename list box, and then click **Paste** on the shortcut menu. A copy of Expenses, with the filename Copy of Expenses, appears in the filename list.

Because Copy of Expenses isn't a very descriptive filename, you'll change the filename to Inca Expenses.

6. Right-click on the filename **Copy of Expenses**, click **Rename** on the shortcut menu, and then type **Inca Expenses**.

7. Select **Inca Expenses** so it is highlighted, and then click the **OK** button. The pathname for Inca Expenses appears in the File text box of the Insert Object dialog box.

8. Click the **Link** check box, and then click the **OK** button. After a few moments, the chart appears on slide 5. You have linked the Excel chart with the PowerPoint presentation. See Figure 4-13.

Figure 4-13 ◀
Slide 5 with
linked object

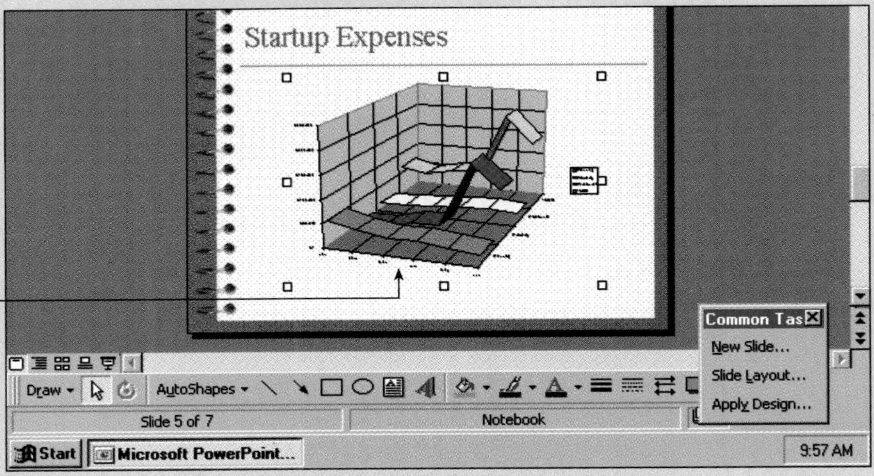

linked Excel chart ——————

Another method for linking the Excel chart with the PowerPoint presentation is to use the Paste Special command. To perform this operation, you select the Excel chart that you want to link from within the Excel program, click the Copy button on the Standard toolbar, switch from Excel to PowerPoint, and then use the Paste Special command on the Edit menu in PowerPoint to link the chart. The Paste Special method is especially handy when you don't want to link an entire file to a PowerPoint presentation.

To link objects, you can use either the Insert Object or the Paste Special method. Linking the Excel chart to Angelena's presentation, using either method, allows you to change the format of the Excel chart or to change any of the data in the worksheet, which in turn changes the graph.

Modifying a Linked Chart

Looking at the linked chart, you notice that both the text of the legend and of the axes are too small to read. You'll take advantage of the link between PowerPoint and Excel to modify the chart by changing the axes text font size to 16 points and the legend text font size to 18 points.

To modify the linked chart:

1. Make sure slide 5 is displayed, and then double-click anywhere on the chart. PowerPoint starts Excel with the Expenses workbook opened.

2. If necessary, click the **Maximize** button on the Excel window so that Excel fills the entire screen. See Figure 4-14.

Figure 4-14 ◄
Excel window with linked chart

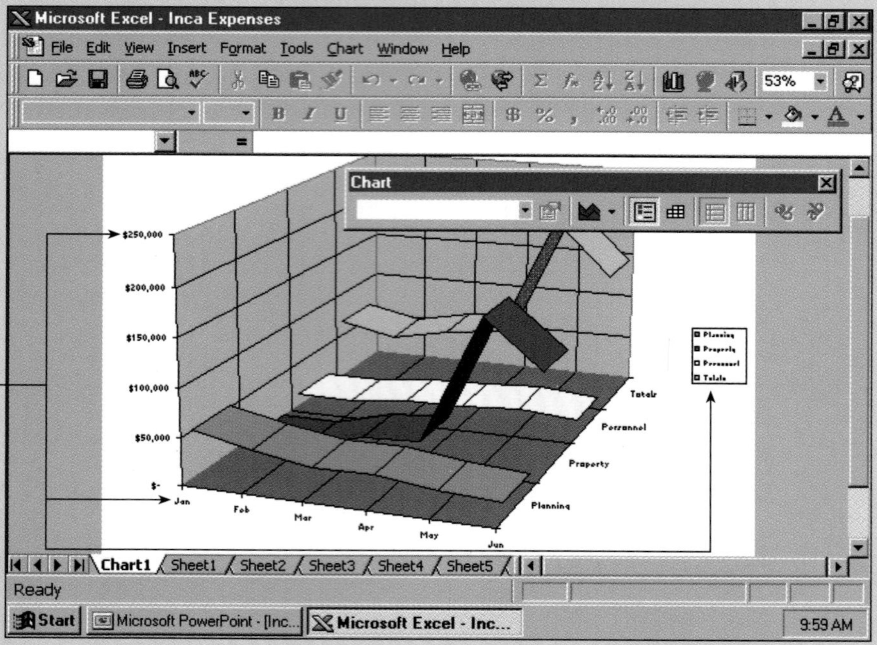

double-click to change font size

3. Double-click **$250,000** (or any of the other numbers along the vertical axis). The Format Axis dialog box opens.

4. Click the **Font** tab, change the **Size** list arrow to **16**, and then click the **OK** button.

5. Double-click one of the months on the horizontal axis to open the Format Axis dialog box, change the font size to **16**, and then click the **OK** button.

6. Double-click one of the 3-D line labels along the right edge of the chart, change the font size to **16**, and then click the **OK** button.

7. Double-click the legend box, change the font size to **18**, and then click the **OK** button.

8. Save the changes to Inca Expenses, and then exit Excel.

Now that you have enlarged the font size to make the slide more readable, you'll enlarge the chart as much as possible.

To resize the chart:

1. Make sure the chart in slide 5 is still selected, drag the bottom-right resize handle to the right and down, all the way to the lower-right corner of the slide area, drag the upper-left resize handle left and up, until the pointer is on the line below the slide title, and then deselect the chart.

2. Click 🖳 to see how the chart looks in full-screen view. See Figure 4-15.

Figure 4-15 ◄
Slide 5 in Slide
Show View

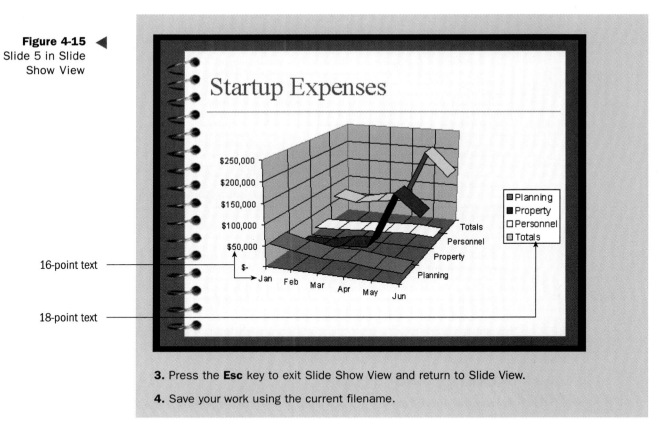

16-point text

18-point text

3. Press the **Esc** key to exit Slide Show View and return to Slide View.

4. Save your work using the current filename.

You have now linked and edited an Excel chart from PowerPoint. If you decide later to make further changes to the data in the workbook, you can do so either by directly starting Excel and opening Expenses or by double-clicking the chart from within PowerPoint. Either way, any changes made to the workbook will be automatically reflected in both files.

You have completed enhancing Angelena's presentation: With its embedded or linked clip-art image, sound clip, video clip, and Excel chart, the presentation will provide valuable information and interest for her audience. To make sure that the slide show will run properly, you now need to view the completed presentation.

Viewing the Completed Slide Show

When you get ready to present a slide show using a presentation with embedded or linked files, those files usually must be available on a disk so that PowerPoint can access them. For example, if you embed a video clip, the video file must be available on the hard drive, on a CD in the CD-ROM drive, or on a floppy in the system on which you're showing the presentation. This is because a copy of the embedded or linked file is often *not* included within the PowerPoint file itself, only the path and filename for accessing the linked file. Therefore, you should view the presentation on the system that will be used for running the slide show to make sure it has the necessary sound clip, video clip, and Excel file.

To view the slide show:

1. Display slide 1 of the presentation in the presentation window, and then click 🖵.
Slide 1 appears, filling the entire screen.

2. Click the left mouse button (or press the spacebar) to advance to slide 2, "Goals," and then click the picture of the basket to view the video clip.

3. Advance to slide 3 and then to slide 4, "General Plan." Click the sound clip icon to hear the fanfare.

TROUBLE? If the embedded sound does not play, check the volume on your computer sound system or check to make sure a sound card is installed on the computer. If you don't have a sound card, you might get an error message. Just click the OK button to close the message dialog box.

4. Advance to slide 5, "Startup Expenses." Here you can see the full-screen view of the Excel chart that is linked to your presentation.

TROUBLE? If the labels and legends aren't large and visible, you have made a mistake in editing and saving the Excel file Inca Expenses. You should return to the section describing how to edit a linked object, and carefully repeat the steps.

5. Continue through the slide show until you reach the end, and then return to Slide View.

Angelena is pleased with how well the embedded and linked objects work in her slide show. However, in reviewing her presentation, Angelena realizes that another slide is needed. She asks you to add a new slide with the timeline for establishing the new office in the Northeast. The new slide will include the four items of the plan, as given in slide 4, along with the proposed month and year in which each item will be accomplished. As you create the slide, you'll need to insert tabs between each item of the plan and its proposed date of accomplishment.

Adding Tab Stops

A **tab** adds space between the left margin and the beginning of the text on a particular line, or between text in one column and the text in another column. (If you were creating several long columns of data, however, you'd probably want to use a table instead of tabs.)

When you press the Tab key, PowerPoint inserts a tab from the current location of the insertion point to the next tab stop. The default tab stops in PowerPoint occur at every 0.5 inch along the slide and are left-aligned. However, you can easily add, remove, or change the location of these tab stops. You can also change the tab stop alignment style from left-aligned to centered, right, or decimal.

In the new slide that Angelena asks you to create, you'll tab between each item in the plan and its proposed date of accomplishment.

To create a new slide and insert tabs:

1. In Slide View, display slide 4, "General Plan," in the presentation window. As you can see, the slide gives four items in the plan for establishing a new office in New York City.

2. Click the **New Slide** button on the Common Tasks toolbar, click **Bulleted List** in the New Slide dialog box, and then click the **OK** button.

3. Click in the slide title placeholder, and then type **Timeline for New Office**.

4. Click in the bulleted list placeholder, type **Relocate Angelena**, press the **Tab** key, type **August 1999**, and then press the **Enter** key. You have typed one of the four items of the plan, and you're now ready to type the others.

5. Type **Establish new office**, press the **Tab** key, type **December 1999**, press the **Enter** key, type **Relocate employees**, press the **Tab** key, type **January 2000**, press the **Enter** key, type **Hire new employees**, press the **Tab** key, and then type **March 2000**. Deselect the text box. Your new slide 5 should now look like Figure 4-16.

Figure 4-16 ◀
New slide 5

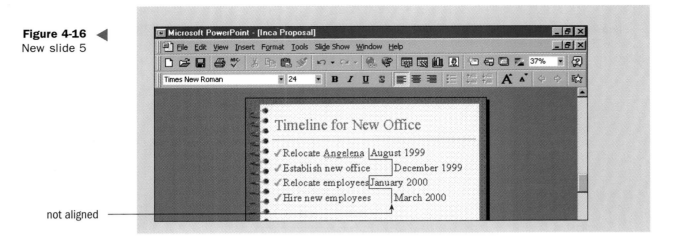

not aligned ────

You can see that, by pressing the Tab key only once between each task and each date, the dates column isn't aligned and some of the dates are too close to the first column. You can easily solve the problem by adding a tab stop. (You could have pressed the Tab key twice to create more space between the task and the date, but you still would have had to change the location of the tab stop.)

To add a tab stop:

    1. Select the bulleted list text box by clicking anywhere in it, click **View** on the menu bar, and then click **Ruler**. The ruler appears below the Formatting toolbar. See Figure 4-17. Notice that the default tab stops are indicated by small tick marks at the bottom of the ruler.

Figure 4-17 ◀
Slide 5
and ruler

left-aligned tab stop ────

ruler ────

current tab stops ────

selected text ────

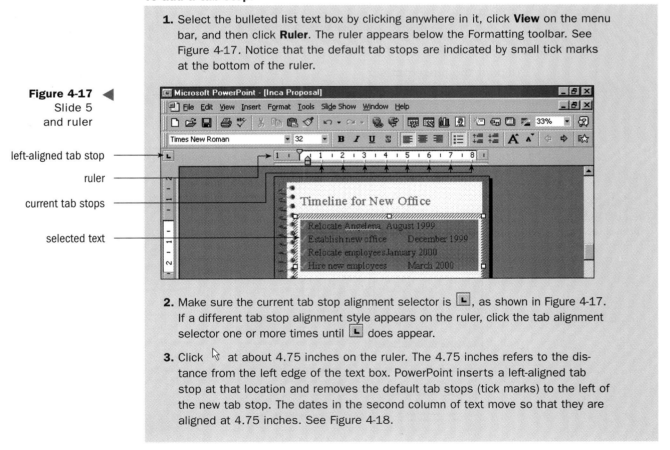

    2. Make sure the current tab stop alignment selector is ⬜, as shown in Figure 4-17. If a different tab stop alignment style appears on the ruler, click the tab alignment selector one or more times until ⬜ does appear.

    3. Click ⬚ at about 4.75 inches on the ruler. The 4.75 inches refers to the distance from the left edge of the text box. PowerPoint inserts a left-aligned tab stop at that location and removes the default tab stops (tick marks) to the left of the new tab stop. The dates in the second column of text move so that they are aligned at 4.75 inches. See Figure 4-18.

Figure 4-18 ◀
Slide 5 with
added tab stop

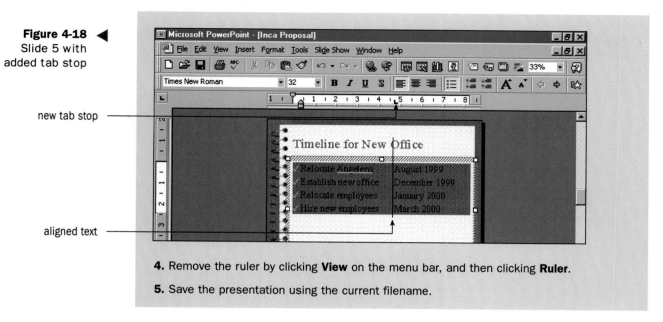

new tab stop

aligned text

4. Remove the ruler by clicking **View** on the menu bar, and then clicking **Ruler**.

5. Save the presentation using the current filename.

If, after you add a new tab stop to the ruler, you decide you want it in a different location, you can drag it to where you want it. If you decide you want to remove a tab stop, you can drag it off the ruler to delete it. You'll continue to practice working with tab stops in Case Problem 1.

Angelena is satisfied with her presentation. She now asks you to print a hard copy of the slides.

To print the presentation:

1. Click **File** on the menu bar, and then click **Print** to open the Print dialog box.

2. In the Print what list box, click **Handouts (6 slides per page)**, click the **Black & white** check box (if necessary), and then click the **OK** button.

3. Switch to Slide Sorter View so you can see all the slides on your screen at once. See Figure 4-19.

Figure 4-19 ◀
The completed
presentation

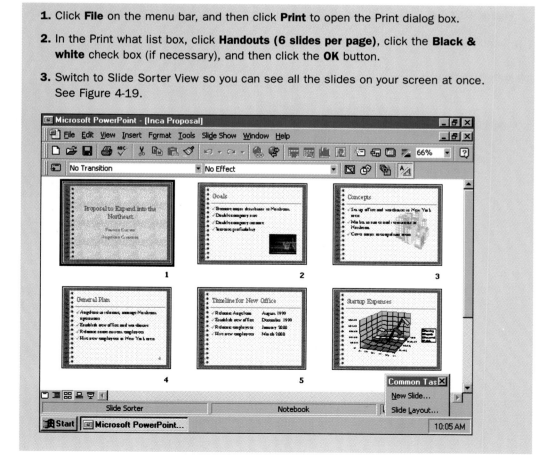

With the PowerPoint presentation completed, Angelena is ready to rehearse giving her presentation. As she goes through the slide show, she realizes that her audience might ask her questions that require her to jump to any slide in the presentation. She can do this easily by using the Slide Navigator.

Using the Slide Navigator

The **Slide Navigator** is a PowerPoint feature that allows the presenter to quickly display any desired slide in the presentation. Angelena asks you to help her rehearse using the Slide Navigator.

To use the Slide Navigator:

1. Click slide **1** in Slide Sorter View (or display slide 1 in Slide View), and then switch to Slide Show View. Angelena now wants you to use the Slide Navigator to go to the slide that presents the "General Plan."

2. Right-click anywhere on the slide to display the shortcut menu.

3. Point to **Go**, and then click **Slide Navigator**. The Slide Navigator dialog box opens. See Figure 4-20.

Figure 4-20 ◄
Slide Navigator
dialog box

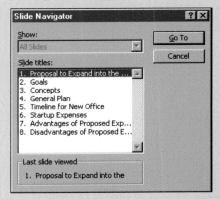

4. Click **4. General Plan** in the Slide titles list box, and then click the **Go To** button. PowerPoint displays slide 4. Now Angelena asks you to go back to slide 2.

5. Again open the Slide Navigator dialog box, click **2. Goals**, and then click the **Go To** button. Angelena is pleased that using the Slide Navigator will allow her to jump so quickly to any slide in the presentation.

6. Press the **Esc** key to exit the slide show and return to Slide Sorter View.

After Angelena rehearses with the Slide Navigator, she realizes that the participants will make various comments and suggestions. You suggest that Angelena learn how to use PowerPoint's Meeting Minder feature.

Generating Meeting Notes and Action Items

PowerPoint's **Meeting Minder** feature allows you to record meeting notes, save the notes with the presentation, and then print the notes. Further, because some comments made during a presentation will be in the form of action items (decisions to be followed up on after the meeting), the Meeting Minder feature also automatically creates a new, final slide in the presentation, listing these action items. You can then review all the action items at the end of the presentation. You can also export the meeting notes and the action items to a Word document. Angelena asks you to help her rehearse creating meeting notes and action items for two of the slides in her presentation.

To create meeting notes and action items:

1. Click slide **2** in Slide Sorter View (you could also display slide 2 in Slide View).

2. Click ⬛ to start the slide show with slide 2. (You could have started with any slide and then moved to slide 2 using the Slide Navigator or used the arrow keys or mouse buttons to advance forward or move backward.)

3. Right-click anywhere in the slide to display the shortcut menu, and then click **Meeting Minder**. The Meeting Minder dialog box opens.

4. If necessary, click the **Meeting Minutes** tab, and then type **Anne Carleton Bradford asked if doubling the company size and income was a realistic goal. Isn't competition in the Northeast worse than in southern California?**

5. Click the **Action Items** tab, type **Arrange ad hoc committee to examine goals** in the Description text box, type **Carl** in the Assigned To text box, and then type **7/15/99** in the Due Date text box. See Figure 4-21.

Figure 4-21 ◄
Meeting Minder
dialog box

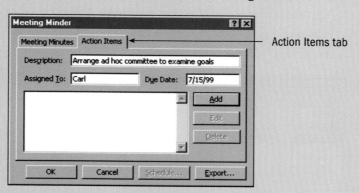

6. Click the **Add** button, and then click the **OK** button.

7. Go to slide 5 ("Timeline for New Office"), open the Meeting Minder, and add an Action Item with the description **Hire a personal secretary for Angelena**, with the task assigned to **Angelena** and a due date of **10/30/99**, click the **Add** button, and then click the **OK** button. The list now has two action items.

While you were creating the action items, PowerPoint was automatically creating a new slide containing these action items. You'll now look at the action items.

8. Go to the last slide (slide 9) in the presentation, the new "Action Items" slide. See Figure 4-22.

Figure 4-22 ◄
Action Items
slide (last
slide)

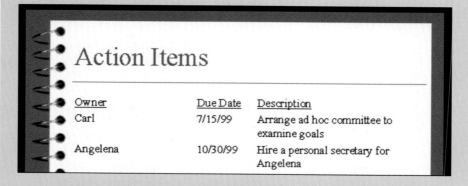

9. Read the slide, return to Slide Sorter View, and then delete the Action Items slide. You don't want to keep this slide because Angelena used it only for rehearsal purposes.

When you save the presentation, the action items will not be saved because you deleted the slide, but the meeting notes will be saved. You can view the meeting notes at any time by opening the presentation, clicking Tools on the menu bar, clicking Meeting Minder, and then clicking the Meeting Minutes tab. The Meeting Minder dialog box also allows you to export the notes to Word by clicking the Export button and following any subsequent instructions.

As she continues to rehearse her presentation, Angelena anticipates that some of the executive officers might want to see some (or all) of the presentation of the Annual Report presentation previously prepared by Patricia Cuevas. To facilitate going from the Inca Proposal presentation to the Annual Report presentation, Angelena asks you to insert a hyperlink into the Inca Proposal presentation.

Creating and Editing Hyperlinks

A **hyperlink** (short for "hypertext link" and also called a "hot link" or just "link") is a word, phrase, or graphic image that you click to "jump to" (or display) another location, called the **target**. Text hyperlinks are usually underlined and appear in a different color than the rest of the document. The target of a hyperlink can be to a location within the document, to a different document, or to a page on the World Wide Web. To use a hyperlink in a PowerPoint slide show, you can click the hyperlink text and the computer will display the target document. In the Inca Proposal presentation, you'll create a hyperlink from one PowerPoint presentation to another.

To insert a hyperlink:

1. Switch to Slide View, and then go to slide 2, "Goals." This slide, Angelena believes, is the most likely slide from which the executive officers would like to see the Annual Report, so this is where you will insert the hyperlink. You can create the hyperlink in any existing text box—for example, the bulleted list box—but usually you'll want to insert the hyperlink in its own text box.

2. Click the **Text Box** button 📰 on the Drawing toolbar, click the pointer ↓ near the bottom-left corner of the slide, about one inch from the left and bottom edges, and type **Annual Report**.

3. Drag I over the text "Annual Report" to select it, and then click the **Insert Hyperlink** button 🔗 on the Standard toolbar. The Insert Hyperlink dialog box opens. See Figure 4-23.

Figure 4-23 ◀
Insert
Hyperlink
dialog box

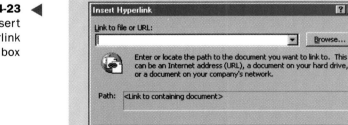

click to locate
file to link

You'll now use the Browse button to find the file Annual Report in the Tutorial.04 folder on your Student Disk.

4. Click the **Browse** button to open the Link to File dialog box, change the Look in folder to **Tutorial.04** on your Student Disk (if necessary), click **Annual Report** in filename list, and then click the **OK** button. The path to the Annual Report appears in the Link to file or URL text box.

5. Click the **OK** button in the Insert Hyperlink dialog box, and then deselect the text box on the slide. See Figure 4-24. The underlining of "Annual Report" indicates that it is a hyperlink.

Figure 4-24 ◀
Slide 2 with
hyperlink

text of hyperlink ——

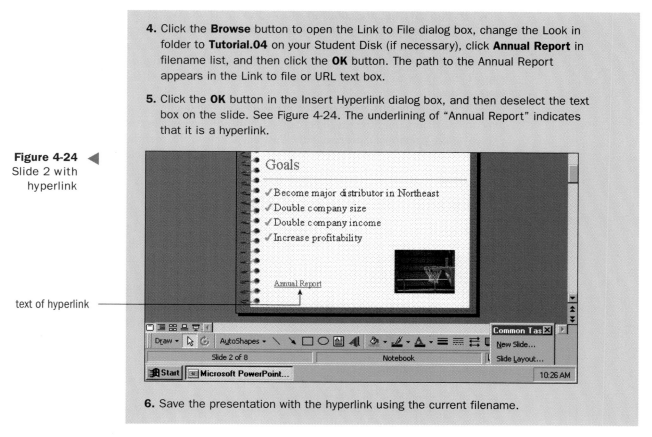

6. Save the presentation with the hyperlink using the current filename.

Now, when you run the slide show, you can click this hyperlink text to open the Annual Report presentation file. When you then close the Annual Report file, the current presentation will return to the screen. You'll see how this works now.

To test the hyperlink:

1. With slide 2 in the presentation window, click ⬚. Slide 2 fills the screen in Slide Show View.

2. Click the hyperlink "Annual Report." PowerPoint now loads the Annual Report presentation and displays slide 1 of that presentation on the screen.

3. Go through as much of the Annual Report slide show as you want, and then press the **Esc** key to exit it and return to the Inca Proposal slide show.

   TROUBLE? If the Annual Report presentation doesn't appear on the screen, press the Esc key to exit the current presentation, and then edit the hyperlink, as explained below.

4. Press the **Esc** key to exit the slide show.

If the hyperlink is incorrect or if you want to modify it, you can do so by selecting the text of the hyperlink and clicking the Insert Hyperlink button 🔗. The Edit Hyperlink dialog box opens, showing the path to the current link. You can then edit the current link as desired.

Angelena is pleased with the slide show and with her ability to use the Slide Navigator, Meeting Minder, and hyperlinks to give her presentation. Angelena is confident that her presentation to the executive officers will go smoothly and successfully.

Now that she's finished rehearsing the slide show, Angelena decides that it would be helpful to have the slide show run continuously on a computer in one of Inca Imports' corporate headquarters offices, so that other Inca Imports' employees can view it before the executive council meeting. She asks you to show her how to set up a self-running presentation.

Setting Up a Self-Running Presentation

To set up a self-running presentation, you use two PowerPoint features: **automatic slide timing**, which allows you to specify how long each slide appears on the screen during a slide show, and **loop continuously**, which sets up the slide show so it automatically starts over with the first slide after displaying the last slide. You'll now set up Inca Proposal as a self-running presentation.

To set up a self-running presentation:

1. In Slide Sorter View, select all the slides by clicking **Edit** on the menu bar and then clicking **Select All**. (Or you could press the **Ctrl + A** keys.)

2. Click the **Slide Transition** button 🔲 on the Slide Sorter toolbar. The Slide Transition dialog box opens.

3. Click the **Automatically after** check box, and set the Automatically after value to **5** seconds.

4. Set the slide transition effect to **Dissolve**. See Figure 4-25.

Figure 4-25 ◀
Completed
Slide Transition
dialog box

transition effect ——————

slide timing ——————

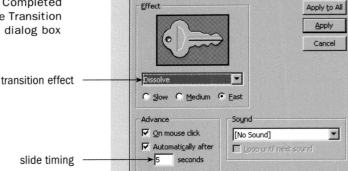

5. Click the **Apply** or **Apply to All** button. The dialog box closes and ":05" appears in the lower-left corner of each slide miniature in Slide Sorter View. Now you'll set PowerPoint to loop through the slide show continuously, until the Esc key is pressed.

6. Click **Slide Show** on the menu bar, and then click **Set Up Show** to open the Set Up Show dialog box.

7. Click the **Browsed at a kiosk (full screen)** option button. (A **kiosk** is an unattended booth that displays advertisements or provides information for people to view on their own. The computer on which Angelena wants to present the Inca Proposal slide show serves as a kiosk.) Notice that PowerPoint checks and dims the Loop continuously until 'Esc' check box option. See Figure 4-26.

Figure 4-26
Set Up Show
dialog box

selected to loop
continuously in kiosk

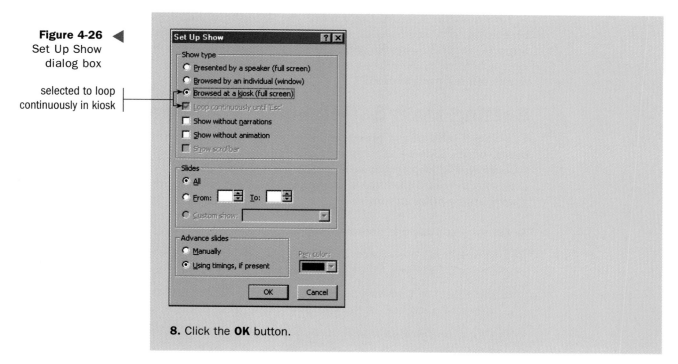

8. Click the **OK** button.

The slide show is now set up to be self-running. You'll now test it to see how it works.

To run the slide show continuously:

1. Deselect the slides, select slide 1, and then click 🖳 to start the slide show.

2. Watch the entire slide show, until you get back to slide 2 or 3, the second time around.

3. Press the **Esc** key to stop the slide show and return to Slide Sorter View.

Satisfied that you or Angelena can easily set up the presentation as a self-running slide show, you'll now return its setting for a normal slide show.

4. Click **Slide Show** on the menu bar, and then click **Set Up Show** to open the Set Up Show dialog box.

5. Click the **Presented by a speaker (full screen)** option button.

6. If necessary, click the **Loop continuously until 'Esc'** check box to deselect it so that the slide show won't run continuously.

7. Click the **OK** button, select all the slides in Slide Sorter View, click the **Slide Transition** button 🖻 on the Slide Sorter toolbar, click the **Automatically after** check box to deselect it, and then click the **Apply to All** button. You'll keep the Dissolve slide transition effects so that they'll appear during a regular slide show.

Angelena sets up a self-running presentation of Inca Imports, and then gives her presentation. Her presentation is very successfully received, but unfortunately, two members of the executive council could not attend the meeting. Angelena therefore decides to give them her presentation over the Internet using PowerPoint's Presentation Conference feature.

Running a Presentation Conference

The **Presentation Conference** feature allows you to present your PowerPoint slide show through other computers connected via a network, a modem, or the Internet. For a presentation conference to work, you need the following:

- PowerPoint installed on all the computers involved in the presentation conference

- Capabilities to make a telephone conference call, so you can talk to all the members of the conference, to coordinate the presentation conference and to provide voice messages during the conference

- Connection to the other computers through a local-area or wide-area network, through a modem connected to the Internet, or through a direct connection to the Internet

A conference presentation consists of the **presenter**, who runs the slide show, and the **participants**, who view the slide show. During the conference presentation, the presenter determines who can use the Slide Navigator to control the show, the Slide Meter (a feature that allows you to monitor the timing of your presentation), speaker notes, and the Meeting Minder. The participants don't have access to these features but are able to use an annotation pen to write and draw on the slides. The presenter can also view a slide show on one computer while controlling it from another. For example, the presenter might want to run the slide show from a laptop computer while viewing it on a large-screen monitor.

During a presentation conference, note that the participants can't view multimedia objects such as sound or video clips, or embedded or linked objects such as an Excel graph. Therefore, Angelena would need to convert the linked Excel chart to a normal graphic. To do this, she would start Excel, open the file Inca Expenses, select the chart, copy it, and then paste it into the presentation using the normal Paste feature, not the Paste Special feature.

Because your particular computer might not have the necessary connection or you might not be able to coordinate a presentation conference with other PowerPoint users, you will not actually hold a presentation conference in this tutorial. The following Reference Window provides you with the instructions necessary to set up and run a conference presentation.

REFERENCE window

SETTING UP AND RUNNING A CONFERENCE PRESENTATION

- As presenter, get all the participants on a telephone conference call.
- Open the PowerPoint presentation you want to run. Instruct the participant to run PowerPoint. When the PowerPoint dialog box opens, have them click the Cancel button so that the presentation window is blank.
- As presenter or participant, click Tools on the menu bar, click Presentation Conference, and then follow the instructions in the Presentation Conference Wizard. The presenter will need to know the names or Internet addresses of all the computers in the conference. The necessary addresses will appear on a participant's Presentation Conference Wizard dialog box.
- As a participant, complete the Presentation Conference Wizard, and then click the Finish button. Each participant must click the Finish button before the presenter does. As presenter, complete the Presentation Conference Wizard, and then click the Finish button, but only after all the participants have finished the Presentation Conference Wizard. Once you as the presenter click the Finish button, the slide show begins on your and the participants' computers.
- As presenter, you can now right-click, and then use the Stage Manager tools to control the show, monitor your timing, review notes, and record notes and action items.

Now that she's given her presentation to the executive officers both in the company boardroom and over the Internet, Angelena asks you to prepare the Inca Proposal presentation for publication on the World Wide Web. That way, any of Inca Imports' employees and stockholders, no matter where in the world they are located, can easily read the proposal over the Internet.

Publishing a Presentation on the World Wide Web

The **World Wide Web** (also called the "**Web**" or "**WWW**") is a global information-sharing system that allows you to find and view electronic documents, called **Web pages**. Organizations and individuals make their Web pages available by placing them on high-capacity hard disks called **Web servers**, which users can access electronically by specifying the address in a **Web browser**, software that retrieves and displays Web pages on a computer screen. The electronic location of a Web page is called a **Web site**. Most companies and many private computer users operate their own Web sites.

Most Web sites contain a **home page**, a Web page that contains general information about the site. Home pages are like "home base"—they are a starting point for online viewers. They usually contain hyperlinks targeting other documents or Web pages that online viewers can click to locate the information they need.

To prepare Angelena's PowerPoint presentation (or any presentation) for viewing on the World Wide Web, you first have to convert it to a special format called HTML (Hypertext Markup Language).

Saving a Presentation as an HTML Document

HTML (**Hypertext Markup Language**) is a special language for describing the format of a Web page so it can be viewed by a Web browser. The HTML markings in a file tell the browser how to format the text. Fortunately, you don't have to learn the Hypertext Markup Language to create HTML documents; PowerPoint does the work for you. You can easily save any PowerPoint presentation as an HTML document using PowerPoint's Save as HTML Wizard. The **Save as HTML Wizard** automatically creates a set of HTML documents (or pages), one page for each slide, plus an index HTML page. The index page includes hyperlinks to all the slides in the presentation. If your presentation includes any type of graphics, PowerPoint usually converts them to separate files, in .GIF or .JPEG format, depending on which format you specify. All these files are stored in a separate folder, which is given the name of the original PowerPoint presentation file.

If you want to edit the resulting HTML documents, you'll have to use a word processor that supports HTML editing (for example, Microsoft Word 97), or better still, use a dedicated HTML editor (for example, Microsoft FrontPage 97). PowerPoint doesn't support direct editing of HTML documents.

You'll now save the PowerPoint presentation as a set of HTML documents using the Save as HTML Wizard.

To save a presentation as a set of HTML documents:

1. Click **File** on the menu bar, and then click **Save as HTML**. The Save as HTML Wizard dialog box opens.

2. Read the information on the first page of the wizard, and then click the **Next** button; make sure the **New layout** option button is selected, and then click the **Next** button.

3. Make sure the **Standard** option button is selected on the Layout selection page of the wizard, and then click the **Next** button.

4. Make sure the **GIF - Graphics Interchange Format** option button is selected on the Graphic type page of the wizard, click the **Next** button, make sure the **640 by 480** option button is selected on the Graphic size page of the wizard, click the **Width of graphics** list box, and then click **3/4 width of screen**. See Figure 4-27.

Figure 4-27 ◄
Save as HTML
Wizard

select resolution ———

select size ———

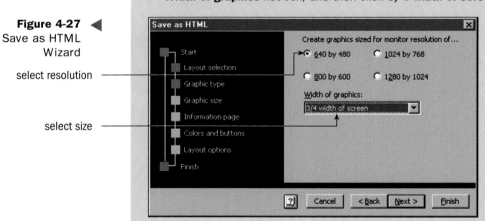

5. Click the **Next** button to go to the Information page. If you have an e-mail address, type it into the appropriate text box; otherwise, leave it blank. In the Your home page text box, type **Inca Proposal**. Leave the rest of this wizard page blank, and then click the **Next** button.

6. Make sure the **Use browser colors** option button is selected, click the **Next** button, click the option button next to the smaller rectangular button in the upper-right corner, and then click the **Next** button.

7. Click the option button to place the navigator buttons below the slide, that is, the upper-right layout, and then click the **Next** button.

8. Insert your Student Disk if necessary, make sure the Folder list box displays the correct disk drive letter, and then click the **Next** button.

9. Read the final page of the wizard, and then click the **Finish** button. When you are asked if you want to save these HTML conversion settings, click the **Don't Save** button. PowerPoint then saves the presentation as HTML documents (this could take a few minutes), and then displays a message that the save was successful. Click the **OK** button.

The HTML documents, with the accompanying GIF files (graphics files) are saved in the Inca Proposal folder within the Tutorial.04 folder on your Student Disk.

Viewing the Presentation in a Web Browser

You're now ready to see how the HTML presentation will appear in a Web browser. When you have finished viewing the HTML presentation, you'll then exit PowerPoint.

To view the presentation in a Web browser and exit PowerPoint:

1. Click **View** on the menu bar, point to **Toolbars**, and then click **Web**. The Web toolbar appears on your screen below the Formatting toolbar.

2. Click the **Go** list arrow on the Web toolbar, and then click **Open**. The Open Internet Address dialog box opens.

3. Click the **Browse** button, change the Look in list box to **Tutorial.04** on your Student Disk, double-click the **Inca Proposal** folder, click **index** (if necessary), click the **Open** button, and then click the **OK** button on the Open Internet Address dialog box. The index to your presentation appears in the browser document window. See Figure 4-28. Notice that the index page lists the slide titles from the original presentation as hyperlinks to Web pages (you may have to scroll down to see all the hyperlinks).

Figure 4-28 ◄
Microsoft
Internet
Explorer with
presentation
Web page

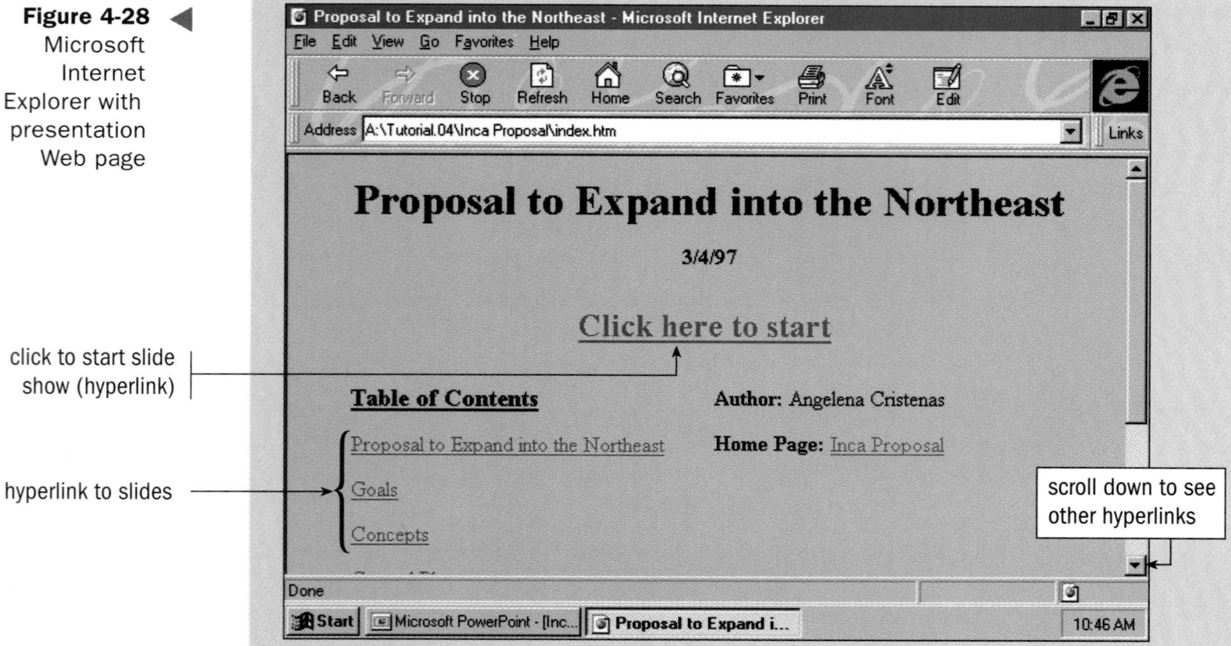

click to start slide
show (hyperlink)

hyperlink to slides

scroll down to see
other hyperlinks

TROUBLE? If PowerPoint opens another program, such as Microsoft Word, or if you receive an error message, a Web browser might not be installed on your computer. Consult your instructor or technical support person for assistance.

4. Click the **Click here to start** hyperlink. The browser opens the HTML document containing the first slide in your presentation. See Figure 4-29.

Figure 4-29 ◀
HTML page of
slide 1

click to go
to last slide

click to advance
to next slide

click to go to
previous slide

click to go
to first slide

click to return to
index page

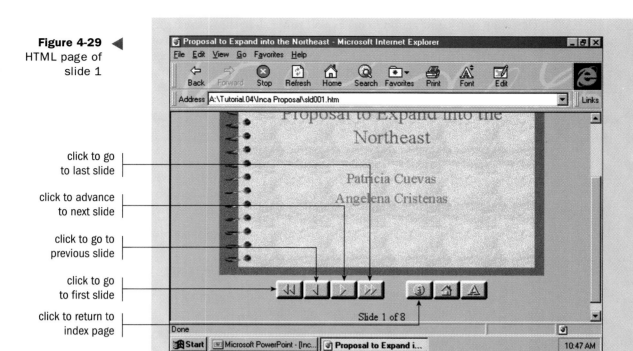

5. Click the **Next** navigation button to go to slide 2. Although you can see the pic-ture of the basketball basket video clip, you can't actually run the video clip here, because when you converted the presentation to an HTML document, the video clip picture was converted to a GIF graphic.

6. Use the navigation buttons below each slide to go to the next slide, go back to the previous slide, go to the first or last slide, or return to the index HTML document.

7. After you have seen the entire presentation, exit your Web browser, and then exit PowerPoint.

Quick Check

1. Why would you link an object rather than embed it?

2. What is the Slide Navigator? How do you use it?

3. How do you generate a new slide with the action item?

4. How would you set a self-running slide show to loop continuously?

5. In general terms, how do you hold a presentation conference?

6. Define the following:
   a. hyperlink
   b. World Wide Web
   c. Web browser

7. How do you save a presentation as an HTML document?

8. In general terms, describe what a presentation looks like in a Web browser. (In your description, answer the questions, What is the first HTML page? What are the subse-quent pages?)

In this session, you completed creating Angelena's presentation by linking an Excel chart and then modifying it. You then leaned how to use the Slide Navigator, generate meeting notes and action items as you run a slide show, create hyperlinks within a presentation, and save the presentation as an HTML document. You also learned how to run a presentation conference. Due to your help creating this presentation, Patricia and Angelena received the go-ahead for expanding Inca Imports. Angelena thanks you for your help and offers you a position in the New York City office.

Tutorial Assignments

After seeing how effective Angelena's presentation was in informing her audience about Inca Imports' proposed expansion, Enrique Hoffmann, Director of Marketing, decides to use it as a model for his upcoming presentation on Inca Imports' competition. He asks you to help him create his presentation by doing the following:

1. If necessary, start PowerPoint and make sure your Student Disk is in the disk drive.

2. Open a new, blank presentation and create a title slide.

3. On the title slide, type the title "Potential Competition in the Northeast" and the subtitle "Inca Imports International."

4. Import the Word file Compete from the Tutorial.04 TAssign folder on your Student Disk.

5. Format the presentation by applying the design template Serene.

6. Into slide 3, embed an appropriate clip-art image that suggests international business, such as a group of people in a meeting. If necessary, resize the clip-art image to appropriately fit on the slide.

7. Make sure Snap to Grid is turned on, and then turn on the Guides feature. Move the horizontal guide up to 1.50 and the vertical guide right to 1.75.

8. Move the clip-art image so that its left edge is aligned along the vertical guide and its top is aligned along the horizontal guide.

9. Recolor the clip-art image as needed so that it fits the color scheme of the design template.

10. On slide 4, change the slide layout to Object, and then link the Excel chart from the Sales file found in the Tutorial.04 TAssign folder on your Student Disk. Enlarge it to maximum size without covering the title of the slide.

11. Double-click the linked Excel chart and, within Excel, change the font color for the axes to a medium blue and the font style to bold, save your changes, and then exit Excel to return to PowerPoint.

12. Make sure the chart is updated in PowerPoint. *Hint*: Right-click on the selected chart.

13. Embed in slide 3 the sound wave file Applause, located in the Tutorial.04 TAssign folder on your Student Disk. Display the sound wave icon in the lower-right corner of the slide.

14. With the sound icon still selected, use the Copy command to copy the embedded sound clip to slides 4 and 5.

15. On the Summary slide, embed the video clip Arrowhit. Position it so it doesn't cover any of the text on the slide. Double-click it to play the video clip.

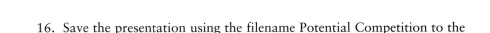

16. Save the presentation using the filename Potential Competition to the Tutorial.04 TAssign folder on your Student Disk.

17. At the bottom of slide 1, create a hyperlink to the Inca Proposal presentation located in the Tutorial.04 folder on your Student Disk. Test the hyperlink.

18. Print a copy of the presentation as black-and-white handouts (six slides per page).

19. Save the presentation as a set of HTML documents to the Tutorial.04 TAssign folder on your Student Disk. View the document in a Web browser.

20. Print the HTML page that contains the first slide of the presentation and then close the file. *Hint:* You can print a HTML page in the same way you print a document from any Windows program.

Case Problems

1. Magic Carpet, Inc. Erturu Ergos is Director of Marketing for Magic Carpet, Inc., a company that manages over 300 independent retail carpet franchises. The company provides information to retailers on the best buys in carpets and coordinates volume discount purchases. Magic Carpet also provides consumer information services through a toll-free hotline. Erturu has decided to prepare a short presentation to introduce new sales representatives to the company's marketing system. Do the following:

1. Open a blank presentation and create a title slide. Use the title "Introduction to Magic Carpet Marketing" and the subtitle "Training for Sales Representatives."

2. Import the Microsoft Word file System located in the Tutorial.04 Cases folder on your Student Disk to create the text for the remainder of the slides.

3. Apply the design template Fans to the presentation. If necessary, reapply the slide layout to each of the slides with bulleted lists so that the design colors are correct.

4. Move slide 3, "Purpose of Telemarketing," so that it comes after slide 5.

5. Export the outline to a Word document, and save it (as a Word Document) to the Tutorial.04 Cases folder on your Student Disk using the filename System Outline.

6. Embed the sound wave Chime, found in the Tutorial.04 Cases folder on your Student Disk, so that you can play it on all slides except slide 1. *Hint:* After you've embedded the sound waves into one slide, use the Copy and Paste commands to copy the sound wave icon to all the other slides.

7. On slide 2,"Overview of Marketing Procedure," insert tabs and then add the proposed dates for the marketing plan. The first mailing is set for 1/99, second mailing for 3/99, telemarketing phone calls for 4/99, and visit by field representatives in 5/99. Select the right-aligned tab stop, and position it at 8.0 inches. Then, drag the tab stop so that it's positioned as closely as possible to the right edge of the text box.

8. On slide 7, "Effectiveness of System," change the format to Object, and then link in the Excel chart named Success, found in the Tutorial.04 Cases folder on your Student Disk. Resize the chart to its maximum size within the slide.

9. To demonstrate the power of a linked object, change the data in cell B5 of Sheet1 of the Excel workbook from 7.4 to 27.4. Before you exit Excel, return to Chart1 so that the chart will appear as an object when you return to PowerPoint. After saving your changes and exiting Excel, right-click on the chart, and then select Update Link. Notice that the chart is updated to reflect the new Second Mailing value in Sheet1 of "Success."

10. Save the presentation as Magic Carpet Marketing to the Tutorial.04 Cases folder on your Student Disk, and then print the slides as black-and-white handouts, six slides to a page.

11. Save the presentation as a set of HTML documents to the Tutorial.04 Cases folder on your Student Disk, and then view the document in a Web browser.

12. Print the HTML page that contains slide 2, "Overview of Marketing Procedure," and then close the file. *Hint:* You can print a HTML page in the same way you print a document from any Windows program.

2. Xpressions, Inc. Margaret Decicco is Vice President of Xpressions, Inc., a small company that designs logos for other companies, clubs, and organizations. Through a manufacturer in Hong Kong, Xpressions makes T-shirts, mugs, pens, pencils, and other items that contain an imprint of the logo. Margaret is preparing a presentation for prospective clients to inform them of the products and services of Xpressions, Inc. Do the following:

1. Open a blank presentation and create a title slide. Use the title "Products and Services" and the subtitle "Margaret Decicco" on one line and "Xpressions, Inc." on a second line.

2. Import the Microsoft Word file XMission located in the Tutorial.04 Cases folder on your Student Disk to create the text for the remainder of the slides.

3. In the Slide Master, change the background color to a shade of yellow, make the shade style Diagonal up, and select the variant that is light along the middle diagonal and dark in the upper-left and lower-right corners.

4. While still in Slide Master, change the title font to blue, 54-point Arial. Keep the text in the object area black, but change the highest-level bullet symbol to blue (remember that you may need to reapply the slide layout).

5. Insert a graphic image, the logo for Xpressions, Inc., into the Slide Master. Use the file XLogo located in the Tutorial.04 Cases folder on your Student Disk, which was created in CorelDRAW and exported as a Windows Metafile (.WMF). Position the logo near the lower-right corner of the slide, so that the text of the logo is just outside the boundaries of the object area. Return to Slide View.

6. On slide 3, "Our Mission," delete the last two items, which begin "Complete refund."

7. On slide 4, "Our Expression," move "Hats and T-Shirts" so it is the first bulleted item in the list.

8. Export the outline to a Word document, and save it (as a Word Document) to the Tutorial.04 Cases folder on your Student Disk using the filename Xpressions Outline.

9. From within Word, print the new outline.

10. Into slide 1, embed the sound wave XIntro, which is an introduction by Stephen Zabriskie, President of Xpressions, Inc. Move the sound wave icon so that it covers the "X" in the company logo. Select the Play Settings tab in the Custom Animation dialog box so that sound plays during the transition to the slide. Make sure the icon is hidden during the slide show.

11. In slide 2, "Our Mission," insert a clip-art image of people interacting, such as shaking hands.

12. Reduce the size of the clip-art image so that you can position it just below the main text and next to the logo.

13. In slide 4, "Our Expressions," embed a clip-art image of an item listed on the slide, such as a mug or a banner. Position the item to the right of the main text and resize as necessary.

14. Remove the Xpressions logo from the background of slide 4, and then insert the picture again into that slide. This time reduce its size so that it can fit on the clip-art image you just inserted, and then position it there to give the appearance that the item is imprinted with the Xpressions logo.

15. Add a new slide 5 to your presentation, using the Object layout. Use the slide title, "Our Success."

16. In the new slide 5, link the Excel worksheet XSales from the Tutorial.04 Cases folder on your Student Disk. The worksheet containing Xpressions sales will appear.

17. Change the chart title font style to bold italic, and the color to blue.

18. To the three slides with bulleted lists, add the Dissolve build effect, with gray as the dimming color.

19. To all the slides, add the Box Out transition effect.

20. Save the presentation as Xpressions Products to the Tutorial.04 Cases folder on your Student Disk, print the slides as black-and-white handouts, six slides to a page, and then close the file.

3. Seeds for All Seasons Rosanna Carillo is Director of Marketing for a seed-catalog business that caters to gardeners nationwide. She's recently created a Web publication that highlights their best-selling seeds. However, some seeds have proved to be less popular, so next month Rosanna plans to have a sale on these items. Rosanna has already created a presentation about the sale, and asks you to create a Web publication based on her slide show. Do the following:

1. Open the Seeds presentation found in the Tutorial.04 Cases folder on your Student Disk.

2. Save the presentation as an HTML document with the following options: include an e-mail address of sales@seeds_seasons.com; include the following other information text: "Special this month! Items from the Seeds for All Seasons catalog 15-20% off. Order yours today!"; and name the layout options you've chosen "Sales."

3. Save the subfolder containing your HTML documents to the Tutorial.04 Cases folder on your Student Disk.

4. Open the Index.htm file in Microsoft Word. *Hint:* This file is located in the Seeds subfolder on your Student Disk.

5. Change the hyperlink from "Click here to start" to "This month's special."

6. Format the background using a Papyrus textured background. *Hint:* Use the same method you would use in PowerPoint. In the Fill Effects dialog box, click the Texture tab.

7. Make any other design or formatting changes that you think improve the appearance and readability of the Web index page.

8. Open Index.htm in your Web browser, and verify that the Web publication is working properly.

9. Save your changes to the Index.htm file, print it, and then close the file.

4. Report on Local Recycling Your school's administration would like to increase student compliance with local recycling efforts. They have asked you to prepare a presentation, to be given as an on-screen slide show as well as published on the World Wide Web, that will inform students about the benefits and procedures of recycling in your area. Do the following:

1. Create an outline (except for the title slide) of your presentation using Word. Include at least five first-level headings. Save the document as Presentation Outline to the Tutorial.04 Cases folder on your Student Disk. Possible slide titles include "What Is Recycling?" "Benefits of Recycling," "What Can Be Recycled?" "How to Recycle," and "Recycled Items." Title the last first-level heading "Summary," and then include second-level headings that summarize your report.

2. Check the spelling of your outline.

3. Save the outline, print a copy of the outline, and then exit Word.

4. Create a blank presentation with a title slide. Choose your own title, but use your name as the subtitle.

5. Import the Word outline into your presentation.

6. Pick an appropriate template or create your own design for the presentation.

7. Include in your presentation one or more of the sound wave files that appear in the Tutorial.04 Cases folder on your Student Disk.

8. Embed clip-art images or other pictures on two or more slides.

9. Include at least one Excel chart. For example, you might want to display an Excel pie chart showing the percentage of materials that are handled by your local recycling center. If you can't find that information, use reasonable estimates.

10. Add appropriate transitions and animation effects to your presentation.

11. Add a hyperlink to the final slide ("Summary") to one of the earlier slides in your presentation. *Hint:* In the Insert Hyperlink dialog box, click the Browse button in the Named location in file section.

12. Save your presentation as Local Recycling to the Tutorial.04 Cases folder on your Student Disk.

13. Print your presentation as black-and-white handouts, six slides per page.

14. Save the presentation as a set of HTML documents to the Tutorial.04 Cases folder on your Student Disk and then view the document in a Web browser.

15. Print the HTML index page, and then close the file.

Answers to Quick Check Questions

SESSION 3.1

1 Major items you should include when preparing for a presentation meeting are: (1) prepare an agenda; (2) prepare the presentation; (3) check the physical arrangements; (4) check the equipment; and (5) prepare other items as needed.

2 Click Insert, click Slides from Files, click the Find Presentation tab, click the Browse button, locate the presentation file to be inserted and select it, click the Open button, click the Display button, select the slides to insert, click the Insert button, and then click the Close button.

3 If you've created your own design or modified a PowerPoint design template to fit your own tastes or needs, you can use that modified design in other presentations.

4 The Slide Master is a slide that contains text and graphics that appear on all the slides (except the title slide) in the presentation and controls the format and color of the text and background on all slides. You would use the Slide Master any time you want to make a change, such as adding a graphic or text, that would affect all the slides in the presentation.

5 a. Press and hold down the Shift key, and then click the Slide View button.
  b. Click Format, click Slide Color Scheme, click the Standard tab, click the desired background, and then click the Apply or Apply to All button.
  c. Click an edge of the title text box, and then click the desired alignment button on the Formatting toolbar.
  d. Display the Slide Master, click anywhere within the text of the bulleted item, click Format, click Bullet, select a font using the Bullets from list arrow, click the desired bullet character, and then click the OK button.

6 Click Insert, click Picture, change the drive and folder as necessary and select the filename, click the OK button, and then resize and move the image as necessary.

7 The Replace command searches through a presentation for a sequence of characters and then substitutes one or more occurrences of this sequence with a specified replacement sequence. You would use it whenever you want to replace a word or phrase throughout the presentation file.

8 You would hide a slide because you may not want to show the slide to one audience but you may want to show it to another one.

SESSION 3.2

1 Display the datasheet, click in the cell that you want to edit, and then type in the new information.

2 Gridlines show the cell boundaries but do not appear in the slide show or in the printed presentation. You would draw rules along certain gridlines to make the table more attractive and readable.

3 a. A transition effect is a method of moving one slide off the screen and bringing another slide onto the screen during a slide show.
  b. An animation effect is the special visual or sound effect of an object (such as graphics or bulleted text).
  c. A sound effect is part of an animation effect so that when you click the left mouse button (or press the spacebar) to display a bulleted item, a sound, such as a "whoosh," will also occur.

4 a. Switch to Slide Sorter View and select the slide(s) to which you want to add a transition effect, click the Slide Transition Effects list arrow on the Slide Sorter toolbar to display a list of transition effects, and then click the desired transition effect.
  b. Display the desired slide in Slide View, click Slide Show on the menu bar, click Custom Animation, click the Effects tab, click the Sound list arrow, click the desired sound, and then click the OK button.

5 One advantage is that if you accidentally misspell words, the Style Checker can find the errors. However, the Style Checker often changes the case of phrases that should stay as you originally typed them or warn you of conditions that aren't really problems. The strengths of the Style Checker, however, greatly outweigh the weaknesses.

6 Click File, click Page Setup, click the Slides sized for list arrow, click Overhead, click the Portrait option button, and then click the OK button.

7 The Genigraphics Wizard automatically creates a special file that you can send to Genigraphics to order 35mm slides of the presentation.

8 The Viewer disk contains the PowerPoint Viewer files and a copy of the presentation. You use it to install and run the presentation on any computer, even those that don't have PowerPoint installed on them.

SESSION 4.1

1 a. An object is a word processing file, spreadsheet chart, graphic, organization chart, or some other type of data or information from another program that appears within a presentation.
   b. To import means to insert a file that was created using one program into another program's file.
   c. To embed means to insert a file that will allow a one-way connection to be maintained with the source program.
   d. To link means to insert a file that will maintain a two-way connection between the source program and the destination program.
   e. OLE (Object Linking and Embedding) supported programs let you embed or link objects from one program to another.

2 The original Word outline is not affected.

3 Click File, point to Send To, click Microsoft Word, click the Outline only option button, and then click the OK button.

4 Guides consist of two visible lines, one horizontal and one vertical, and help you position objects, such as clip-art images. Guides differ from the grid as the guides are visible, not invisible, lines, and the Guides feature needs to be turned on, whereas the Snap to Grid feature is turned on by default.

5 In the Microsoft Clip Gallery 3.0 dialog box, click the Clip Art tab, click the Find button, type an appropriate description word(s) in the Keywords list box, and then click the Find Now button.

6 Select the clip-art image, click the Draw list arrow on the Drawing toolbar, point to Order, and then click Send to Back.

7 Click the Insert Clip Art button on the Standard toolbar, click the Videos tab, click the desired video clip, and then click the Insert button. To play the video clip, you double-click on the video picture in Slide View, and click the picture only once in Slide Show View.

8 An advantage of using a wave file rather than a MIDI file is that it will produce sound without disturbing the appearance of a PowerPoint on-screen slide. However, a wave file is large in size and requires significant disk space.

SESSION 4.2

1 You may want any changes made to the linked file to take effect in both the source program and the destination program.

2 The Slide Navigator allows the presenter to quickly display any slide in the presentation. To use it, switch to Slide Show View, right-click anywhere on the slide, point to Go, click Slide Navigator, click the slide you want to display, and then click the Go To button.

3 First create action items in Slide Show View by right-clicking on the slide, clicking the Meeting Minutes tab, clicking the Action Items tab, typing the action item(s), clicking the Add button, and then clicking the OK button; the new slide with the action items is automatically created and added as the last slide in the presentation.

4 In Slide Sorter View, select all the slides, click the Slide Transition button on the Slide Sorter toolbar, click the Automatically after check box, set the Automatically after value and slide transition effect, click the Apply button, click Slide Show on the menu bar, click Set Up Show, click the Browsed at a kiosk (full screen) option, and then click the OK button.

5 Get all the participants on a telephone conference call. To run PowerPoint, follow the instructions in the Presentation Conference Wizard, and then use the Stage Manager tools to control the show, monitor your timing, review notes, and record notes and action items.

6 a. A hyperlink is a word, phrase, or graphic image that you click to display another location.
   b. The World Wide Web is a global information-sharing system that allows you to find and view electronic documents.
   c. A Web browser is software that retrieves and displays Web pages on a computer screen.

7 Use the Save as HTML Wizard, which automatically creates a set of HTML documents, one page for each slide, plus an index HTML page.

8 In a Web browser, the first page is the index page, which lists the slide titles from the original presentation as hyperlinks to Web pages; subsequent pages are the slides from the original presentation.

If you are using this text as part of our Custom Edition Program, you will find entries in the Index and Task Reference that do not apply to your custom tutorials.

A

action items, generating, P 4.23–4.25
alignment, text, P 3.12–3.13
animation, P 3.27–3.28
applications, integrating. *See* embedding;
    embedding clip-art images; importing; inte-
    grating PowerPoint; linking
Apply Design dialog box, P 1.22–1.23
AutoContent Wizard, P 1.7–1.10
AutoContent Wizard dialog box, P 1.8–1.9
automatic slide timing, P 4.27
AutoShapes feature, P 2.17–2.18
.AVI files, embedding in slides, P 4.13–4.14
axis titles, charts, P 3.19–3.20

B

Background dialog box, P 2.6–2.7
background graphics, removing from slides,
    P 2.6–2.7
black slides, P 3.16
browsers. *See* Web browsers
bullet(s), color, P 3.11–3.12
Bullet dialog box, P 3.11–3.12
bulleted items, moving, P 1.15–1.16

C

center alignment, P 3.12
charts, P 3.17–3.20. *See also* graphics;
    organization charts
    axis titles, P 3.19–3.20
    editing, P 3.18–3.19
    Excel, linking to slides, P 4.16–4.19
    inserting in slides, P 3.17–3.18
clip art, P 2.10–2.13
    adding to slides, P 2.10–2.12
    editing, P 2.12–2.13
    embedding. *See* embedding clip-art images
    ungrouping, P 2.12
Clip Gallery, P 4.7–4.9
color
    bullets, P 3.11–3.12
    printing presentations, P 3.33–3.34
color scheme, P 3.9–3.10
Color Scheme dialog box, P 3.9–3.10
continuously looping presentations, P 4.27–4.28
Custom Animation dialog box, P 3.28
cutting and pasting text, P 1.19–1.20

D

deleting. *See also* removing
    slides, P 1.17–1.18
demoting outline text, P 1.17
design templates, P 1.22
    applying from another presentation, P 3.7
    changing, P 1.22–1.23
destination program, P 4.2
displaying. *See also* previewing presentations;
    viewing; viewing presentations
    Slide Master, P 3.8
documents, saving presentations as HTML
    documents, P 4.30–4.32
dragging and dropping text, P 1.21

E

Edit Hyperlink dialog box, P 4.26
editing
    charts. *See* editing charts
    clip art, P 2.12–2.13
    presentations. *See* editing presentations in
        Outline View; editing presentations in
        Slide View
    tables, P 3.24–3.25
editing charts, P 3.18–3.19
    linked charts, P 4.17–4.19
editing presentations in Outline View, P 1.14–1.17
    moving text up and down, P 1.15–1.16
    promoting and demoting text, P 1.16–1.17
editing presentations in Slide View, P 1.19–1.22
    adding slides, P 1.21–1.22
    moving text, P 1.19–1.21
embedding, P 4.3
    clip-art images. *See* embedding clip-art
        images
    sound files into presentations, P 4.14–4.15
    video clips into presentations, P 4.13–4.14
embedding clip-art images, P 4.7–4.13
    finding images, P 4.7–4.9
    positioning images, P 4.9–4.11
    recoloring images, P 4.11–4.12
    stacking order of objects, P 4.12–4.13
errors
    finding and replacing text, P 3.14–3.15
    Style Checker, P 3.29–3.31
Excel, linking charts to slides, P 4.16–4.19
exiting
    Microsoft Organization Chart window, P 2.16

PowerPoint, P 1.14, P 1.29
exporting outlines from Word, P 4.5, P 4.6–4.7

F

Find command, P 3.14–3.15
Find dialog box, P 3.14–3.15
finding
    clip-art images, P 4.7–4.9
    text, P 3.14–3.15
flipping objects, P 2.19–2.20
fonts, P 3.10–3.12
formatting tables, P 3.22–3.24
Formatting toolbar, P 1.10

G

Genigraphics Corporation, P 3.31
graphics, P 2.1–2.22
    adding scanned images to Title Masters,
      P 3.13–3.14
    clip art. *See* clip art; embedding clip-art images
    flipping, P 2.18–2.19
    inserting pictures into slides, P 2.7–2.8
    inserting shapes into slides, P 2.17–2.18
    organization charts. *See* organization charts
    removing from slides, P 2.6–2.7
    Slide Layout, P 2.8–2.10
    text boxes. *See* text boxes
graphs. *See* graphics
grid, P 4.9–4.11
gridlines, tables, P 3.22
guides
    moving, P 4.10
    positioning images, P 4.9–4.11

H

Help system, P 1.24–1.25
hiding slides, P 3.16
highlighting placeholders, P 1.11
home pages, P 4.30
hyperlinks, P 4.25–4.26
    testing, P 4.26
Hypertext Markup Language (HTML), P 4.30
    saving presentations as HTML documents,
      P 4.30–4.32

I

importing, P 4.2, P 4.3. *See also* importing
  outlines from Word
importing outlines from Word, P 4.3–4.7
    exporting outlines, P 4.6–4.7
    modifying outlines, P 4.5–4.6
Insert Hyperlink dialog box, P 4.25
inserting
    charts in slides, P 3.17–3.18
    clip art into slides, P 2.10–2.12
    organization charts into slides, P 2.16–2.17
    pictures into slides, P 2.7–2.8
    shapes into slides, P 2.17–2.18
    slides from another presentation, P 3.4–3.6
    subordinate levels in organization charts,
      P 2.15–2.16
    text boxes into slides, P 2.19–2.20

text into outlines, P 1.12–1.13
integrating PowerPoint, P 4.1–4.33. *See also*
  embedding; embedding clip-art images;
  importing; importing outlines from Word;
  linking techniques, P 4.2–4.3

L

left alignment, P 3.12, P 3.13
linking, P 4.3
    Excel charts to slides, P 4.16–4.19
    hyperlinks, P 4.25–4.26
locating. *See* finding
logos, P 2.4
looping continuously, P 4.27–4.28

M

main text, P 1.11
Meeting Minder dialog box, P 4.24
Meeting Minder feature, P 4.23–4.25
meeting notes, generating, P 4.23–4.25
Microsoft Clip Gallery 3.0 dialog box,
  P 2.11–2.12, P 4.8
Microsoft Internet Explorer, P 4.32
Microsoft Organization Chart window,
  P 2.14–2.15
    exiting, P 2.16
.MID files, embedding in slides, P 4.14–4.15
moving
    guides, P 4.10
    positioning images, P 4.9–4.11
    text. *See* moving text
    text boxes, P 2.5–2.6, P 2.20–2.21
moving text
    Outline View, P 1.15–1.16
    Slide View, P 1.19–1.21

N

New Slide dialog box, P 1.21
Notes Pages View button, P 1.10

O

object(s), P 2.3, P 4.2. *See also specific objects*
    flipping, P 2.19–2.20
    stacking order, P 4.12–4.13
Object Linking and Embedding (OLE), P 4.3
Office Assistant, P 1.24–1.25
Office Assistant dialog box, P 1.24
Office Shortcut Bar, P 1.6
OLE. *See* Object Linking and Embedding
  (OLE)
opening presentations, P 1.15, P 2.2–2.3, P 3.5
organization charts, P 2.14–2.17
    adding subordinate levels, P 2.15–2.16
    adding to slides, P 2.17
    creating, P 2.14–2.15
outlines
    adding text, P 1.12–1.13
    AutoContent Wizard for creating, P 1.7–1.10
    editing. *See* editing presentations in Outline
      View
    importing from Word. *See* importing out-
      lines from Word

replacing text, P 1.11–1.12
Outline View
    deleting slides, P 1.17–1.18
    editing outlines. *See* editing presentations in
        Outline View
Outlining toolbar, P 1.10
overheads, preparing, P 3.32–3.33

P Pack and Go Wizard, P 3.34
participants, P 4.29
pasting text, P 1.19–1.20
pictures. *See* graphics
placeholders, P 1.11
    adding text, P 2.9–2.10
    selecting, P 1.11
planning, presentations, P 3.4, P 4.2
planning presentations, P 1.5, P 2.2
points, P 3.10
positioning images, P 4.9–4.11
PowerPoint
    description, P 1.5
    exiting, P 1.14, P 1.29
    starting, P 1.6–1.7, P 1.15
PowerPoint dialog box, P 1.7
PowerPoint window, P 1.10
preparing presentation materials, P 3.31–34
    overheads, P 3.32–3.33
    printing in color, P 3.33–3.34
    running presentations on another computer,
        P 3.34
    35mm slides, P 3.31
Presentation Conference feature, P 4.29–4.30
presentations
    checking style, P 3.29–3.31
    design templates. *See* design templates
    editing. *See* editing presentations in Outline
        View; editing
presentations in Slide View
    effective, P 3.35
    principles for creating, P 1.11
    integrating programs, P 4.1–4.33. *See also*
        embedding; embedding clip-art images;
        importing; importing outlines from Word;
        linking
    opening, P 1.15, P 2.2–2.3, P 3.5
    outlines. *See* editing presentations in Outline
        View; outlines
planning, P 1.5, P 2.2, P 3.4, P 4.2
preparing materials, P 3.31–3.34
previewing in black and white, P 1.27–1.28
printing. *See* printing presentations
publishing on World Wide Web. *See* publishing
    presentations on World Wide Web
    running on another computer, P 3.34
    saving. *See* saving presentations
    self-running, P 4.27–4.28
    slides. *See* slide(s)
    starting in middle, P 3.28–3.29

tips, P 3.25
    viewing. *See* viewing presentations
presenters, P 4.29
previewing presentations, P 1.27–1.28
Print dialog box, P 1.28
printing
    color, P 3.33–3.34
    presentations, P 4.22
printing presentations, P 1.28, P 2.22, P 4.22
    color, P 3.33–3.34
programs, integrating. *See* embedding; embed-
    ding clip-art images; importing; integrating
    PowerPoint; linking
promoting outline text, P 1.16–1.17
publishing presentations on World Wide Web,
    P 4.30–4.33
    saving presentations as HTML documents,
        P 4.30–4.32
    viewing presentations in Web browsers,
        P 4.32–4.33

R ragged alignment, P 3.12
Recolor Picture dialog box, P 4.11–4.12
Reference Windows, P 1.4
removing. *See also* deleting
    background graphics, P 2.6–2.7
Replace command, P 3.14, P 3.15
Replace dialog box, P 3.15
resizing text boxes, P 2.4–2.5
right alignment, P 3.12
rotating text boxes, P 2.20–2.21
rules, tables, P 3.22–3.24

S Save as HTML Wizard, P 4.31
saving presentations, P 1.13
    HTML documents, P 4.30–4.32
    new name, P 2.3
scanned images, adding to Title Masters,
    P 3.13–3.14
selecting placeholders, P 1.11
self-running presentations, P 4.27–4.28
Set Up Show dialog box, P 4.28
shapes, inserting in slides, P 2.17–2.18
sizing
    linked charts, P 4.18–4.19
    text boxes, P 2.4–2.5
slide(s). *See also* presentations
    adding clip art, P 2.10–2.12
    adding in Slide View, P 1.21
    adding organization charts, P 2.17
    adding text boxes, P 2.19–2.20
    automatic timing, P 4.27
    black, P 3.16
    deleting, P 1.17–1.18
    hiding, P 3.16
    inserting from another presentation, P 3.4–3.6
    inserting shapes, P 2.17–2.18
    integrating programs, P 4.1–4.33

See also embedding; embedding clip-art images; importing; importing outlines from Word; linking
  looping continuously, P 4.27–4.28
  new, adding, P 3.20–3.21
  removing background graphics, P 2.6–2.7
  text boxes. *See* text boxes
  35mm, preparing, P 3.31
  viewing, P 1.18–1.19
Slide Finder dialog box, P 3.6
Slide Layout, P 2.8–2.10
  adding text to placeholders, P 2.9–2.10
  existing slides, changing, P 2.8–2.9
Slide Layout dialog box, P 2.9
Slide Master, P 1.5, P 3.7–3.14
  adding scanned images to Title Masters, P 3.13–3.14
  color scheme, P 3.9–3.10
  displaying, P 3.8
  fonts and bullets, P 3.10–3.12
  text alignment, P 3.12–3.13
Slide Navigator dialog box, P 4.23
Slide Navigator feature, P 4.23
Slide Show button, P 1.10
slide shows. *See* presentations
Slide Sorter View button, P 1.10
Slide Transition dialog box, P 4.27
slide transitions, P 3.26
Slide View
  adding slides, P 1.21
  editing presentations. *See* editing presentations in Slide View
  viewing slides, P 1.18–1.19
Slide View button, P 1.10
Snap to Grid feature, P 4.9–4.11
sound effects, P 3.27–3.28
sound files, embedding in slides, P 4.14–4.15
source program, P 4.2
speaker notes, P 1.23
  creating, P 1.25–1.26
special effects, P 3.25–3.28
  animation and sound, P 3.27–3.28
  slide transitions, P 3.26
stacking order, objects, P 4.12–4.13
Standard toolbar, P 1.10
starting PowerPoint, P 1.6–1.7, P 1.15
Style Checker, P 3.29–3.31
Style Checker Options dialog box, P 3.29–3.30

T tables, P 3.21–3.25. *See also* graphics
  creating, P 3.21–3.22
  editing, P 3.24–3.25
  formatting, P 3.22–3.24
Tables and Borders toolbar, P 3.23
tab stops, P 4.20–4.22
targets, hyperlinks, P 4.25
templates. *See* design templates
testing hyperlinks, P 4.26

text, P 2.19–2.21
  adding to placeholders, P 2.9–2.10
  alignment, P 3.12–3.13
  finding and replacing, P 3.14–3.15
  moving. *See* moving text
  outlines. *See* editing presentations in Outline View; outlines
text boxes, P 2.3–2.6
  adding to slides, P 2.19–2.20
  aligning text, P 3.12–3.13
  moving, P 2.5–2.6, P 2.20–2.21
  resizing, P 2.4–2.5
  rotating, P 2.20–2.21
35mm slides, preparing, P 3.31
timing, automatic, P 4.27
titles, P 1.11
toolbars, P 1.10
ToolTips, P 1.10
transition effects, P 3.26
TROUBLE? paragraphs, P 1.4
tutorials, effective use, P 1.4

U ungrouping clip art, P 2.12

V video clips, embedding in slides, P 4.13–4.14
view(s), P 1.10. *See also specific views*
Viewer, P 3.34
viewing
  presentations. *See* viewing presentations
  slides, P 1.18–1.19
viewing presentations, P 1.26, P 2.22, P 4.19–4.20. *See also* previewing presentations
  Web browsers, P 4.32–4.33
View toolbar, P 1.10

W .WAV files, embedding in slides, P 4.14–4.15
Web, publishing presentations. *See* publishing presentations on World Wide Web
Web browsers, P 4.30
  viewing presentations, P 4.32–4.33
Web pages, P 4.30
Web servers, P 4.30
Web sites, P 4.30
What's This? command, P 1.24
Word, importing outlines. *See* importing outlines from Word
World Wide Web (WWW), publishing presentations. *See* publishing presentations on World Wide Web

Microsoft PowerPoint 97 **Task Reference**

TASK	PAGE #	RECOMMENDED METHOD
35mm Slides, prepare	P 3.31	Click File, click Page Setup, click Slides sized for list arrow, click 35mm Slides, click OK, send copy of file to service bureau or click File, point to Send To, click Genigraphics, follow Wizard
Animation, add	P 3.27	In Slide Sorter View, select desired slides, click Text Preset Animation list arrow, select desired animation effect
AutoContent Wizard, use	P 1.8	Click AutoContent wizard radio button on PowerPoint startup dialog box; or click File, click New, click Presentations tab, click AutoContent Wizard, click OK
Background graphic, remove	P 1.27	Click Format, click Background, click Omit background graphics from master check box, click Apply or Apply to all
Black & White, view	P 1.27	Click
Borders, table, modify	P 3.23	Click , select desired line style and line weight, drag pointer along table gridlines
Bulleted item, dim previous	P 3.27	Click Slide Show, click Custom Animation, click Effects tab, click desired Animation Order item, click After Animation list arrow, click tile of desired color, click Sound list arrow, click desired sound, click OK
Bullet style, modify	P 3.11	Click in text of bulleted item, click Format, click Bullet, click desired bullet character and color, click OK
Chart, insert	P 3.17	Change slide layout to Text & Chart or Chart & Text, double-click chart placeholder, edit information in datasheet, click anywhere outside chart to deselect it
Clip art, insert	P 2.11	Click , click desired clip-art layout, click Apply, double-click clip-art placeholder, click desired clip-art category, click desired clip-art image, click OK
Color scheme, modify	P 3.9	Click Format, click Slide Color Scheme, change colors as desired, click Apply or Apply to All
Conference, Presentation, set up and run	P 4.30	Click Tools, click Presentation Conference, follow Wizard (participants must click Finish before presenter)
Design template, change	P 1.22	Click , click name of desired template file, click Apply
Guides, use	P 4.9	Click View, click Guides, drag guides to desired location, drag object to guides
Hyperlink, create	P 4.25	Select phrase, click , insert pathname or URL into Link to file or URL text box, type bookmark into Names location in file (optional) text box, click OK
Meeting Minder, create slide using	P 4.24	In Slide Show View, right-click in slide, click Meeting Minder, click desired tab, add desired items, click OK

Microsoft PowerPoint 97 **Task Reference**

TASK	PAGE #	RECOMMENDED METHOD
Next or previous slide, go to	P 1.19	In Slide View, click ⬇ or click ⬆
Notes Page View	P 1.25	Click 🖥
Object, link	P 4.16	Click Insert, click Object, click Link check box, click Create from File option button, type filename, click OK
Organization chart, add co-worker	P 2.16	Click ⬜⁻:Co-worker or Co-worker⁻⬜, click existing box
Organization chart, add subordinate	P 2.15	Click Subordinate:⬜, click existing box
Organization chart, insert	P 2.14	Change slide layout to Organization Chart; double-click organization chart placeholder; type names, positions, etc.; add subordinates and co-workers
Outline, export	P 4.6	Click File, point to Send To, click Microsoft Word, click Outline only option button, click OK, save Word file
Outline text, demote	P 1.17	Place insertion point in text of slide title or bulleted item, click ➡
Outline text, move	P 1.15	Position ✛ on slide icon or bullet, click ⬆ or ⬇
Outline text, promote	P 1.16	Place insertion point in text of slide title or bulleted item, click ⬅
Outline View	P 1.10	Click ☰
Overheads, prepare	P 3.32	Click File, click Page Setup, click Slides sized for list arrow, click Overhead, select desired options, click OK
Pack and Go Wizard, use	P 3.34	Place blank, formatted disk in drive, click File, click Pack And Go, follow Wizard
Picture(s), group or ungroup	P 2.12	Select picture(s), click Draw list arrow, click Group or click Ungroup
Picture, insert	P 2.7	Click Insert, click Picture, select disk and folder, click name of picture file, click OK
Picture, recolor	P. 4.11	Select picture, click 🖼, modify colors, click OK
Presentation, open	P 1.15	Click 📂, select disk and folder, click filename in Name list box, click Open
Presentation, print	P 1.27	Click File, click Print
Presentation, save	P 1.13	Click 💾; if necessary, select disk and folder, type name in File name text box, click Save
Presentation, save with a new filename	P 2.3	Click File, click Save As, enter new filename in File name text box, click Save
Presentation Style, check	P 3.29	Click Tools, click Style Checker, click Options, specify desired options, click OK, click Start button, accept or ignore each suggested style change

Microsoft PowerPoint 97 **Task Reference**

TASK	PAGE #	RECOMMENDED METHOD
Self-running presentation, set up	P 4.27	Click ⬚, click Automatically after check box, set time for each slide, click Apply to All, click Slide Show, click Set Up Show, click Browsed at a kiosk (full screen), click OK
Shape, create	P 2.17	Click AutoShapes list arrow, click desired shape, drag ╋ to draw and size shape
Shape, flip	P 2.18	Select shape, click Draw list arrow, point to Rotate or Flip, click Flip Vertical or Flip Horizontal
Slide, delete	P 1.17	In Outline View, click slide icon, press Delete. In Slide View, click slide icon, click Edit, click Delete
Slide, hide	P 3.16	Click ⬚, select slide(s) to hide, click ⬚
Slide, insert from another presentation	P 3.5	Click Insert, click Slides from Files, select folder and filename, select desired slides, click Insert button
Slide, insert new	P 3.20	Click ⬚, select desired layout, click OK
Slide layout, change	P 2.8	Click Format, click Slide Layout, click desired layout, click Apply or Reapply
Slide Master, modify	P 3.8	Shift-click ⬚, modify formatting features as desired, click ⬚
Slide Show, exit	P 1.26	Press Esc
Slide Show, view	P 1.26	Click ⬚; press spacebar or click left mouse button to advance; press Backspace or click right mouse button to go back
Slide Sorter View	P 1.28	Click ⬚
Slide View	P 1.19	Click ⬚
Sound file, embed	P 4.15	Click Insert, point to Movies and Sounds, click Sounds from File, select folder and filename, click OK
Spelling, check	P 1.27	Click ⬚
Table, create	P 3.21	Click ⬚, click Table layout, click OK, double-click table placeholder, set the number of columns and rows, click OK, fill in and format cells as desired
Tab stops, add	P 4.21	Select text box, click View, click Ruler, click tab stop alignment selector button to select desired tab stop style, click desired location on ruler
Template, apply from another presentation	P 3.7	Click Apply Design on Common Tasks toolbar, select folder, click Files of type list arrow, click Presentations and Shows, click filename, click Apply
Text boxes, align	P 2.6	Click to select first text box, press and hold Shift, click to select other text box(es), click Draw list arrow, point to Align or Distribute, click alignment position
Text box, create	P 2.19	Click ⬚, click pointer on slide, type text

Microsoft PowerPoint 97 **Task Reference**

TASK	PAGE #	RECOMMENDED METHOD
Text box, resize	P 2.4	Click text box to select it, drag a resize handle
Text box, rotate	P 2.20	Select text box, click ⟳, drag a resize handle
Text, change alignment	P 3.12	Click in text or select text box, click a text alignment button
Text, find	P 3.14	Click Edit, click Find, type search string in Find what text box, click Find Next button
Text, replace	P 3.15	Click Edit, click Replace, type search string in Find what text box, type replacement string in Replace with text box, click Find Next or Replace All button
Transition effects, add	P 3.26	In Slide Sorter View, select desired slides, click Slide Transition Effects list arrow, select desired effect
Video, embed	P 4.13	Click ▣, click Videos tab, click desired video clip, click Insert
Viewer, start	P 3.34	Place Pack and Go disk in drive, click Windows 95 Start button, click Run, type a:\pngset, click OK, follow instructions
Web page, publish	P 4.31	Click File, click Save as HTML, follow Wizard
Word Outline, import	P 4.4	Create and save outline in Word, in PowerPoint click Insert, click Slides from Outline, select folder and outline filename, click Insert button